Williams o

First Supplement to Ninth Edition

Publisher's Note

Paragraphs in this supplement update and replace in their entirety those published in the Ninth edition mainwork of Williams on Wills. To highlight specifically those points which have changed, a note is provided at the beginning of each reprinted paragraph to indicate what the changes are. The exception to this is in Volume 2, Part G, the statutes, where it will be clear from the annotations what are the new amendments.

Williams on Wills

First Supplement to Ninth Edition

Consultant Editor

FRANCIS BARLOW
MA (OXON)
One of Her Majesty's Counsel, a Bencher of Lincoln's Inn
10 Old Square, Lincoln's Inn, London WC2A 3SU

Editors

CHRISTOPHER SHERRIN
LLM PHD
Professor of Law, Department of Professional Legal Education, University of Hong Kong

RICHARD WALLINGTON
MA (CANTAB)
Barrister, a Bencher of Lincoln's Inn
10 Old Square, Lincoln's Inn, London WC2A 3SU

SUSANNAH L MEADWAY
MA (OXON)
of the Middle Temple and Lincoln's Inn, Barrister
10 Old Square, Lincoln's Inn, London WC2A 3SU

MICHAEL WATERWORTH
MA (CANTAB)
of Lincoln's Inn, Barrister
10 Old Square, Lincoln's Inn, London WC2A 3SU

Members of the LexisNexis Group worldwide

United Kingdom	LexisNexis, a Division of Reed Elsevier (UK) Ltd, Halsbury House, 35 Chancery Lane, London, WC2A 1EL, and London House, 20–22 East London Street, Edinburgh EH7 4BQ
Australia	LexisNexis Butterworths, Chatswood, New South Wales
Austria	LexisNexis Verlag ARD Orac GmbH & Co KG, Vienna
Benelux	LexisNexis Benelux, Amsterdam
Canada	LexisNexis Canada, Markham, Ontario
China	LexisNexis China, Beijing and Shanghai
France	LexisNexis SA, Paris
Germany	LexisNexis Deutschland GmbH, Munster
Hong Kong	LexisNexis Hong Kong, Hong Kong
India	LexisNexis India, New Delhi
Italy	Giuffrè Editore, Milan
Japan	LexisNexis Japan, Tokyo
Malaysia	Malayan Law Journal Sdn Bhd, Kuala Lumpur
New Zealand	LexisNexis NZ Ltd, Wellington
Poland	Wydawnictwo Prawnicze LexisNexis Sp, Warsaw
Singapore	LexisNexis Singapore, Singapore
South Africa	LexisNexis Butterworths, Durban
USA	LexisNexis, Dayton, Ohio

Published by LexisNexis

A CIP Catalogue record for this book is available from the British Library.

ISBN 9781405726672

Typeset by Columns Design Ltd, Reading, England
Printed in the UK by CPI William Clowes Beccles NR34 7TL

Visit LexisNexis at www.lexisnexis.co.uk

PREFACE

This First Supplement to the 9th edition of Williams on Wills is based on new material which has arisen since December 2007. A qualification of that statement is that IHT nil-rate band transfer does not figure prominently in this Supplement. This is because although it was only enacted by the Finance Act 2008, it was announced on 9 October 2007 as taking effect from that date, and a draft of the legislation for it was then published, and so it was taken into account in the preparation of the 9th edition. The legislation subsequently enacted differed from the original draft only in a few minor respects which are not particularly significant for will drafting.

The new materials incorporated in this Supplement are mostly new case law, though there has also been new legislation in the form of the Human Fertilisation and Embryology Act 2008, the Cremation (England and Wales) Regulations 2008, and the statutory instruments amending the intestacy rules. Also certain parts of the Charities Act 2006 have come into force. The rate of interest provided under the Civil Procedure Rules for pecuniary legacies given by will has been reduced to 2 per cent (see para **[32.4]**) but, curiously, the rate of interest under the intestacy rules on the fixed net sum for a surviving spouse or civil partner remains at 6 per cent.

The will-drafting professions need to prepare themselves for two major changes in the law which are likely to happen in the next year or two. These are the introduction of a single perpetuity period of 125 years, and the repeal of the statutory restrictions on accumulation: see the Perpetuities and Accumulations Bill now before Parliament. Under the Bill as currently drafted these changes will apply to a will only if it is executed after the Act comes into force, and the Act is likely to come into force some time after it receives the Royal Assent. At the moment the Bill is not in its final form, and the time is not ripe to take account of it in a Supplement, but this legislation is likely to be the big news in the next Supplement.

This Supplement incorporates material to hand by 31 May 2009.

June 2009

The Editors

Contents

VOLUME 1 – THE LAW OF WILLS

PART P FAMILY PROVISION

VOLUME 2 – PRECEDENTS AND STATUTES

PART A INTRODUCTORY NOTE

PART B CLAUSES IN WILLS

PART G STATUTES

Table of abbreviations

Abbreviation	Full Title
AA 1976	Adoption Act 1976
AA 1984	Anatomy Act 1984
ACA 2002	Adoption and Children Act 2002
AEA 1925	Administration of Estates Act 1925
AJA 1982	Administration of Justice Act 1982
CA 1985	Companies Act 1985
CCA 1984	County Courts Act 1984
CDPA 1988	Copyright, Designs and Patents Act 1988
ChA 1989	Children Act 1989
CLSA 1990	Courts and Legal Services Act 1990
CPA 2004	Civil Partnership Act 2004
FA 1984	Finance Act 1984
FA 2002	Finance Act 2002
FA 2003	Finance Act 2003
FA 2004	Finance Act 2004
FA 2005	Finance Act 2005
FA 2006	Finance Act 2006
FA 2008	Finance Act 2008
FAA 1976	Fatal Accidents Act 1976
FoA 1982	Forfeiture Act 1982
FLRA 1969	Family Law Reform Act 1969
FLRA 1987	Family Law Reform Act 1987
FPA 1966	Family Provision Act 1966
GRA 2004	Gender Recognition Act 2004
HA 1996	Housing Act 1996
HFEA 1990	Human Fertilisation and Embryology Act 1990
HFEA 2008	Human Fertilisation and Embryology Act 2008
HRA 1998	Human Rights Act 1998
HTA 1961	Human Tissue Act 1961
HTA 2004	Human Tissue Act 2004
IA 1978	Interpretation Act 1978
ICTA 1988	Income and Corporation Taxes Act 1988
IEA 1952	Intestates' Estates Act 1952
I(PFD)A 1975	Inheritance (Provision for Family and Dependants) Act 1975
IHTA 1984	Inheritance Tax Act 1984
ITA 2007	Income Tax Act 2007

ITTOIA 2005	Income Tax (Trading and Other Income) Act 2005
LA 1976	Legitimacy Act 1976
LLPA 2000	Limited Liability Partnerships Act 2000.
LP(MP)A 1989	Law of Property (Miscellaneous Provisions) Act 1989
LRA 2002	Land Registration Act 2002
LR(S)A 1995	Law Reform (Succession) Act 1995
MCA 2005	Mental Capacity Act 2005
MeHA 1983	Mental Health Act 1983
MFPA 1984	Matrimonial and Family Proceedings Act 1984
MGACA 1972	Museums and Galleries Admissions Charges Act 1972
MGA 1992	Museum and Galleries Act 1992
MHA 1959	Mental Health Act 1959
PLMA 1964	Public Libraries and Museums Act 1964
RA 1977	Rent Act 1977
SL(R)A 1981	Statute Law (Repeals) Act 1981
TA 1925	Trustee Act 1925
TCGA 1992	Taxation of Chargeable Gains Act 1992
TLATA 1996	Trusts of Land and Appointment of Trustees Act 1996
TrA 2000	Trustee Act 2000
WA 1837	Wills Act 1837
WA 1968	Wills Act 1968

VOLUME 1

The law of wills

PART A

Nature of wills

CHAPTER 2

Joint and mutual wills

[Updated in the text and at footnote 7 for *Olins v Walters* [2009] Ch 212.]

[2.5]

Agreements relating to mutual wills. In order for the doctrine of mutual wills to apply there has to be, what amounts to, a contract at law between the two testators that both wills will be irrevocable and will remain unaltered.[1] A mere mutual desire that both wills should remain unaltered could not, in the absence of an express agreement, of itself prevent the survivor from departing from the arrangement.[2] Such agreements vary according to the circumstances of particular cases and the wishes of the parties. The wills may be executed upon an agreement that they shall not be revoked or altered.[3] On the other hand, they may be made in pursuance of an agreement that they shall be freely revocable by any party.[4] In a modern case such wills and the accompanying agreement were construed so that as to one part of the residuary estate revocation was allowed, but not as to the other part.[5] In some cases no agreement at all is made, or at least none is proved.[6]

The 'irreducible core' of the doctrine has been described as a contract between two testators, T1 and T2, that in return for T1 agreeing to make a will in form X and not to revoke it without notice to T2, then T2 will make a will in form Y and agree not to revoke it without notice to T1. If such facts are established then upon the death of T1 equity will impose upon T2 a form of constructive trust (shaped by the exact terms of the contract that T1 and T2 have made.) The constructive trust is imposed because T1 has made a disposition of property on the faith of T2's promise to make a will in form Y, and with the object of preventing T1 from being defrauded.[7]

1 *Re Goodchild* [1997] 3 All ER 63, CA; affirming Carnwath J [1996] 1 All ER 670; applying *Gray v Perpetual Trustee Co Ltd* [1928] All ER Rep 758 at 762 and *Re Dale, Proctor v Dale* [1993] 4 All ER 129 at 133. In *Re Goodchild* the absence of proof of such an agreement meant that the mutual wills were not established.

2 *Re Goodchild* [1997] 3 All ER 63.

3 Such an agreement was held proved in *Stone v Hoskins* [1905] P 194. In *Re Oldham, Hadwen v Myles* [1925] Ch 75, it was only proved that the parties agreed to make mutual wills and nothing was proved as to any agreement to revoke.

4 This is commonly evidenced by making the gift to the other 'absolutely and beneficially and without any sort of trust or obligation'. It may also be evidenced by a recital that the will, though made as a mutual will, is made without any agreement that it or any of its provisions shall be irrevocable and that the intention is that either party shall have full liberty to revoke or alter all or any of the provisions of his or her will. This clearly leaves it open to the survivor to revoke his will and make other provisions, which, indeed, may often be necessary in altered circumstances, such as remarriage, or the marriage of some children while others remain unmarried. It is apprehended that an agreement not to revoke leaves the

testator free to dispose of his property during his lifetime (see para **[2.3]**, above, n 1), and this is clearly so where there is no such agreement. Where the agreement is in special terms (see e g *Re Green, Lindner v Green* [1951] Ch 148, [1950] 2 All ER 913, more fully discussed in n 5, below) it may be that the terms of the agreement prevent his disposing of his own property or property coming from the first to die or some other specified source. If the agreement relates to specific property, the right of disposition is fettered as to that property, but, if the agreement has been ignored, it may be that only a remedy in damages is available against the estate of the testator so ignoring it: see Chapter 3.

5 *Re Green, Lindner v Green* [1950] 2 All ER 913. In this case the survivor remarried and made a new will giving the whole of the residue to his second wife. Certain property which by his former will he had disposed of as property belonging to his first wife was held to be taken by the personal representatives upon trust to give effect to the first will. Certain legatees were given pecuniary legacies under both wills but not of identical amounts. As these legacies had in the first will been given out of property notionally regarded as the first wife's property, the legatees were entitled to take under both wills. Apparently the legacies under the first will were in the special circumstances of the case subject to abatement.

6 *Re Oldham, Hadwen v Myles* [1925] Ch 75; *Gray v Perpetual Trustee Co Ltd* [1928] AC 391; *Garioch's Trustees v Garioch's Executors* 1917 SC 404. In such case the will may be revoked by one of the parties by a holograph will: *Saxby v Saxby Executors* 1952 SC 352.

7 *Olins v Walters* [2009] Ch 212 at [38].

[Updated reference to the Law of Property (Miscellaneous Provisions) Act 1989, in footnote 4.]

[2.6]

Proof of agreement. The agreement may be incorporated in the will by recital or otherwise,[1] or it may be proved outside the will.[2] It may be oral or in writing,[3] but it would seem that in so far as such agreement affects a disposition of land, it must be in writing.[4] The mere simultaneity of the wills and the similarity of their terms are not enough taken by themselves to establish the necessary agreement,[5] which must be established by clear and satisfactory evidence on the balance of probabilities.[6] Proof of the precise terms of the agreement is essential, for any subsequent limitation of the powers of disposition of any party is dependent upon the precise restriction being proved to have been agreed between the parties.[7] The key issue in the proof of mutual wills is that each of the parties has agreed with the other not to alter his or her testamentary dispositions on the death of the first to die.[8]

1 *Re Hagger, Freeman v Arscott* [1930] 2 Ch 190. This is certainly the better course because, if any question arises, it may well arise many years after the execution of the will and evidence of an oral agreement may be either unobtainable or it may be difficult to establish its precise terms. See *Re Ohorodnyk* (1980) 102 DLR (3d) 576 on proof of the agreement.

2 *Re Heys' Estate, Walker v Gaskill* [1914] P 192 at 194.

3 See *Stone v Hoskins* [1905] P 194; *Re Oldham, Hadwen v Myles* [1925] Ch 75; *Gray v Perpetual Trustee Co Ltd* [1928] AC 391.

4 It would seem that this must be so since 1989 by virtue of the Law of Property (Miscellaneous Provisions) Act 1989, s 2. As to cases before that Act see *Humphreys v Green* (1882) 10 QBD 148. It seems there is no distinction between the law applicable to an ordinary agreement not to revoke a will and a mutual agreement not to revoke a mutual will; indeed, it was said in *Dufour v Pereira* (1769) 1 Dick 419, as reported in 2 Hargrave Juridicial Arguments 304 at 309, that 'there is no difference between promising to make a will in such a form and making a will with a promise not to revoke it', and this has been cited with approval in *Stone v Hoskins* [1905] P 194 at 196, 197; *Re Oldham* [1925] Ch 75 at 84, and in *Gray v Perpetual Trustee Co Ltd* [1928] AC 391 at 399.

5 *Gray v Perpetual Trustee Co Ltd* [1928] AC 391 at 399–400 per Viscount Haldane; *Dufour v Pereira* (1769) 1 Dick 419, cited with approval by Nourse J in *Re Cleaver, Cleaver v Insley* [1981] 2 All ER 1018 at 1022. See also *Re Oldham, Hadwen v Myles* [1925] Ch 75 at 87; *Re Skippen, Hodgson v Armstrong and MacInnes* [1947] 1 DLR 858; *Re Gillespie* (1969) 3 DLR (3d) 317.

6 Per Nourse J in *Re Cleaver, Cleaver v Insley* [1981] 2 All ER 1018 at 1024, applying *Birmingham v Renfrew* (1937) 57 CLR 666; clear and satisfactory evidence of the agreement was found in *Re Cleaver, Cleaver v Insley* [1981] 2 All ER 1018. See *Re Goodchild* [1997] 3 All ER 63 where these points were emphasised by Leggatt LJ at 67–72: a 'common understanding' will not suffice, 'clear and satisfactory evidence' is required. The crucial difference between *Re Cleaver* and *Re Goodchild* was that in the former case there was specific evidence as to the testator's mutual intentions at the time the wills were made, whereas in the latter case there was not: *Re Goodchild* [1997] 3 All ER 63 at 71c. Similarly in *Birch v Curtis* [2002] EWHC 1158 (Ch), [2002] 2 FLR 847, where it was emphasiSed that the doctrine of mutual wills derived from a contract between the parties making the wills, the crucial ingredient being the contracting out of the right to revoke the wills. And in *Lewis v Cotton* [2001] WTLR 1117 it was held that a contention that wills were mutual required very careful scrutiny and proof beyond a balance of probabilities; the contention failed in that case.

7 This seems to follow from the decision in *Re Oldham*, where it was held that an agreement to make mutual wills was proved but there was no proof of an agreement not to revoke such wills. In *Re Green, Lindner v Green* [1951] Ch 148, [1950] 2 All ER 913, the agreement was set out in the wills which were in identical terms *mutatis mutandis*. At the time of making the wills the parties had little property but were entitled in reversion to a substantial estate given to them in equal shares or to the survivor as the case might be. The wife died and the husband succeeded to the whole of her estate, then the reversionary interest fell in. The husband remarried, made a subsequent will and later died. It was held that the effect of the mutual wills was that the wife's moiety was impressed with a trust binding on the testator, while the testator's moiety remained at his free disposition; *Dufour v Pereira* (1769) 1 Dick 419 applied; *Re Oldham, Hadwen v Myles* [1925] Ch 75, distinguished. See also *Re Grisor* (1980) 101 DLR (3d) 728. See also para **[2.8]**, n 1.

The principle has been extended to the case where the agreement is that if one party makes a change in his will, the other will make a corresponding change and the court will compel him to do so: *Re Fox* [1951] 3 DLR 337.

8 *Estate of Brynelsen v Verdeck* (2001–02) 4 ITELR 857 (BC CA). In this case there was no evidence that the parties had bound themselves in that way and thus the essential foundation of mutual wills was absent; *Dufour v Pereira* (1769) 1 Dick 419 and Lord *Walpole v Orford* (1797) 3 Ves 402, applied. A similar result was reached in *Osborne v Estate of Osborne (2001–02)* 4 ITELR 804 (Vic CA). The mere making of similar or identical wills was not sufficient to prove that they were mutual wills. Mutual wills were the result of an arrangement or contract which obliged the survivor not to dispose of his estate in any way other than that agreed with the deceased. In this case there was no evidence, other than the making of the wills, that the parties intended to bind each other for the lifetime of the survivor; *Birmingham v Renfrew* (1936) 57 CLR 666 applied.

[Updated at footnote 2 for *Olins v Walters* [2009] Ch 212.]

[2.8]

Effect of first to die abiding by agreement. Where the first to die has left his will unaltered and unrevoked in pursuance of the agreement, the survivor is bound by the agreement, and, though it is not strictly true to say that he cannot alter or revoke his will, the court, if asked, will ultimately refuse to give effect to such alteration or revocation.[1] The agreement is enforced by means of a constructive trust. Nourse J has stated the position as follows:[2]

> 'The principle of all these cases[3] is that a court of equity will not permit a person to whom property is transferred by way of gift but on the faith of an agreement or clear understanding that it is to be dealt with in a particular way for the benefit of a third person, to deal with that property inconsistently with that agreement or understanding. If he attempts to do so after having received the benefit of the gift equity will intervene by imposing a constructive trust on the property which is the subject matter of the agreement or understanding.'[4]

In a more recent case the principles were expressed as follows. The doctrine of mutual wills is to the effect that where two individuals have agreed as to the disposal of their property and have executed mutual wills in pursuance of the agreement, on the death of the first (T1) the property of the survivor (T2), the subject matter of the agreement, is held on an implied trust for the beneficiary named in the wills. The survivor may thereafter alter his will, because a will is inherently revocable, but if he does so his personal representatives will take the property subject to the trust.[5]

The agreement or understanding must be such as to impose on the donee a legally binding obligation to deal with the property in the particular way and certainty as to the subject matter of the trust and the persons intended to benefit under it must be present.[6] Giving effect to such a mutual will is an indirect process because probate must be granted of a testator's last will. If, therefore, the survivor has revoked the mutual will by making a new will, it is the new will which is admitted to probate.[7] If he has altered the will by duly executing a codicil, the codicil must be admitted to probate with the will.[8] It is, however, open to those benefiting under the mutual will to apply to a court of construction,[9] and then in a proper case an order will be made upon the personal representatives to hold the estate upon trust to give effect to the provisions of the mutual will.[10] Where the trusts are for the survivor for life with absolute remainders over, the remainders vest on the first death and the remainderman's interest does not lapse where he survives the first deceased but dies before the death of the second.[11] The parties might intend that the mutual wills should only affect those assets which are in existence before the death of the first party to the agreement.[12]

1 *Re Heys' Estate, Walker v Gaskill* [1914] P 192 at 200. The doctrine is not confined to cases in which the surviving testator receives a benefit under the will of the first to die but extends to cases where both testators leave their estates to beneficiaries other than themselves: *Re Dale, Proctor v Dale* [1994] Ch 31, [1993] 4 All ER 129.

2 In *Re Cleaver, Cleaver v Insley* [1981] 2 All ER 1018 at 1024; see also Clauson J in *Re Hagger, Freeman v Arscott* [1930] 2 Ch 190 at 195, on the authority of Lord Camden in *Dufour v Pereira* (1769) 1 Dick 419. See also *Re Dale, Proctor v Dale* [1993] 4 All ER 129, where the fraud giving rise to a constructive trust approach was followed. In *Healy v Brown* [2002] WTLR 849, A and F were joint tenants of the matrimonial home. They had made mutual non-revocable wills under which the survivor would receive the entirety of the other's estate with an ultimate gift to H on the death of the survivor. A died first and F became entitled to the whole of the property. Subsequently, by inter vivos gift, F transferred the property from his sole name to the joint names of himself and B, so that when F died the property passed by survivorship to B. H claimed that B held the property on trust for H in accordance with the scheme of the mutual wills. It was held that the disposition of the property by F had been intended to defeat H's legitimate expectations under the mutual wills and, since F had accepted A's share of the property on the basis of the mutual wills agreement, it was unconscionable, and a constructive trust was imposed in respect of A's one half undivided share on B in favour of H; *Yaxley v Gotts* [2000] Ch 162 referred to and *Lloyds Bank plc v Rosset* [1991] 1 AC 107, distinguished. It was held that the trust only affected A's half share and not the original interest of F, because the declarations contained in the mutual wills of A and F had no legal effect as a contract for the disposition of land because they failed to satisfy the requirements of LP(MP)A 1989, s 2 and therefore the doctrine of mutual wills did not apply; *Goodchild v Goodchild* [1997] 1 WLR 1216 applied. In *Olins v Walters* [2007] EWHC 3060 Norris J (at first instance) held that a direction by the testatrix to her executors to convert her estate, and after directing them to pay her testamentary and funeral expenses, debts and taxes, to dispose of the residue so realised does not require any formalities and is not within the rule applied in *Healy v Brown*. *Olins v Walters* was upheld on appeal ([2009] Ch 212).

3 *Birmingham v Renfrew* (1936) 57 CLR 666; *Ottaway v Norman* [1972] Ch 698, [1971] 3 All ER 1325.

4 Nourse J equated mutual wills with analogous situations such as secret trusts, in which a court of equity will intervene to impose a constructive trust, referring to *Ottaway v Norman* [1971] 3 All ER 1325, and *Re Pearson Fund Trusts* (21 October 1977, unreported).

5 Per Morritt J in *Re Dale, Proctor v Dale* [1993] 4 All ER 129 at 132. The judge continued: 'The basic doctrine is not in dispute. The dispute is as to the circumstances in which the doctrine applies.' In *Re Goodchild* [1996] 1 All ER 670, Carnwath J referred to the trust as a 'floating trust'; see affirmed [1997] 3 All ER 63, CA but mutual wills were not made out: see para **[2.4]** above.

6 *Re Goodchild*, n 5 above. It was held in *Re Dale, Proctor v Dale* [1993] 4 All ER 129, that the doctrine will apply not only where the parties each take a benefit but also where both leave their property to particular beneficiaries.

7 *Hobson v Blackburn and Blackburn* (1822) 1 Add 274; *Re Heys' Estate, Walker v Gaskill* [1914] P 192. In the case of *Re O'Connor's Estate* [1942] 1 All ER 546, it was part of the agreement to make separate wills after the execution of the joint will and one testatrix dying very shortly after the other, the court made a grant of the joint will and ignored the separate will of the second to die as conditional on her predeceasing the first to die.

8 See n 7, above.

9 That is the Chancery Division of the High Court.

10 *Stone v Hoskins* [1905] P 194; *Re Hagger, Freeman v Arscott* [1930] 2 Ch 190; *Re Green, Lindner v Green* [1951] Ch 148, [1950] 2 All ER 913 as in *Re Cleaver, Clever v Insley* [1981] 2 All ER 1018, [1981] 1 WLR 939.

11 *Re Hagger, Freeman v Arscott* [1930] 2 Ch 190.

12 *Re Gillespie* (1969) 3 DLR (3d) 317.

PART B

Capacity and disposing intent

CHAPTER 4

Testamentary capacity

VI. SOUND DISPOSING MIND

[Updated in the text and footnotes 2 to 4 for *Scammell v Farmer* [2008] WTLR 1261.]

[4.9]

Mental Capacity Act 2005 The test for mental capacity, whether to make a will or do any other act, has previously been established by a series of judicial decisions, the most significant of which are noted in the following paragraphs. The Mental Capacity Act 2005, sections 1 to 4 of which were brought into force on 1 April 2007, [1] puts the test for mental capacity on a statutory footing. The Act is not retrospective and is of no consequence in considering the validity of wills made prior to 1 April 2007.[2] The Act was intended to be a codification of the existing law and it does not purport to deal with all areas in which mental capacity may be relevant. There is some doubt as to whether the Mental Capacity Act 2005 has any relevance to wills made outside the statutory jurisdiction[3] and it is plain[4] that, in the case of wills, the existing authorities discussed in the remainder of this section will continue to be relevant.

Nonetheless, the Mental Capacity Act 2005 and the Code of Practice under it, provide a new definition of capacity and judges might use the new statutory definition to develop common law rules in particular cases. Medical experts are expected to find the statutory definition easier to use and may ignore the existing rules. The Mental Capacity Act 2005 provides that the starting point should be that there is a presumption of capacity: s 1(2); this reflects the common law presumption.

Lack of capacity is catered for in s 2 by reference to a 'functional' approach which is 'decision specific'. The section provides that:

> 'For the purposes of this Act, a person lacks capacity in relation to a Matter if at the material time he is unable to make a decision for himself in relation to the matter because of an impairment of, or a disturbance in the functioning of, the mind or brain. It does not matter whether the impairment or disturbance is permanent or temporary.'

The provisions which, in reality, provide the test for capacity are to be found in s 3(1) which provides that:

> 'For the purposes of section 2, a person is unable to make a decision for himself if he is unable—
>
> (a) to understand the information relevant to the decision,
>
> (b) to retain that information,

(c) to use or weigh that information as part of the process of making the decision or
(d) to communicate his decision (whether by talking, using sign language or any other means).'[5].

That is qualified by the remainder of s 3 so that:

'(2) A person is not to be regarded as unable to understand the information relevant to a decision if he is able to understand an explanation of it given to him in a way that is appropriate to his circumstances (using simple language, visual aids or any other means).

(3) The fact that a person is able to retain the information relevant to a decision for a short period only does not prevent him from being regarded as able to make the decision.

(4) The information relevant to a decision includes information about the reasonably foreseeable consequences of—
(a) deciding one way or another, or
(b) failing to make the decision.'[6]

As these new rules are adopted and applied in wills cases there should be less reliance on the previous case law tests of testamentary capacity as embodied in such time–honoured cases as *Banks v Goodfellow*.[7]

1 SI 2007/563. The remainder of the Act came into force on 1 October 2007 (SI 2007/1897).
2 *Scammell v Farmer* [2008] WTLR 1261 at [21] to [30].
3 For doubts as to the application of the Mental Capacity Act 2005 to the making of wills see *Scammell v Farmer* [2008] WTLR 1261 at [26]. The Code of Practice provides (at para 4.32) that: 'The Act makes clear that the definition of "lack of capacity" and the two-stage test for capacity set out in the Act are "for the purposes of this Act". This means that the definition and test are to be used in situations covered by this Act.' For statutory wills see para **[4.21]** below.
4 See paras 4.31 to 4.33 of the Code of Practice and, in particular para 4.33: 'The Act's new definition of capacity is in line with the existing common law tests, and the Act does not replace them'.
5 The Code of Practice explains that the Mental Capacity Act 2005, s 3 sets out the test for assessing whether a person is unable to make a decision for him/herself and therefore lacks capacity. This is a 'functional' test, focussing on how the decision is made rather than the outcome of it and is primarily aimed at inter vivos decisions. The Act says that a person is unable to make a decision if he is unable to satisfy any of the tests at (a) to (d) above.
6 Only time will tell the extent to which these new provisions will affect the nature of the test to ascertain mental capacity in the context of probate claims and the peculiar nature of certain rules peculiar to probate claims, such as the rule in *Parker v Felgate* (1883) 8 PD 171, see para **[4.10]** below.
7 (1870) LR 5 QB 549, see para **[4.11]** below.

[Updated in footnote 5 for *Re Baker, Baker v Baker* [2008] WTLR 565.]

[4.10]
The relevant time. It must be shown that the testator was of sound disposing mind at the time when the will or codicil was made.[1] The law requires that there should be sound disposing mind both at the time when the instructions for the will are given and when the will is executed, but it would appear that if the will is shown to have been drawn in accordance with instructions given while the testator was of sound disposing mind, it is sufficient that, when he executes it, he appreciates that he is being asked to execute as his will a

document drawn in pursuance of those instructions though he is unable to follow all its provisions.[2] Supervening insanity will not revoke the will[3] nor will a recovery validate a will or codicil made during absence of testamentary capacity.[4] A will has been admitted to probate although a codicil made shortly after has been refused on the ground of want of sound disposing mind at the time of its execution.[5]

1 *Arthur v Bokenham* (1708) 11 Mod Rep 148; *Palmer and Brown v Dent* (1850) 2 Rob Eccl 284 (where a later will made while not of sound mind was rejected). This paragraph and others in the 7th edition, of *Williams on Wills*, were cited extensively and applied in *Re Wilkes dec'd, Wilkes v Wilkes* [2006] WTLR 1097 in which it was held by the Deputy Judge (Terence Etherton QC), upholding the will under challenge, that allegations of incapacity, want of knowledge and approval and undue influence had not been made out.

2 *Perera v Perera* [1901] AC 354; *Kenny v Wilson* (1911) 11 SRNSW 460; *Wilkie v Wilkie* (1915) 17 WALR 156; *Thomas v Jones* [1928] P 162; *Battan Singh v Amirchand* [1948] AC 161, [1948] 1 All ER 152. This is so even though the testator is unable to remember the instructions previously given and his signature was affixed by another person on his behalf: *Parker v Felgate* (1883) 8 PD 171. This case was applied in *Clancy v Clancy* [2003] EWHC 1885 (Ch), where a testatrix had testamentary capacity when she gave instructions for her will to be drafted and the will was properly drafted in accordance with those instructions and executed by the testatrix, the will was held to be valid if the testatrix understood that she was signing a will which she believed gave effect to her earlier instructions, even if there was some doubt as to her capacity at that time.

See *Re Flynn, Flynn v Flynn* [1982] 1 All ER 882, [1982] 1 WLR 310, per Slade J at 890, 891 and *Re Rodziszewski's Estate* (1982) 29 SASR 256. As to cases where testator is too ill to sign, see para **[11.21]** below. *Forse and Hembling's Case* (1588) 4 Co Rep 60 b at 61 b; *Warn v Swift* (1832) 1 LJ Ch 203 (incapacity developing shortly after execution); *Re Crandon's Goods* (1901) 84 LT 330. Since any testamentary disposition must be made while the testator is of sound disposing mind, supervening insanity will ex hypothesi prevent his varying any will made while sane, and since the same sound disposing mind is required for revocation (see Chapter 18, para **[18.4]** below) it also prevents any revocation of a will made while sane.

3 *Arthur v Bokenham* (1708) 11 Mod Rep 148 at 157; *Public Trustee v Prisk* (1896) 14 NZLR 306.

4 *Brouncker v Brouncker* (1812) 2 Phillim 57.

5 *Harwood v Baker* (1840) 3 Moo PCC 282; *Banks v Goodfellow* (1870) LR 5 QB 549 at 569; *Re Sever's Will* (1887) 13 VLR 572; *Boreham v Prince Henry Hospital* (1955) 29 ALJ 179. See also *Baker Estate v Myhre* [1995] 6 WWR 410 and *Webb v Webb Estate* [1995] 6 WWR 52. There is a simple statement of the essentials in a very early case; *Re Marquess Winchester's Case* (1598) 6 Co Rep 23a, in these words:

> 'It is not sufficient that the testator be of memory when he makes his will to answer familiar and unusual questions, but he ought to have a disposing memory, so that he is able to make a disposition of his lands with understanding and reason.'

The equivalent paragraph in the eighth edition was approved in *Re Baker, Baker v Baker* [2008] WTLR 565.

[Updated in footnotes 2 and 7 for *Blackman v Man* [2008] WTLR 389, in the text and footnote 3 for *Sharp v Adam* [2006] WTLR 1059 (CA), and in footnote 7 for *Ledger v Wooton* [2008] WTLR 235; *Re Barker-Benfield, Hansen v Barker-Benfield* [2006] WTLR 1141 and *Scammell v Farmer* [2008] WTLR 1261.]

[4.11]

Criterion of sound disposing mind. At common law[1] sound testamentary capacity means that four things must exist at one and the same time: (i) The testator must understand that he is giving his property to one or more objects of his regard; (ii) he must understand and recollect the extent of his property;[2] (iii) he must also understand the nature and extent of the claims upon him both of those whom he is including in his will and those whom he is excluding from his will; (iv) no insane delusion shall influence his will in disposing of his property and bring about a disposal of it which, if the mind had been sound, would not have been made.[3] The testator must realise that he is signing a will and his mind and will must accompany the physical act of execution.[4] It is said that perversion of moral feeling does not constitute unsoundness of mind in this respect,[5] but this is really a matter of degree.[6] The criterion to be applied has been thus stated by Cockburn CJ, in *Banks v Goodfellow*:[7]

> 'It is essential to the exercise of such a power that a testator shall understand the nature of the act and its effects; shall understand the extent of the property of which he is disposing; shall be able to comprehend and appreciate the claims to which he ought to give effect; and with a view to the latter object, that no disorder of the mind shall poison his affections, pervert his sense of right, or prevent the exercise of his natural faculties—that no insane delusion shall influence his will in disposing of his property and bring about a disposal of it which, if the mind had been sound, would not have been made.'

The mere fact that the testator was eccentric or was subject to one or more delusions is not of itself sufficient.[8] It must be shown that the delusion had, or was calculated to have, an influence on testamentary dispositions.[9] A will has been held good subject to the deletion of a clause affected by a delusion.[10]

1 See para **[4.9]** above.
2 But precise knowledge of the value of property is not necessary: *Blackman v Man* [2008] WTLR 389.
3 *Sharp v Adam* [2006] WTLR 1059 (CA) at [68]. For a statement of the essentials by the Supreme Court of Canada, see *Re Poirier Estate, Leger v Poirier* [1944] 3 DLR 1.
4 *Langlais v Langley* [1952] 1 SCR 28.
5 *Frere v Peacocke* (1846) 1 Rob Eccl 442 at 456.
6 *Sutton v Sadler* (1857) 3 CBNS 87; *Burdett v Thompson* (1873) LR 3 P & D 72n.
7 LR 5 QB 549 at 565; applied in *Wood v Smith* [1993] Ch 90, [1991] 2 All ER 939, affirmed on this point by Court of Appeal [1993] Ch 90, [1992] 3 All ER 556, where capacity was lacking. In *Richards v Allan* [2001] WTLR 1031 the testatrix's condition was described as having moments of lucidity interspersed between periods of confusion. She was found to have been confused earlier in the day the will was executed and she was subsequently admitted to hospital having been found in a collapsed state and observed there to be confused. The testatrix was found to lack capacity and knowledge and the will was held to be invalid. *Banks v Goodfellow* and other cases were cited in *McClintock v Calderwood* [2005] EWHC 836 (Ch), [2005] All ER (D) 356 (Apr) where an allegation that the testator lacked testamentary capacity was held not to have been made out. In *Sharp v Adam* [2006] WTLR 1059 the Court of Appeal upheld the decision of the Deputy Judge (Nicholas Strauss QC) ([2005] EWHC 1086 (Ch)) that a testator paralysed by advanced multiple sclerosis was held to lack the capacity to make a will because he was not capable of making a rational judgment. See also *Westendorp v Warwick* [2006] EWHC 915 (Ch); *Re Laxston dec'd* [2006] WTLR 1567; *Turner v Turner* [2007] All ER (D) 238 (May); *Rutland v Rutland* [2007] All ER (D) 326 (Mar); *Blackman v Man* [2008] WTLR 389; *Ledger v Wooton* [2008] WTLR 235; *Re Barker-Benfield, Hansen v Barker-Benfield* [2006] WTLR 1141 and *Scammell v Farmer* [2008] WTLR 1261.

The corresponding paragraph in the seventh edition of *Williams on Wills* was cited in its entirety and applied in *Re Wilkes dec'd, Wilkes v Wilkes* [2006] WTLR 1097; see also the Note to para **[4.9]**. See para **[11.10]** below on the formalities aspect of this case. See also *Brown v Pourau* [1995] 1 NZLR 352 where a number of points relating to capacity are set out, *Banton v Banton* (1998) 164 DLR (4th) 176 (lacked capacity) and *Longmuir v Holland* (2000) 192 DLR (4th) 62 (will invalid on grounds of incapacity).

8 *Banks v Goodfellow* (1870) LR 5 QB 549; *Murfelt v Smith* (1887) 12 PD 116. It had been laid down at one time that a mind unsound on one subject could not be called sound on any subject (*Waring v Waring* (1848) 6 Moo PCC 341) and that proof of such unsoundness of mind on one subject, though quite irrelevant to any testamentary disposition, completely negatived testamentary capacity, but this doctrine has long been not only departed from but definitely overruled.

9 *Boughton v Knight* (1873) LR 3 P & D 64; *Smee v Smee* (1879) 5 PD 84; *Montreal Trust Co v McKay* (1957) 21 WWR 611. This passage of the text was cited with approval by White J in *O'Connell v Shortland* (1989) 51 SASR 337, at 350, 351, where despite the near approach of death and no medical evidence of the testator's capacity at the time, the testator was held to have capacity.

10 *Re Bohrmann's Estate, Caesar and Watmough v Bohrmann* [1938] 1 All ER 27 l. There are two old decisions in which part of a will was admitted to probate: *Billinghurst v Vickers* (1810) 1 Phillim 187; *Wood v Wood* (1811) 1 Phillim 357.

[Amended for provisions of the Mental Health Act 2007 brought into force on 3 November 2008.]

[4.12]

Mental disorder. The law relating to persons suffering from mental disorders is now governed by the Mental Health Act 1983 (MeHA 1983) as heavily amended by the Mental Health Act 2007.[1]

Under the Mental Health Act 2007 there is only one definition of 'mental disorder' meaning any disorder or disability of the mind and the term 'mentally disordered' is to be construed accordingly.[2] Dependence on alcohol or drugs is not considered to be a disorder or disability of the mind for these purposes.[3] A person with a learning disability[4] is not to be considered by reason of that disability to be suffering from mental disorder unless that disability is associated with abnormally aggressive or seriously irresponsible conduct on his part.[5]

The provisions of the Mental Health Acts govern the classification and treatment of persons suffering from mental disorders but, since 1 October 2007, they no longer govern the management of property', which is now subject to the provisions of the Mental Capacity Act 2005.[6]

However, simply because a person is deemed to be suffering from mental disorder within the meaning of the MeHA 1983, or even that he is detained pursuant to the powers contained in the MeHA 1983, does not necessarily mean that he is incompetent to make a will. Each case must, it seems, be considered with reference to the general definitions noted above; and medical and psychiatric evidence will be important.[7]

1 The MeHA 1983 came into force on 30 September 1983 repealing and consolidating the previous legislation, notably the Mental Health Act 1959. MeHA 1983 is substantially amended by Mental Health Act 2007 and the definitions referred to here have been amended by Mental Health Act 2007 with effect from 3 November 2008: Mental Health Act 2007 (Commencement No 7 and Transitional Provisions) Order 2008 (SI 2008/1900).

2 MeHA 1983, s 1(2), which derives from the Mental Health (Amendment) Act 1982, ss 1, 2. This is now amended by Mental Health Act 2007 which replaces the four categories of mental disorder previously identified by MeHA 1983. These were:

'mental disorder' which means mental illness, arrested or incomplete development of mind, psychopathic disorder and any other disorder or disability of mind and 'mentally disordered' shall be construed accordingly;

'severe mental impairment' which means a state of arrested or incomplete development of mind which includes severe impairment of intelligence and social functioning and is associated with abnormally aggressive or seriously irresponsible conduct on the part of the person concerned and 'severely mentally impaired' shall be construed accordingly;

'mental impairment' which means a state of arrested or incomplete development of mind (not amounting to severe mental impairment) which includes significant impairment of intelligence and social functioning and is associated with abnormally aggressive or seriously irresponsible conduct on the part of the person concerned and 'mentally impaired' shall be construed accordingly; and

'psychopathic disorder' which means a persistent disorder or disability of mind (whether or not including significant impairment of intelligence) which results in abnormally aggressive or seriously irresponsible conduct on the part of the person concerned.

3 Mental Health Act 1983, s 1(3).

4 The term 'learning disability' means a state of arrested or incomplete development of the mind which includes significant impairment of intelligence and social functioning: MEHA 1983, s 1(4).

5 It is expressly provided by MeHA 1983, s 1(2A)–(2B), that a person shall not be deemed to be suffering from any form of mental disorder as described above, by reason only of promiscuity or other immoral conduct, sexual deviancy or dependence on alcohol or drugs. Under Mental Health Act 2007 the references to promiscuity, immoral conduct and sexual deviancy have been removed.

6 Mental Capacity Act 2005, ss 16 to 18 came into force on 1 October 2007 (SI 2007/1897) and, from that date, the repeal of MeHA 1983, ss 96 and 97 took effect. See the power to make wills for mentally disordered persons: Mental Capacity Act 2005, ss 16 and 18(1), Sch 2, paras 1–4, paras **[4.21]–[4.23]** below.

7 This passage of the text was cited with approval by White J in *O'Connell v Shortland* (1989) 51 SASR 337.

[A reference to *Blackman v Man* [2008] WTLR 389 has been added to footnote 1.]

[4.17]

Senile decay and illness. Unsoundness of mind may be occasioned by physical infirmity or advancing years as distinguished from mental derangement and the resulting defect of intelligence may be a cause of incapacity, but the intelligence must be reduced to such an extent that the proposed testator does not appreciate the testamentary act in all its bearings.[1] In particular, the instructions for the will may have been given when the testator was of far better understanding than when the will was actually executed, and in these cases the will is generally pronounced for.[2] Where it is shown that the testator was incapable of reading the will and it is not read over to him, it is generally rejected but the criterion in such cases is whether he was really aware of the contents.[3] A will has been found for where the testatrix could only answer the drawer by means of nods and pressure of the hand in answer to questions as to her intentions,[4] but where the testatrix had suffered from delusions, the dispositions being probable and made when her medical attendant stated that she had recovered from her delusions, it was held that the onus of showing capacity had not been discharged.[5] The infirmity of the testator will strengthen certain presumptions which arise against the will in any case, eg where the will is contrary to the previously expressed intentions of the testator as to his testamentary dispositions[6] or where the will is drawn by the propounder and is wholly or largely in his favour.[7] Old age, or the near approach of death at any age, lend strength to suggestions that the testator had no proper knowledge of the contents of the will,[8] or that there was undue influence,[9] or the suspicion arising from the fact that the will is largely in favour of the person drawing or procuring it.[10] A desirable safeguard in such circumstances is for the will to be witnessed by a medical practitioner who satisfies himself as to the capacity and understanding of the testator and makes a record of his examinations and findings.[11] This has been described as the 'golden rule'.[12] although that is not, of itself a touchstone of validity, but only a means of minimising disputes.[13] It has been said that the grand criterion by which to judge whether the mind is injured or destroyed is to ascertain the state of the memory, for without memory the mind cannot act.[14]

1 *Banks v Goodfellow* (1870) LR 5 QB 549 at 566; *Emes v Emes* (1865) 11 Gr 325 (there must be some evidence of mental incapacity); *Re Munn, Hopkins v Warren* [1943] SASR 304; *Re Smith's Estate* [1945] 3 WWR 216; *Re Schwartz* (1970) 10 DLR (3d) 15; on appeal (1971) 20 DLR (3d) 313. In *Tchilingirian v Ouzounian* [2003] EWHC 1220 (Ch) the testatrix was found to be showing signs of confusion and dementia in everyday matters prior to making the challenged wills. It was held that she lacked mental capacity. Further there was even less evidence that she knew and approved the contents of the wills. The corresponding paragraph in the 7th edition of *Williams on Wills* was cited in its entirety and applied in *Re Wilkes dec'd, Wilkes v Wilkes* [2006] WTLR 1097. See also *Blackman v Man* [2008] WTLR 389.

2 *Parker v Felgate* (1883) 8 PD 171; *Perera v Perera* [1901] AC 354; *Thomas v Jones* [1928] P 162; *Re Wallace's Estate, Solicitor of the Duchy of Cornwall v Batten* [1952] 2 TLR 925; *Re Flynn, Flynn v Flynn* [1982] 1 All ER 882, [1982] 1 WLR 310.

3 *Mitchell v Thomas* (1847) 6 Moo PCC 137; *Durnell v Corfield* (1844) 1 Rob Eccl 51. For a case where the will was read over to the testatrix but was not admitted to probate, see *Tyrrell v Painton* [1894] P 151. See also *Fulton v Andrew* (1875) LR 7 HL 448; *Re Martin, MacGregor v Ryan* (1965) 53 DLR (2d) 126. For a case where the will was not read over but admitted to probate, see *Re Wallace's Estate, Solicitor of the Duchy of Cornwall v Batten* [1952] 2 TLR 925.

4 *Re Holtham's Estate, Gillett v Rogers* (1913) 108 LT 732. See also *Re Souch* [1938] 1 DLR 563 (loss of power of speech and writing due to epileptic fit).

5 *Johnson v Blane* (1848) 6 Notes of Cases 442; *Batten Singh v Amirchand* [1948] AC 161, [1948] 1 All ER 152 (testator stating he had no relations when in fact he had nephews); *Re Morrison's Estate* [1953] 3 DLR 274 (changes in dispositions made on advice of solicitor); *Re Nightingale, Green v Nightingale (No 2)* (1974) 119 Sol Jo 189 (testator suffering from cancer made a second will shortly before he died excluding his son, who was the principal beneficiary under the first will, from benefiting. This exclusion was prompted by a belief founded on fanciful evidence that the son was trying to kill him. Held, executors had failed to discharge onus of proof of capacity and first will pronounced for).

6 *Harwood v Baker* (1840) 3 Moo PCC 282.

7 *Reece v Pressey* (1856) 2 Jur NS 380; *Mackenzie v Handasyde* (1829) 2 Hag Ecc 211.

8 *Durnell v Corfield* (1844) 1 Rob Eccl 51.

9 *Ashwell v Lomi* (1850) LR 2 P & D 477.

10 See cases cited in n 3.

11 *Re Simpson, Schaniel v Simpson* (1977) 121 Sol Jo 224; *Kenward v Adams* [1975] CLY 3591, and *Buckenham v Dickinson* [1997] CLY 4733; see para **[4.21]** below.

12 See n 11.

13 *Cattermole v Prisk* [2006] 1 FLR 693.

14 *Murphy v Lamphier* (1914) 20 DLR 906.

[Updated in footnote 1 for *Re Baker, Baker v Baker* [2008] WTLR 565, and in the text and footnote 16 for *Blackman v Man* [2008] WTLR 389.]

[4.20]

Evidence of sound disposing mind. Both oral and documentary evidence is admissible to show that the testator was of sound disposing mind at the relevant time.[1] All statements made by him at the time of making the will or preparatory thereto are admissible to prove that he knew the character of the act he was undertaking.[2] The fact that the will is in his own handwriting is strongly in favour of his capacity.[3] The evidence of an attesting witness, since it must impeach his own act of attestation, is admissible but in general requires corroboration.[4] Evidence of the manner in which the act of making the will was performed is admissible, and also evidence of its accord with natural affection and moral duty, and its conformity to past and subsequent declarations of intention.[5] Evidence of conduct before and after the actual making of the will is admissible,[6] but it carries little weight where there is satisfactory evidence of sound disposing mind at the actual time of making the will,[7] and its importance varies with the nature of the mental disease from which the testator is alleged to be suffering.[8] Generally, evidence of the general habits and course of life is of a greater weight than that of particular acts.[9] It has been doubted whether the fact that unsoundness of mind has existed or exists in the testator's family is admissible.[10] The treatment of the testator by his friends and relations is admissible as for or against them, but not as against third parties, such evidence being admissible to introduce what the testator did with regard to it but not otherwise.[11] General reputation that a person is suffering from unsoundness of mind is not admissible.[12] The evidence of a medical witness who has attended the testator is admissible but such a witness cannot be asked to give his opinion as to the existence of facts which he has not himself observed.[13] The evidence of experts, however, has been held not to outweigh that of eye-witnesses who had opportunities for observation and knowledge of the testatrix[14] but a scientific witness who did not see the testator may be asked his opinion upon the facts proved in evidence[15] but the court should be wary of placing too much reliance on the evidence of medical experts who did not have the opportunity of seeing the deceased.[16]

1 *Wheeler and Batsford v Alderson* (1831) 3 Hag Ecc 574; *Jenkins v Morris* (1880) 14 Ch D 674; *Bannatyne v Bannatyne* (1852) 2 Rob Eccl 472; *Snook v Watts* (1848) 11 Beav 105. Subsequent letters are admissible but of little value: *Bootle v Blundell* (1815) 19 Ves 494. This paragraph of the text was cited with approval by White J in *O'Connell v Shortland* (1989) 51 SASR 337 at 353. The corresponding paragraph in the 7th edition of *Williams on Wills* was cited extensively and applied in *Re Wilkes dec'd, Wilkes v Wilkes* [2006] WTLR 1097. The equivalent paragraph in the eighth edition was approved in *Re Baker, Baker v Baker* [2008] WTLR 565.

2 *Hall v Warren* (1804) 9 Ves 605 at 610; *Levy v Lindo* (1817) 3 Mer 81; *Filmer v Gott* (1774) 4 Bro Parl Cas 230; *Fane v Duke of Devonshire* (1718) 6 Bro Parl Cas 137; *Wheeler and Batsford v Alderson* (1831) 3 Hag Ecc 574; *Butlin v Barry* (1837) 1 Curt 614 at 629; *Durling and Parker v Loveland* (1839) 2 Curt 225.

3 *Cartwright v Cartwright* (1793) 1 Phillim 90 at 100; *Rutherford v Maule* (1832) 4 Hag Ecc 213 at 216; *Clarke v Leare and Scarwell* (1791), cited in 1 Phillim at 119.

4 *Bootle v Blundell* (1815) 19 Ves 494 at 504; *Howard v Braithwaite* (1812) 1 Ves & B 202; *Kinleside v Harrison* (1818) 2 Phillim 449 at 499; *Young v Richards* (1839) 2 Curt 371; *Pennant v Kingscote* (1843) 3 Curt 642.

5 *Wrench v Murray* (1843) 3 Curt 623; *Boughton v Knight* (1873) LR 3 P & D 64; *Arbery v Ashe* (1828) 1 Hag Ecc 214; *Brouncker v Brouncker* (1812) 2 Phillim 57; *Evans v Knight and Moore* (1822) 1 Add 229; *Brydges v King* (1828) 1 Hag Ecc 256. But a change in dispositions may be accounted for: *Williams v Goude* (1828) 1 Hag Ecc 577. In *King v Farley* (1828) 1 Hag Ecc 502, there was a change of dispositions and a subsequent reversion to the former dispositions.

6 *Rodd v Lewis* (1755) 2 Lee 176; *Re Watts' Goods* (1837) 1 Curt 594; *Beavan v M'Donnell* (1854) 10 Exch 184.

7 *Ferguson v Borrett* (1859) 1 F & F 613; *Prinsep and East India Co v Dyce Sombre* (1856) 10 Moo PCC 232.

8 *Mudway v Croft* (1843) 3 Curt 671.

9 *Snook v Watts* (1848) 11 Beav 105; *Smith v Tebbitt* (1867) LR 1 P & D 398; *Boughton v Knight* (1873) LR 3 P & D 64 at 75.

10 *M'Adam v Walker* (1813) 1 Dow 148; *Doe d Mather v Whitefoot* (1838) 8 C & P 270.

11 *Re Windham* (1862) 4 De G F & J 53; *Wright v Doe d Tatham* (1834) 1 Ad & El 3; *Wheeler and Batsford v Alderson* (1831) 3 Hag Ecc 574; *Bannatyne v Bannatyne* (1852) 2 Rob Eccl 472.

12 *Greenslade v Dare* (1855) 20 Beav 284.
13 *Doe d Bainbrigge v Bainbrigge* (1850) 16 LTOS 245; *Martin v Johnston* (1858) 1 F & F 122; *Lovatt v Tribe* (1862) 3 F & F 9 (evidence of medical men who gave certificates on which person confined. Such medical men should give the grounds on which they base their certificates). As to the advisability of having a medical man at hand to hear a person critically ill approve the contents of a will, see *Re Johnson's Estate* [1946] 3 WWR 424.
14 *O'Neil v Royal Trust Co and McClure* [1946] 4 DLR 545; *Boughton v Knight* (1873) LR 3 P&D 64.
15 *Papijans v Gudowski* [1963] Tas SR 183; *Re Schwartz* (1970) 10 DLR (3d) 15; on appeal (1971) 20 DLR (3d) 313.
16 *Blackman v Man* [2008] WTLR 389.

[Revised generally as a result of *Scammell v Farmer* [2008] WTLR 1261 and the light it sheds on previous decisions.]

[4.21]

Solicitor's duty. It has been suggested that a solicitor taking instructions for a will or supervising the execution of a will, has a duty to satisfy himself that the client has testamentary capacity.[1] The extent of such duty as might exist is limited. A duty is owed to the testator to procure a legally effective will in favour of the beneficiaries of the last will but not to beneficiaries taking under an earlier will who suffered a loss (costs) in successfully arguing that the later will was not valid.[2] A solicitor who hesitates because of unfounded doubts about a testator's capacity will breach his duty to the testator and potentially incur liabilities to the intended beneficiaries of the will that is not made as a result.[3]

Where capacity is in doubt it might be useful for the solicitor to record his or her impressions of the testator's state of mind, at the time.[4] It has been suggested that solicitors should follow the 'golden rule' that when a solicitor is drawing up a will for an aged testator or one who has been seriously ill it should be witnessed or approved by a medical practitioner, who ought to record his examination of the testator and his findings.[5] Other precautions were that if there was an earlier will it should be examined and any proposed alterations should be discussed with the testator[6] and solicitors should at least ask the testator open questions such as 'why, what, who or when' to establish that the testator can hear and understand the provisions of a will which was being read aloud.[7] It has also been said that it is desirable that an elderly, infirm testator should be seen by a solicitor who knows him.[8] This so-called 'golden rule' contains prudent guidance for solicitors and does not purport to lay down the law,[9] it only provides guidance as to how disputes may be avoided but is not a touchstone of validity or a substitute for established tests of capacity or knowledge and approval.[10]

1 *Murphy v Lamphier* (1914) 31 OLR 287; affd 32 OLR 19; *Re Carvell Estate* (1977) 21 NBR (2d) 642; *Re Worrell* (1970) 8 DLR (3d) 36.
2 See *Worby v Rosser* [2000] PNLR 140, *Corbett v Bond Pearce* [2001] PNLR 739. Two New Zealand decisions shed further light on the extent of a solicitor's duty in respect of the liability for the unrecovered costs of Probate Claims. These concerned a Mr. Hooker who made a series of wills between 1990 and 1992. In a probate action the last two wills (made in 1992) were held invalid for want of capacity but the last 1991 will was upheld. The costs of the probate action were substantial and both the beneficiary and executor of the 1991 will brought claims against the solicitor who prepared the 1992 wills. In *Knox v Till* [2002] WTLR 1147, the beneficiary under the 1991 will had alleged that the solicitor had a duty to ensure that the testator had testamentary capacity and, thus, to refuse to act for the testator in 1992. The New Zealand Court of Appeal had little difficulty in holding that the solicitor owed no duty of care to the beneficiary of the 1991 will because the overriding duty was to

carry out the testator's instructions and he could not go behind the testator's back to establish capacity; the question of capacity was outside the solicitor's expertise; and there was a conflict between different beneficial interests. In *Public Trustee v Till* [2002] WTLR 1169 the Public Trustee sought to recover the estate's costs of the probate action. This claim also failed, principally because there was nothing in the circumstances when the testator instructed the solicitor that would have alerted a reasonably competent solicitor to the testator's lack of capacity.

3 See, for example, *Ryan v Public Trustee* [2000] 1 NZLR 700.

4 *Maw v Dickey* (1974) 52 DLR (3d) 178 at 190–191; *Ross v Caunters* [1980] Ch 297, [1979] 3 All ER 580; *Whittingham v Crease & Co* (1978) 88 DLR (3d) 353; *Orles and Kruger v R* (1958) 38 Sask LR 38.

5 *Kenward v Adams* [1975] CLY 3591 followed in *Re Simpson* (1977) 121 Sol Jo 224. For a summary of the cases see *Scammell v Farmer* [2008] WTLR 1261 at [117] to [124].

6 *Kenward v Adams* [1975] CLY 3591; *Hoff v Atherton* [2005] WTLR 99 at [49].

7 *Buckenham v Dickenson* [2000] WTLR 1083 (testator very old, partially blind and deaf, held not to have capacity).

8 *Re Belliss, Polson v Parrott* (1929) 141 LT 245 per Lord Merrivale P.

9 *Hoff v Atherton* [2005] WTLR 99 at [49] per Peter Gibson LJ.

10 *Cattermole v Prisk* [2006] 1 FLR 693 at 699. In that case the will of an elderly and infirm testatrix was upheld despite the failure to observe the rule. Contrast *Westendorp v Warwick* [2006] EWHC 915 (Ch), [2006] All ER (D) 248 (Apr).

[This is a new paragraph.]

[4.21A]

Costs in probate disputes. The normal rule (apart from the special position of executors) is that costs should follow the event so that the losing party pays the costs of the winning party.[1] The importance of this general rule cannot be overstated. Unless an unsuccessful party can make out an alternative case he should expect to pay the successful party's costs. There are three exceptions to the general rule as to costs in probate claims. One of these (Defendant's notice to cross-examine only) is expressly acknowledged in the Civil Procedure Rules.[2] The other two are of common law origin. They are:

(a) When the facts reasonably required investigation, the unsuccessful party might sometimes be entitled to his costs out of the estate or be left to bear his own costs but is not ordered to pay another party's costs.[3]

(b) When the deceased or those interested in residue have been the cause of the litigation, the costs of those who unsuccessfully opposed probate may be ordered to be paid out of the estate.[4]

The application of the exceptions is less likely (but not impossible) when coercion ('undue influence') has been alleged unsuccessfully.[5]

1 CPR 44.3(1), (2)(a).

2 At CPR 57.5(5).

3 *Spiers v English* [1907] P 122 at 123 per Sir Gorell Barnes P; *Wylde v Culver* [2006] 1 WLR 2674; *Kostic v Chaplin* [2007] EWHC 2909 (Ch), where the older authorities are thoroughly discussed.

4 *Kostic v Chaplin* [2007] EWHC 2909 (Ch); *Spiers v English* [1907] P 122; *Re Cutcliffe's Estate* [1959] P 6; *Hoff v Atherton* [2005] WTLR 99; *Broughton v Knight* [1873] LR 3 P7 D 64; *Twist v Tye* [1902] P 92.

5 *Spiers v English* [1907] P 122; *Re Cutcliffe's Estate* [1959] P 6; *Re Fuld (No 3)* [1968] P 675.

VII. POWER TO MAKE WILLS FOR MENTALLY DISORDERED PERSONS

[Updated in the text and footnotes 3, 5 and 6 for *Re P* [2009] EWHC 163 (Ch).]

[4.22]

The jurisdiction. The Mental Health Act 1959 (MHA 1959) conferred in s 102 a wide general power on the court with respect to the property and affairs of a mentally disordered person ('a patient') to do all such things as appear necessary or expedient in order to provide maintenance for the patient or his or her family, or otherwise for administering the patient's affairs. Without prejudice to this general provision s 103(1) conferred specific powers to manage and deal with the patient's property in the patient's name; and to make settlements and gifts of the patient's property.[1] However, the MHA 1959 did not confer the power to make a will for the patient a deficiency which was remedied by the Administration of Justice Act 1969, s 17, which added a new provision, as paragraph (dd), to this effect to the MHA 1959, s 103(1). This new power was considered in a number of reported decisions[2] and guidelines relating to the law and practice were laid down by Vice-Chancellor Megarry in *Re D(J)*.[3] The MHA 1959 was repealed and the legislation consolidated in the Mental Health Act 1983, the relevant parts of which are themselves repealed by the Mental Capacity Act 2005 with effect from 1 October 2007 and the jurisdiction is now to be found in the Mental Capacity Act 2005, ss 16, 18(1) and Sch 2, paras 1–4.[4] The former practice as laid down in *Re D(J)* was reconsidered by Lewison J in *Re P*[5] in the light of the Mental Capacity Act 2005 and it is clear that a new regime[6] is in place.

Under the Mental Capacity Act 2005, if a person (referred to as 'P') lacks capacity in relation to a matter or matters concerning P's property and affairs,[7] the court may, by making an order, make the decision or decisions on P's behalf in relation to the matter or matters.[8] The powers as respects P's property and affairs extend in particular to the execution for P of a will[9] although no will may be made under subsection (1)(i) at a time when P has not reached 18.[10] The jurisdiction can only be exercised where the judge has reason to believe that the patient is incapable of making a valid will for himself.[11] It will be appreciated that it is possible for a person subject to the Court of Protection to have capacity to make a personal will and in such cases that should be done subject to guidance and advice.

The will may make any provision (whether by disposing of property or exercising a power or otherwise) which could be made by a will executed by P if he had capacity to make it.[12]

The details relating to the formalities governing the exercise of this jurisdiction are to be found now in the Mental Capacity Act 2005 Sch 2.[13] This provides that the will must state that it is signed by P acting by the authorised person, should be signed by the authorised person with the name of P and with his own name, in the presence of two or more witnesses present at the same time, and these witnesses attest and subscribe in the usual way and the will is then authenticated with the official seal of the Court of Protection.[14] Where these formalities are complied with then it is provided that the will shall have the same effect for all purposes as if the patient were capable of making a valid will and the will had been executed by him in the manner required by the Wills Act 1837 (WA 1837).[15]

However, this does not apply to the will in so far as it disposes of immovable property outside England and Wales, or in so far as it relates to any other property or matter if, when the will is executed P is domiciled outside England and Wales, and, under the law of P's domicile, any question of his testamentary capacity would fall to be determined in accordance with the law of a place outside England and Wales.[16].

With the exception, of course, of s 9, the WA 1837 applies to such wills.[17] The will so made, often referred to as a 'statutory will' (although judicial will would seem more apt) becomes the patient's will for all purposes and thus precludes the Court of Protection from jurisdiction to make a different distribution.[18]

1 It was this power to make settlements for the patient which was invoked in *Re L(WJG)* [1966] Ch 135, [1965] 3 All ER 865, to provide, in effect, a substitute for a will; an inter vivos settlement was ordered by the court on behalf of a 68-year-old bachelor patient, who would otherwise have died intestate with assets of over £130,000.
2 See *Re HMF* [1976] Ch 33, [1975] 2 All ER 795, and *Re Davey* [1980] 3 All ER 342, [1981] 1 WLR 164.
3 [1982] Ch 237, [1982] 2 All ER 37. In *Re R (Execution of Statutory Will)* [2003] WTLR 1051 Ferris J emphasised that, in exercising its powers under MHA 1983, the Court of Protection should be satisfied that such decisions reflected the intention of the patient. In that case a statutory will made on the application of a nephew whereby he was given a substantial legacy to the disadvantage of his brother, was set aside on appeal. Following *Re P* [2009] EWHC 163 (Ch), that approach is no longer justified.
4 Mental Capacity Act 2007 came into force on 1 October 2007: SI 2007/1897.
5 [2009] EWHC 163 (Ch), [2009] All ER (D) 160 (Feb).
6 See para **[4.23]** below.
7 Section 16(1)(b) of the Mental Capacity Act 2005.
8 Mental Capacity Act 2005, s 16(2)(a).
9 Mental Capacity Act 2005, s 18(1)(i).
10 Mental Capacity Act 2005, s 18(1)(ii).
11 Thus in many cases the court will require a report from one of the Lord Chancellor's visitors as to this and such further medical evidence as the Master may direct; *Practice Direction* [1983] 3 All ER 255.
12 Mental Capacity Act 2005, Sch 2, para 2.
13 Mental Capacity Act 2005, Sch 2, para 4.
14 Mental Capacity Act 2005, Sch 2, para 4(1).
15 Mental Capacity Act 2005, Sch 2, para 4(3).
16 Mental Capacity Act 2005, Sch 2, para 4(4)–(5)
17 Mental Capacity Act 2005, Sch 2, para 4.
18 This can be achieved by revoking the statutory will and making a new will in its place–which is impossible if (as in *Re Davey* [1980] 3 All ER 342, [1981] 1 WLR 164; see Fox J at 349) the patient were then dead since it is not possible to make a will for, or to revoke the will of, a deceased person.

[Updated in the text and footnotes 5 to 9 for *Re P* [2009] EWHC 163 (Ch), [2009] All ER (D) 160 (Feb) and MCA 2005.]

[4.23]

Guidelines governing the exercise of the jurisdiction. Under MeHA 1983 all statutory will applications were decided in accordance with the guidance laid down by the Vice-Chancellor in *Re D(J)*.[1] The continuity of these guidelines assisted not only the masters concerned with making the order but more importantly the patient's relatives and their legal advisers in formulating a set of agreed proposals that could form the basis of the application. The crucial consideration under the approach adopted in *Re D(J)* was that the court would regard the disposition of the estate subjectively from the patient's point of view and would, so to speak sit in his armchair and make for him a will that he or she was likely to have made.[2] This meant that it was to be assumed that the patient was having a brief lucid interval at the time when the will is made and that, during the lucid interval the patient had a full knowledge of the past and a full realisation that as soon as the will was executed he or she would relapse into the actual mental state that previously existed with the prognosis as it actually was. These two propositions although recognised to be somewhat curious assumptions were consistent with the accepted practice regarding making of settlements for the patient under MeHA 1983.[3] The court would assume, thirdly, that during the hypothetical lucid interval the patient was to be envisaged as being advised by a competent solicitor. Finally, the patient was assumed to take a fairly broad view of any claims upon his bounty and the court would not be concerned with examinations analogous to a profit and loss account. Although, recognised by the Vice-Chancellor not to be either exhaustive or precise these principles for factors did provide useful guidance on the judicial attitude to the power vested in them.[4]

Under the Mental Capacity Act 2005 the counter-factual assumptions concerning a brief lucid interval with complete knowledge of the past and the substituted judgment of the court are not part of the test which requires the court to act in the best interests of the patient.[5] The Mental Capacity Act 2005 does not require the counter-factual assumption that P is not mentally disordered. The facts must be taken as they are. It is not therefore necessary to go through the mental gymnastics of imagining that P has a brief lucid interval and then relapses into his former state. The goal of the enquiry is not what P 'might be expected' to have done; but what is in P's best interests. This is more akin to the 'balance sheet' approach than to the 'substituted judgment' approach. The code of practice[6] makes this clear in that it points out that the test of best interests was one that was worked out by the courts mainly in decisions relating to the provision of medical care. The previous guidance was concerned with deciding what P would have wanted if he were not mentally disordered. But the Mental Capacity Act 2005 requires the decision maker to consider P's present wishes and feelings, which ex hypothesi are wishes and feelings entertained by a person who lacks mental capacity in relation to the decision being made on his behalf. The same structured decision making process applies to all decisions to be made on P's behalf, whether great or small, whereas the previous guidance was specific to the making of a will, gift or settlement. Moreover, it is a decision making process which must be followed, not only by the court, but by anyone who takes decisions on P's behalf. In making his decision the decision maker must consider 'all relevant circumstances'. The Act expressly directs the decision maker to take a number of steps before reaching a decision. These include encouraging P to participate in the decision. He must also 'consider' P's past and present wishes, and his beliefs and values and must 'take into account' the views of third parties as to what would be in P's best interests.[7] In reaching a decision a third party decision maker will, if appropriate, take legal or other advice. The other advice may be medical, financial, or advice of any other kind. The court will, of course, act according to the law, and be assumed to have sufficient knowledge of the law (either before or after assistance from advocates) to make whatever decision it is called upon to make. But there is, no need (as envisaged by *Re D(J)*) to assume (a) that P has taken legal advice (which he has not) and then (b) to attempt to decide what P would have done with that advice if he had had capacity (which he does not). If P's wishes have been formed without having taken legal advice in circumstances where a person with capacity would have taken legal advice, that may be a reason for giving them less weight than might otherwise have been the case.[8] Furthermore, in deciding what provision should be made in a will to be executed on P's behalf and which, ex hypothesi, will only have effect after he is dead, the court is entitled to take into account, in assessing what is in P's best interests, how he will be remembered after his death.[9]

1 [1982] Ch 237, [1982] 2 All ER 37. Although expressed with reference to the jurisdiction in the MHA 1959 the comments are equally applicable to the consolidating MeHA 1983.
2 See Sir Robert Megarry, VC, [1982] Ch 237, [1982] 2 All ER 37 at 43; disagreeing with the previous remarks of Fox J in *Re Davey* [1980] 3 All ER 342 at 348, [1981] 1 WLR 164. It should be noted that the making of a statutory will by the court does not preclude an application under the Inheritance (Provision for Family and Dependants) Act 1975 (I(PFD)A 1975) and as Fox J emphasised in *Re Davey*, any objective unfairness can be remedied by an application under that Act. However, on the other hand it is not helpful for the court to make a totally unreasonable will consistent perhaps with the arbitrary prejudices of the patient when sane, if that will inevitably gives rise to an immediate application under the I(PFD)A 1975 on the death. It is inevitable perhaps that the court will try to effect … the will which the actual patient, *acting reasonably*, would have made …' per Sir Robert Megarry VC, [1982] Ch 237, [1982] 2 All ER 37 at 43.
3 See Cross J in *Re WJGL* [1965] 3 All ER 865 at 871–872.
4 Sir Robert Megarry VC, [1982] Ch 237, [1982] 2 All ER 37 at p 43.
5 MCA 2005, s 1(5).
6 At paragraph 5.1.
7 *Re P* [2009] EWHC 163 (Ch), [2009] All ER (D) 160 (Feb) at [38] per Lewison J.
8 [2009] EWHC 163 (Ch) at [43].
9 [2009] EWHC 163 (Ch) at [44].

[Updated in the text and footnote 1 for *Re P* [2009] EWHC 163 (Ch), [2009] All ER (D) 160 (Feb).]

[4.24]

Illustrations of the exercise of the jurisdiction. Aside from *Re P*,[1] the power has been invoked to remedy an injustice caused by effect of ademption on a specific devise[2] or an emergency or salvage jurisdiction to avoid an undesirable intestacy.[3] The court has exercised the jurisdiction to make a will for a person who had been mentally disabled since birth and who had inherited a substantial estate. The will made provision for such persons and purposes for whom/which the patient might have been expected to provide if she had not been mentally disordered on the assumption that she would have been a normal decent person who would have acted in accordance with contemporary standards of morality.[4]

1 *Re P* [2009] EWHC 163 (Ch), [2009] All ER (D) 160 (Feb).
2 See *Re D(J)* [1982] Ch 237, [1982] 2 All ER 37 which was concerned with an elderly woman patient whose mental condition had deteriorated to such an extent that her affairs were made subject to the control of the Court of Protection. Whilst of full capacity the patient had devised the house in which she lived to one of her daughters and the residue of her estate to her five children in equal shares. Subsequently, the patient moved in with the daughter and remained with her, selling her own house and thus adeeming the devise. The

patient purchased a new house near to her daughter but never lived in that house but remained with her daughter and her husband. The daughter (and another daughter who had been appointed to be patient's receiver) applied to the Court of Protection under the MHA 1959, s 103(1)(dd) for the execution of a codicil to the original will specifically devising the new house to the daughter in place of the adeemed legacy of the old house and contents. The patient's new house was then sold for £22,000 and her estate was likely to be valued at about £50,000. The daughter was, no doubt, now looking for a legacy equal to the sale price of the house but the deputy master was less generous, ordering the execution of a will giving her a legacy of £10,000 with an equal share with the other children in the residue. The daughter appealed to the Vice-Chancellor, who decided that he did have a power of review, and ordered a new will which increased the legacy to £15,000.

3 A striking illustration is provided by *Re Davey* [1980] 3 All ER 342, [1981] 1 WLR 164, where a 92-year-old woman described as suffering from senile mental deterioration to a degree which rendered her incapable of properly managing her affairs, went through a ceremony of marriage with a much younger male employee of the nursing home in which she resided. That marriage, though voidable, had the effect of revoking an earlier will which the woman had made in favour of her two nephews who were her nearest relatives (see *Re Roberts, Roberts v Roberts* [1978] 3 All ER 225, [1978] 1 WLR 653, CA and Chapter 17). Her affairs were made subject to the Court of Protection and the Official Solicitor applied to the court for an order for the execution under the MHA 1959, s 103(1)(dd) of a will for the woman in the same terms as the earlier will that had been revoked by the marriage. The matter was regarded as one of great urgency (which, in fact, proved to be the case since the woman died six days later) and the will was made by the deputy master without notice being given to the other party to the marriage or to the beneficiaries under the earlier will. The court (Fox J) decided that, in the circumstances, this was an acceptable procedure since although normally notice should be given to parties adversely affected by the exercise of the jurisdiction, the urgency of the matter precluded that course in this case. The judge thought that any delay might result in an undesirable intestacy and that any unfairness to the other party to the marriage could be remedied by an application by him to the court, during the patient's lifetime, for a new statutory will, or, after her death, for provision out of her estate under the Inheritance (Provision for Family and Dependants) Act 1975. See also the Administration of Justice Act 1982, s 49 which facilitates the presentation of petitions for matrimonial relief on behalf of the patient and thus might provide an alternative, although more protracted, solution to cases like *Re Davey* [1980] 3 All ER 342, [1981] 1 WLR 164.

4 *Re C (a patient)* [1991] 3 All ER 866. On that basis it was thought that the patient would have felt a moral obligation to show recognition to the community and to her family since she had spent the whole of her life in the care of the community, as embodied in the national health service, the hospital and voluntary mental health charities, and had derived her fortune from being a child of a family. *Inter vivos* gifts of £100,000 to charity and £400,000 to her family were made, with a will drawn leaving her estate equally between charity and the family. The difficulty in such a case where the patient has been disabled since birth is that there is no subjective indication of her wishes. See also *Re S* [1997] 1 FLR 96 where inter vivos dispositions under the MeHA 1983, s 95, and a statutory will under the MeHA 1983, s 103, were made for a mental patient. See also *Re R (Execution of Statutory Will)* [2003] WTLR 1051.

CHAPTER 5

Knowledge and approval

I. KNOWLEDGE AND APPROVAL

[Updated in footnote 1 for *Re Baker, Baker v Baker* [2008] WTLR 565 and in footnote 2 for *Boudh v Boudh* [2008] WTLR 411.]

[5.1]

Knowledge and approval. Before a paper is entitled to probate[1] the court must be satisfied that the testator knew and approved of the contents at the time he signed it.[2] It has been said[3] that this rule is evidential rather than substantive and that in the ordinary case proof of testamentary capacity and due execution suffices to establish knowledge and approval,[4] but that in certain circumstances the court requires further affirmative evidence.[5] It was at one time thought that the fact that the will had been duly read over to a capable testator on the occasion of its execution, or that its contents had been brought to his notice in any other way, should when coupled with his execution thereof, be held conclusive evidence that he approved as well as knew the contents thereof.[6] However, the better view now seems to be that such a circumstance raises but a prima facie presumption of knowledge and approval.[7] In *Fuller v Strum*[8] the proposition that a testator can have knowledge and approval of part of his will but not of another part was affirmed. An obvious example would be where a person preparing a will for another fraudulently included wording in the will which was contrary to the testator's instructions but which were not noticed by the testator when the will was executed. The court has always had power to omit words from a will which were inserted per incuriam, quite apart from the more recently conferred jurisdiction to rectify wills under s 20 of AJA 1982.[9]

In some cases where the testator employs an expert draftsman to provide the appropriate wording to give effect in law to the testator's intentions, the testator has to accept the phraseology selected by the draftsman without himself really understanding its esoteric meaning and in such a case he adopts it and knowledge and approval is imputed to him.[10] This principle is carried further by the so-called rule in *Parker v Felgate*[11] to the effect that a will which has been prepared in accordance with previous instructions given when the testator fully understands the contents and effect thereof is valid, notwithstanding that at the time of execution the testator does not in fact have that understanding.[12]

1 The paragraph in the 7th edition of *Williams on Wills* corresponding with para **[5.1]** of the current edition was cited in its entirety and applied in *Re Wilkes dec'd, Wilkes v Wilkes* [2006] WTLR 1097. The equivalent paragraph in the eighth edition was approved in *Re Baker, Baker v Baker* [2008] WTLR 565.

2 *Guardhouse v Blackburn* (1866) LR 1 P & D 109 at 116; *Barry v Butlin* (1838) 2 Moo PCC 480; *Wintle v Nye* [1959] 1 All ER 552, [1959] 1 WLR 284; *Re Morris, Lloyds Bank Ltd v Peake* [1971] P 62, [1970] 1 All ER 1057; *Boudh v Boudh* [2008] WTLR 411.

3 *Re Fuld's Estate (No 3), Hartley v Fuld* [1968] P 675 at 697, [1965] 3 All ER 776 at 781.

4 As to the presumption of the execution see Chapter 13.

5 *Barry v Butlin* (1838) 2 Moo PCC 480, at 490; *Re Ireland* (1963) 147 DLR (3d) 480 at 482. Where a major beneficiary gave instructions to a solicitor to draft a will for an elderly aunt with failing eyesight it was held that a suspicion was raised which had to be removed before the will could be admitted to probate: *Re Hall* (1988) 50 DLR (4th) 51. *Tyrrell v Painton* [1894] P 151, CA; *Fulton v Andrew* (1875) LR 7 HL 448 and *Barry v Butlin* (1838) 2 Moo PCC 480 referred to.

6 Per Lord Penzance in *Guardhouse v Blackburn* (1866) LR 1 P & D 109; *Atter v Atkinson* (1869) LR 1 P & D 665; *Harter v Harter* (1873) LR 3 P & D 11 at 22.

7 *Re Morris, Lloyds Bank Ltd v Peake* [1971] P 62, [1970] 1 All ER 1057, tracing the progressive erosion of the rule; *Fulton v Andrew* (1875) LR 7 HL 448 at 449, 460, 461, 469; *Martell v Consett Iron Co Ltd* [1955] Ch 363 at 414, [1955] 1 All ER 481 at 498; *Gregson v Taylor* [1917] P 256 at 261; *Crerar v Crerar* (1956) unreported, see 106 Law Journal 694. See also *Re Ticehurst, Midland Bank Executor and Trustee Co v Hankinson* (1973) Times, 6 March; *Re Schwartz* (1971) 20 DLR (3d) 313 (change of solicitor not a suspicious circumstance that could lead to inference that the testator might not have known and approved of the contents of the will); and *Re Fenwick* [1972] VR 646.

8 [2001] EWCA Civ 1879, [2002] 2 All ER 87. See also *Lau Hau Chu v Ip Kam* [2006] HKLR 100.

9 *Re Morris, Lloyds Bank Ltd v Peake* [1971] P 62, [1970] 1 All ER 1057. There are few case law authorities where part of a will was pronounced for and part against but two such cases are *Re Austin's Estate* (1929) 73 Sol Jo 545 and *Fulton v Andrew* (1875) LR 7 HL 448 (*Fuller v Strum* also contains some helpful statements on the evidence needed to prove knowledge and approval).

10 *Rhodes v Rhodes* (1882) 7 App Cas 192 at 199, 200; *Re Morris, Lloyds Bank Ltd v Peake* [1971] P 62, [1970] 1 All ER 1057 at 79 and 1066 (respectively). But see *Re Ticehurst, Midland Bank Executor and Trustee Co v Hankinson* (1973) Times, 6 March.

11 (1883) 8 PD 171.

12 See also, *Perera v Perera* [1901] AC 354; *Thomas v Jones* [1928] P 162; *Re Wallaces' Estate, Solicitor of the Duchy of Cornwall v Batten* [1952] 2 TLR 925; *Re Flynn, Flynn v Flynn* [1982] 1 All ER 882 at 890, 891.

[Updated in footnote 3 for *Re Bates, Bates v Wheildon* [2008] WTLR 1705 and *Blackman v Man* [2008] WTLR 389.]

[5.2]

When evidence required. The cases referred to above, when affirmative evidence of knowledge and approval of the contents of a will will be required include the following: testators who are deaf and dumb,[1] or blind,[2] and when the person who prepared the will received a benefit under the will.[3]

1 The question is a matter of fact in each case, see *Dickenson v Blisset* (1754) 1 Dick 268; *Re Harper* (1843) 6 Man & G 732; *Re Owston's Goods* (1862) 2 Sw & Tr 461; *Re Geale's Goods* (1864) 3 Sw & Tr 431; *Re Biddulph's Trusts, Re Poole's Trusts* (1852) 5 De G & Sm 469; *Re Souch* [1938] 1 DLR 563; *Re Sellwood's Estates, Heynes v Sellwood* (1964) 108 Sol Jo 523. The paragraph in the 7th edition of *Williams on Wills* corresponding with para **[5.2]** of the current edition, was cited in its entirety and applied in *Re Wilkes dec'd, Wilkes v Wilkes* [2006] WTLR 1097.

2 To establish the will of a testator wholly blind, or so nearly as to be incapable of discerning writing, it must be shown to the satisfaction of the court that the will was read over to him in the presence of the witnesses or that he was otherwise acquainted with its contents: *Fincham v Edwards* (1842) 3 Curt 63; affd 4 Moo PCC 198; *Re Axford* (1860) 1 Sw & Tr 540; *Re Sellwood* (1964) 108 Sol Jo 523. See also *Re Hall* (1988) 50 DLR (4th) 51.

3 *Barry v Butlin* (1838) 2 Moo PCC 480; *Fulton v Andrew* (1875) LR 7 HL 448; *Wintle v Nye* [1959] 1 All ER 552; *Re Stott, Klouda v Lloyds Bank Ltd* [1980] 1 All ER 259; See also *Tchilingirian v Ouzounian* [2003] EWHC 1220 (Ch) applying *Fulton v Andrew* (1875) LR 7

HL 448 and *Re Loxton dec'd* [2006] WTLR 1567. Suspicion was not aroused in *Re Bates, Bates v Wheildon* [2008] WTLR 1705 or in *Blackman v Man* [2008] WTLR 389.

[Updated in footnote 1 for *Re Baker, Baker v Baker* [2008] WTLR 565, in footnote 4 for *Re Bates, Bates v Wheildon* [2008] WTLR 1705 and *Blackman v Man* [2008] WTLR 389, and in footnote 5 for *Boudh v Boudh* [2008] WTLR 411.]

[5.3]

The evidence in support of the plea. The Court of appeal in *Fuller v Strum*[1] set out the law relating to proof of knowledge and approval of the contents of a will. First, the *onus probandi* lies in every case upon the party propounding a will and he must satisfy the Court that the instrument so propounded is the last will of a free and capable testator; *Barry v Butlin*.[2] Second, proof of testamentary capacity of the deceased and the due execution of the will, without more, will give rise to a proper inference of knowledge and approval; *Fuller v Strum*.[3] Third, where the circumstances are such as to arouse the suspicion of the court the propounder must prove affirmatively that knowledge and approval so as to satisfy the court that the will represents the wishes of the deceased; *Fuller v Strum*[4] and *Wintle v Nye*.[5] Fourth, the standard of proof required in relation to knowledge and approval in a probate case is the civil standard – that is, the court must be satisfied, on a balance of probability, that the contents of the will do truly represent the testator's intentions; *Fuller v Strum*.[6] It is possible for the court to infer knowledge and approval from the circumstances. The extent of the evidential burden depends on how grave a suspicion is aroused by the circumstances in which the will was made.

It has been said that where a question is raised concerning knowledge and approval of the contents of a will the circumstances which are held to excite the suspicions of the court must be circumstances attending or at least relevant to, the preparation and execution of the will itself,[7] but it is accepted that the allegations could also be relevant to the testamentary capacity of the deceased or to a plea of undue influence.[8] It is open to a party alleging want of knowledge and approval to cross-examine the person propounding the will on matters which may result in establishing fraud or undue influence on the part of such person, even though fraud or undue influence are not pleaded.[9] Further there is authority to the effect that the failure or deliberate omission of a party, who had raised a plea of want of knowledge and approval in a probate action, also to plead undue influence, does not preclude such a party from introducing in support of his plea matters of fact which would also, at least in a broad sense, be relevant in support of a plea of undue influence.[10] However the defence of want of knowledge and approval is not to be used 'as a screen behind which one man is to be at liberty to charge another with fraud or dishonesty without assuming the responsibility for that charge in plain terms'.[11]

1 [2001] EWCA Civ 1879, [2002] 2 All ER 87, [2002] 1 WLR 1097, where the Court of Appeal upheld the validity of the whole will albeit that it was somewhat eccentric and home made. *Fuller v Strum* was referred to in *Re Good (decd), Carapeto v Good; Brennan v Good* [2002] EWHC 640 (Ch), where it was held that the burden of proof that the testatrix knew and approved the contents of her will had been discharged. The testatrix was described as a highly intelligent woman who had received legal advice prior to the execution of her will and there was no evidence that she had been coerced into making her will. *Fuller v Strum* was also referred to in *Shuck v Loveridge* [2005] EWHC 72 (allegation of want of

knowledge and approval not made out). See also *Hoff v Atherton* [2004] EWCA Civ 1554, [2005] WTLR 99, CA, *Reynolds v Reynolds* [2005] EWHC 6 (Ch), *In the Estate of Sherrington Deceased, Sherrington v Sherrington* [2005] EWCA Civ 326, [2005] WTLR 587, CA.; *Re Johnson's Estate* [2006] All ER (D) (Oct) 146. and *Franks v Sinclair* [2006] EWHC 3365 (Ch). *Fuller v Strum* was applied in *Re Rowinska dec'd, Wyniczenko v Plucinska-Surowka* [2006] WTLR 487 in which the Deputy Judge (Judge Behrens) rejected, on the balance of probability, an allegation of forgery even though there was a real possibility that the will was forged, but held in the light of the suspicious circumstances surrounding the will that the propounder had not shown that the testatrix had known and approved its contents. The equivalent paragraph in the eighth edition was approved in *Re Baker, Baker v Baker* [2008] WTLR 565.

2 (1838) 2 Moo PCC 480, at pp 482–483.

3 [2001] EWCA Civ 1879, [2002] 2 All ER 87, [2002] 1 WLR 1097.

4 Ibid, see Peter Gibson LJ at p 1107; p 96. Suspicion was not aroused in *Re Bates, Bates v Wheildon* [2008] WTLR 1705 or in *Blackman v Man* [2008] WTLR 389.

5 [1959] 1 All ER 552, [1959] 1 WLR 284. See also *Boudh v Boudh* [2008] WTLR 411 where the suspicion was not removed.

6 *Fuller v Strum*, per Chadwick LJ, at p 1120; p 109.

7 Per Willmer J in *Re R* [1951] P 10, [1950] 2 All ER 117 where allegations irrelevant to the plea of want of knowledge and approval were struck out.

8 Per Willmer J in *Re R* [1951] P 10, [1950] 2 All ER 117; see Slade J in *Re Stott, Klouda v Lloyds Bank Ltd* [1980] 1 All ER 259 at 262.

9 See Lord Simonds in *Wintle v Nye* [1959] 1 All ER 552 at 560; Slade J in *Re Stott, Klouda v Lloyds Bank Ltd* [1980] 1 All ER 259 at 264.

10 Scarman J in *Re Fuld's Estate, Hartley v Fuld (No 3)* [1965] 3 All ER 776 at 783. Thus in *Re Stott, Klouda v Lloyds Bank Ltd* [1980] 1 All ER 259, there was an attempt to strike out many of the allegations pleaded in support of a defence of want of knowledge and approval as contravening RSC Ord 76, r 9(3) in that the allegations would also be relevant in support of a plea of undue influence which the defendant had not pleaded. The attempt failed because the judge thought that there will often be an inevitable overlap between evidence in support of want of knowledge and approval and evidence in support of undue influence.

11 Willmer J in *Re R* [1950] 2 All ER 117 at 123. The risk as to costs of a party opposing a will is reduced if he puts his opponent to proof of knowledge and approval instead of making positive allegations of fraud or undue influence which he himself has the burden of proving.

CHAPTER 6

Rectification

[Updated in the text and footnotes 3 and 4 for *Pengelly v Pengelly* [2008] Ch 375.]

[6.2]
Clerical errors. The Administration of Justice Act 1982, s 20[1] provides as follows:

> 'If a court is satisfied that a will is so expressed that it fails to carry out the testator's intentions, in consequence—
>
> (a) of a clerical error … it may order that the will shall be rectified so as to carry out his intentions.'

It has been stated that the term 'clerical error' means an inadvertent error made in the process of recording the intended words of the testator in drafting or in the transcription of his will. Thus where a solicitor failed to include a clause in a later will which was intended to mirror a clause in an earlier will which it replaced, it was held to be an error made in the process of recording the intended words of the testatrix. The will was rectified to include the omitted clause.[2] The introduction of a clause which is inconsistent with the testator's instructions in circumstances in which the draftsman has not applied his mind to its significance or effect is also a 'clerical error' for the purposes of this provision[3] but the introduction of words to which the draftsman has applied his mind with a proper understanding of his instruction but which (perhaps through failure properly to understand the law) do not achieve the objective which he and the testator intended is not.[4]

This provision seems apt to cover cases such as *Re Morris*,[5] where it will be recalled the codicil as written revoked 'clause 7 of the will' whereas the admitted intention had been to revoke 'clause 7(iv) of the will'. The omission of the Roman numeral (iv) was accepted on all sides as a clerical error, and such a case would now be simply resolved by the addition of the missing number, or words as the case might be. In many of these cases the error will be that of the draftsman, typist or amanuensis but the section is not so limited.[6]

1 See Vol 2, Part G, para **[244.98]**.

2 *Wordingham v Royal Exchange Trust Co Ltd* [1992] Ch 412, [1992] 3 All ER 204. In *Wu Man Shan v Registrar of Probate* [2006] 2 HKC 106 a will was rectified under corresponding Hong Kong legislation where the mistake was regarded as clerical and trivial.

3 *Re Segelman* [1996] Ch 171, [1995] 3 All ER 676 at 686 (in which the offending clause was deleted). An order for rectification was granted in *Wong v Wong,* sub nom *Re Munday (dec'd)* [2003] WTLR 1161, to correct an obvious clerical error. Rectification was ordered in *Re Vautier's Estate* (2000–01) 3 ITELR 566 to give effect to the testator's intention in the circumstances described in the note to para **[5.7]** above. See also *Bush v Jouliac* [2006]

EWHC 363 (Ch) (failure to omit WA 1837, s 33); *Hobart v Hobart* [2007] WTLR 1213; *Re Craig (decd), Price v Craig* [2006] EWHC 2561 (Ch); *Clarke v Brothwood* [2007] WTLR 329 and *Pengelly v Pengelly* [2008] Ch 375, in all of which cases, a will was rectified to correct a clerical error.

4 *Re Segelman* [1996] Ch 171 at 184–185; *Pengelly v Pengelly* [2008] Ch 375 at [23]–[24].

5 [1971] P 62, [1970] 1 All ER 1057.

6 The Law Reform Committee 19th Report on the Interpretation of Wills (1973, cmnd 5301), para 19, saw no difference in principle between a slip made by the testator himself, his solicitor or the typist: and there is nothing in the wording in s 20 to introduce such a distinction. This view has been confirmed, obiter, by Nicholls J in *Re Williams, Wiles v Madgin* [1985] 1 All ER 964 at 969.

[Updated in footnote 4 for *Sprackling v Sprackling* [2008] All ER (D) 55 (Nov).]

[6.3]

Failure to understand the testator's instructions. The second situation where the AJA 1982, s 20(1)[1] introduces a power of rectification is as follows:

> 'If a court is satisfied that a will is so expressed that it fails to carry out the testator's intentions, in consequence—
>
> (a) …
>
> (b) of a failure to understand his instructions,
>
> it may order that the will shall be rectified so as to carry out his intentions.'

It will be noticed that this provision is confined to cases where a draftsman fails to understand instructions and thus has a limited scope. The section does not cover the more common type of mistake, i e cases where the testator (and possibly his solicitor as well) fails to understand the legal effect of the words actually used, and thus produces the wrong result although using the intended expression; where in effect, all concerned may know what the testator wants but fail to use the right technique to achieve it.[2]

But where it can be established first, that the will fails to embody the testator's instructions, and secondly, what those instructions were, then it is now open to the court to rectify the will so as to make it embody them.[3] An example of such a case is where for instance, the testator has instructed his solicitor to draw his will in such a way as to leave certain property to X; the solicitor failing to understand what is wanted draws the will in such a way as to leave the property to Y, and the testator, not appreciating the mistake executes the will. Such a will could be rectified under the power in section 20.

It is apparent from the wording, '… a failure to understand his instructions …', that the power of rectification in this second context is available only where there has been the intervention of another person. This will typically be where the testator has instructed another to draft his will, whether that person be a solicitor or a lay person, or where the testator dictates his will to an amanuensis. Thus this power would not be available in the much more common cases where mistakes occur, where a lay testator writes out his whole will using inappropriate or unsatisfactory language.

Further in order for the remedy to be available it must be established not only that the will fails to carry out the testator's instructions but also what those instructions were.[4] This will be a matter of proof and there is no guidance in the section as to the admissibility of the evidence in support. Section 21, which provides for the admissibility of extrinsic evidence as an aid in a will's interpretation, does not assist here, but clearly extrinsic evidence must be admitted to aid rectification since by definition the instructions for a will are not to be found within the will.[5]

1 See Vol 2, Part G, para **[244.96]**.

2 Rectification in such circumstances is sometimes possible in relation to eg settlements: see *Re Butlin's Settlement Trusts, Butlin v Butlin* [1976] Ch 251, [1976] 2 All ER 483. But the Law Reform Committee did not think the power of rectification appropriate to wills in such cases, op cit, para 20.

3 Law Reform Committee, 19th Report on the Interpretation of Wills (1973, cmnd 5301), para 21.

4 See *Walker v Geo H Medlicott & Son (a firm)* [1999] 1 All ER 685 where the plaintiff failed to prove by convincing evidence that the testatrix had instructed the solicitor defendants to include in her will a gift of a house to the plaintiff as alleged. But an application failed in *In the Estate of Grattan (Robin Francis), Grattan v McNaughton* [2001] WTLR 1305 because the evidence was insufficient to show that the testator's will had failed to carry out his instructions; *Walker v Geo H Medlicott & Son* [1999] 1 WLR 727 applied. See also *Goodman v Goodman* [2006] EWHC 1757 (Ch), [2006] WTLR 1807 and *Sprackling v Sprackling* [2008] All ER (D) 55 (Nov), in both of which rectification was ordered on the ground of failure to understand the testator's instructions, and *Racal Group Services Ltd v Ashmore* [1995] STC 1151, CA, upholding Vinelott J [1994] STC 416, a case concerning a claim to rectify a deed of covenant, for the circumstances in which rectification for tax reasons may be obtained.

5 The Law Reform Committee (n 3, above, para 28–30) considered the question and concluded that although the standard of proof should be high, there should be no rigid restrictions on the nature of the evidence admissible (or on its weight) on a claim of rectification of a will (n 3 above, para 65). In the absence of anything in the section to the contrary this is probably the position.

[Updated in footnote 1 for *Price v Craig* [2006] WTLR 1873, *Pengelly v Pengelly* [2008] Ch 375 and *Hobart v Hobart* [2007] WTLR 1213.]

[6.5]

Supplementary. An application for rectification must be made within six months of the date when representation is first taken out (except with the permission of the court).[1] In computing this period certain limited grants (settled land, trust property etc) are left out of account.[2] There is an express provision protecting personal representatives in that they will not be liable for any distribution of the estate, after the six months' period has elapsed, … 'on the ground that they ought to have taken into account the possibility that the court might permit the making of an application for an order under this section after the end of that period'.[3] However, this is without prejudice to the power of the court to recover any part of the estate so distributed.[4]

1 AJA 1982, s 20(2); Vol 2, Part G, para **[244.98]**. In *Price v Craig* [2006] WTLR 1873 the necessary permission was given in a case where the problem requiring rectification had not come to light until after the end of the six month period, and no one had been prejudiced by the delay. In similar circumstances permission was readily granted: *Pengelly v Pengelly* [2008] Ch 375. Permission was also granted after six months in *Hobart v Hobart* [2007] WTLR 1213.

2 AJA 1982, s 20(4).

3 AJA 1982, s 20(3).

4 AJA 1982, s 20(3).

PART C

What dispositions may be made

CHAPTER 7

What may be disposed of by will

[Updated in the text and footnote 5 for *Re Woolnough, Perkins v Borden* [2002] WTLR 595 and *Carr v Isard* [2007] WTLR 409.]

[7.3]

Joint tenancy. Property held under a joint tenancy survives to the surviving joint tenant or joint tenants and one of two or more joint tenants has no power to dispose of his interest by will.[1] The rule is applicable to both legal and equitable joint tenancies and a purely legal joint tenancy (ie where the joint tenant has no beneficial interest and which must be a trust estate) is also governed by the rule that a testator cannot now dispose of a trust estate.[2] A joint tenancy may be severed during the lifetime of the joint tenant,[3] but he cannot sever it by any disposition made by his will.[4] Instructions given by joint owners of property to make wills in terms inconsistent with the continuation of a joint tenancy may be capable of effecting severance by mutual agreement[5] but severance in such a case occurs at the point when the wills are made and is not the result of the operation of the will taking effect on death. Since, however, the will speaks from the death of the testator and he is expressly empowered to devise or bequeath any real or personal estate 'which he shall be entitled to, either at law or in equity, at the time of his death', it is clear that, if there is a severance during the testator's lifetime, a gift in his will made before severance will pass the severed interest in the property and of course a gift made after severance will pass that interest. If there is no severance but the testator by the death of the other joint tenant or tenants becomes the sole survivor, the will can pass the whole interest in the property.[6]

1 *Swift d Neale v Roberts* (1764) 1 Wm Bl 476; *Low v Carter* (1839) 1 Beav 426; *Turner v A-G* (1876) 10 IR Eq 386; *Renouf's Trustees v Haining* 1919 2 SLT 15. The matter is now settled so far as England and Wales is concerned by the Administration of Estates Act 1925, s 3(4), which provides that the interest of a deceased person under a joint tenancy where another tenant survives the deceased is an interest ceasing on his death. It can be noted that by the Trusts of Land and Appointment of Trustees Act 1996, Sch 2, para 4, trusts for sale of land, whether created before or after 1 January 1997, now become trusts of land; statutory trusts for co-owners under Law of Property Act 1925, s 34 (tenants in common) and s 36 (joint tenants) cease to be trusts for sale and become trusts of land.

2 See n 1.

3 Severance would be effected by an assignment of the joint tenant's interest: *Partriche v Powlet* (1740) 2 Atk 54; *Daly v Aldworth* (1863) 15 I Ch R 69; or by a mortgage or charge of his share: *Re Pollard's Estate* (1863) 3 De G J & Sm 541; or by the bankruptcy of the joint tenant: *Re Butler's Trusts, Hughes v Anderson* (1888) 38 Ch D 286; or by a notice in writing given to the other joint tenant or tenants under the Law of Property Act 1925, s 36(2) (as amended by the Trusts of Land and Appointment of Trustees Act 1996, Sch 2, para 4). See *Nielson-Jones v Fedden* [1975] Ch 222, [1974] 3 All ER 38; *Burgess v Rawnsley* [1975]

Ch 429, [1975] 3 All ER 142, CA; and *Harris v Goddard* [1983] 3 All ER 242, [1983] 1 WLR 1203, CA; *Goodman v Gallant* [1986] Fam 106, [1986] 1 All ER 311, CA.

4 2 Cru Dig tit 18 Joint Tenancy, c 2, s 19; but an agreement to devise his share in a mutual will followed by a will carrying out the agreement severs the joint tenancy: *Re Hey's Estate, Walker v Gaskill* [1914] P 192.

5 See *Re Woolnough, Perkins v Borden* [2002] WTLR 595, a decision of Master Moncaster in which the wills were found to have severed the joint tenancy. For this to happen, however, the wills should be 'unequivocably inconsistent with the continuation of the joint tenancy' and made in the presence and with the knowledge (and probably with the mutual agreement) of both joint tenants since 'It will not suffice to rely on an intention with respect to the particular share, declared only behind the backs of the other persons interested' (*Williams v Hensman* (1861) 1 J & Hem 546). See *Carr v Isard* [2007] WTLR 409. Severance in this fashion is more readily inferred in the case of mutual wills, see para **[2.4]** n 6 above.

6 *Re Horton, Lloyd v Hatchett* [1920] 2 Ch 1; *Re Russell, Russell v Chell* (1882) 19 Ch D 432; and see Wills Act 1837, s 24; Vol 2, Part G, para **[244.26]**. Possibly it is necessary that the wording of the gift shall not be such as can only refer to a share in the property.

[Updated in footnote 2 for *Lewisham Hospital NHS Trust v Hamuth* [2007] WTLR 309 and *Hartshorne v Gardner* [2008] 2 FLR 1681, and *Burrows v HM Coroner for Preston* [2008] 2 FLR 1225 and in footnote 6 for *Ghai v Newcastle City Council (Ramgharia Gurdwara, Hitchin and another intervening)* [2009] EWHC 978 (Admin), [2009] All ER (D) 68 (May) and in footnotes 4, 6, 12 and 13 for the Cremation (England and Wales) Regulations 2008.]

[7.33]

Funeral and burial wishes. A binding disposition of the dead body of the testator cannot be made by will so as to oust the executors' or administrators' rights and duties as to its disposal[1] but statutes have allowed some qualification of this position. In the event of a dispute the court may give directions for the disposal of the body.[2]

Cremation is not unlawful at common law unless it is done so as to create a nuisance or to prevent the coroner holding an inquest.[3] A direction, therefore, for cremation is valid apart from the statute[4] and, although under the statute and the regulations made thereunder it is not necessary that written directions for cremation should be given, it is not unlawful to cremate the body of a person who has left written directions to the contrary,[5] and cremation must take place in a recognised crematorium.[6] Although it is a common practice for such directions to be included in a will, it is not the most convenient method of giving such directions as the will may not be found or not be opened before the funeral.

The testator can if he so desires give directions as to funeral[7] or the erection of tombstone or other monument[8] and provide for the maintenance of his grave.[9] He may, where he desires to be cremated, arrange for the disposal of his ashes. These may be buried or scattered on consecrated ground[10] or under a church even after it has been closed for burial subject to a faculty from the ordinary.[11] A fortiori they may be scattered or kept in an urn in any unconsecrated place. In the absence of a direction by the testator, the person who applies for cremation may arrange for such disposal[12] and, in the absence of any such direction, they will be decently interred in a burial ground or land adjoining the crematorium or scattered thereon.[13]

1 *Williams v Williams* (1882) 20 Ch D 659. The doubt expressed in this case as to the legality of cremation has been departed from; see cases in n 3, below: *Hunter v Hunter* [1930] 4 DLR 255.

2 As in *Lewisham Hospital NHS Trust v Hamuth* [2007] WTLR 309 in which the relatives of the deceased could not agree as to how to dispose of his body and the hospital, being in lawful custody of the corpse, sought directions as to the appropriate means for the disposal

by cremation. See also *Hartshorne v Gardner* [2008] 2 FLR 1681 and *Burrows v HM Coroner for Preston* [2008] 2 FLR 1225 where it was held that the wishes of the deceased and what family life he enjoyed must now (in the light of decisions on the European Human Rights Convention) be taken into account in deciding which of more than one claimant should have control of the disposal of his body.

3 *R v Price* (1884) 12 QBD 247; *R v Stephenson* (1884) 13 QBD 331.

4 Cremation Act 1902; Cremation (England and Wales) Regulations 2008, SI 2008/2841, in force with effect from 1 January 2009 and replacing the Cremation Regulations 1930, SR & O 1930/1016, as amended by the Cremation Regulations 1965, SI 1965/1146. The procedure relating to cremation was slightly amended by the Cremation Act 1952.

5 Formerly there was such a prohibition by virtue of reg 4 of the Cremation Regulations 1930, but this regulation was revoked by the Cremation Regulations 1965, SI 1965/1146.

6 Cremation (England and Wales) Regulations 2008, SI 2008/2841, reg 13, replacing, with effect from 1 January 2009, the Cremation Regulations 1930, SR & O 1930/1016, reg 3. Cremation in the open air is prohibited and such prohibition is not a breach of human rights under arts 8, 9 or 14 of the European Convention on Human Rights: *Ghai v Newcastle City Council (Ramgharia Gurdwara, Hitchin and another intervening)* [2009] EWHC 978 (Admin), [2009] All ER (D) 68 (May).

7 Such directions are in general better given in a separate writing to be opened immediately on death; but, if the testator desires any specific arrangement which is likely to increase the funeral expenses beyond what is reasonable for a person of his rank, he should also include them in his will with an authority to pay out of his estate all such expenses as the proper carrying out of such directions shall entail and the executor's decision as to what is reasonable and proper in accordance with the direction should be made conclusive on all parties; see *Re Read, Galloway v Harris* (1892) 36 Sol Jo 626. Where an executrix was directed to spend £300 on the funeral and grave, it was held she was entitled to spend that sum or any smaller sum she thought proper: *Re Pearce* [1946] SASR 118.

8 See *Re Dean, Cooper-Dean v Stevens* (1889) 41 Ch D 552. It would appear that the cost of a monument is not funeral expenses (*Hart v Griffith-Jones* [1948] 2 All ER 729); but as to a tombstone, see *Goldstein v Salvation Army Assurance Society* [1917] 2 KB 291, where the question is said to be one of fact.

9 See para **[9.29]** below.

10 *Re Dixon* [1892] P 386.

11 *Re Kerr* [1894] P 284.

12 Cremation (England and Wales) Regulations 2008, SI 2008/2841, reg 30, replacing, with effect from 1 January 2009, the Cremation Regulations 1930, SR & O 1930/1016, reg 16.

13 Cremation (England and Wales) Regulations 2008, SI 2008/2841, reg 30, replacing, with effect from 1 January 2009, the Cremation Regulations 1930, SR & O 1930/1016, reg 16.

CHAPTER 9

Who may benefit under a will

VI. CHILD BORN AS A RESULT OF FERTILISATION TECHNIQUES

[Updated for Human Fertilisation and Embryology Act 2008.]

[9.27]

Status of such children. The status of children born as a result of artificial insemination or other fertilisation techniques ('assisted reproduction') is governed by the Human Fertilisation and Embryology Act 1990 (HFEA 1990) or the Human Fertilisation and Embryology Act 2008 (HFEA 2008). HFEA 1990 applies where the placing in the woman of embryos or sperm and eggs, or the artificial insemination, occurred before 6 April 2009, and HFEA 2008 applies where it occurred on or after that date. The provisions of the HFEA 1990 and HFEA 2008 are discussed in Chapter 74.

XX. INSOLVENT BENEFICIARIES

[This is a new paragraph.]

[9.46]

Capacity to receive. There is no objection to an insolvent person being a beneficiary under a will, but a bankrupt's estate vests in the trustee in bankruptcy immediately upon his appointment.[1] A bankrupt's estate comprises all property belonging to or vested in the bankrupt at the commencement of the bankruptcy.[2] Property for this purpose includes money, goods, things in action, land and every description of property wherever situated and also obligations and every description of interest, whether present or future or vested or contingent, arising out of or incidental to, property.[3] A specific or pecuniary legatee's entitlement to a legacy is within this definition of property[4] and so vests in the trustee in bankruptcy. The same is true of residuary legatees, even if a residuary legatee's right is limited to a right to compel due administration of the estate, the legatee nevertheless still has an immediate 'interest', being the right to receive the assets comprising residue as and when the administration of the estate is complete, which vests in the trustee in bankruptcy.[5]

1 Insolvency Act 1986, s 306(1).
2 IA 1986, s 283(1).
3 IA 1986, s 436.
4 *Lord Sudeley v Attorney-General* [1897] AC 1.
5 *Raymond Saul & Co (a firm) v Holden* [2008] WTLR 2008; *Official Receiver in Bankruptcy v Schultz* (1990) 170 CLR 306 (concerning the Australian Bankruptcy Act 1966).

PART D

Form of will and execution

CHAPTER 12

Attestation

II. MODE OF ATTESTATION

[Updated at footnote 1 for *Olins v Walters* [2007] EWHC 3060 (Ch).]

[12.4]

Witness must attest the will. It is essential that the witnesses in signing should attest the will and not merely some alteration to it.[1]

1 *Re White, Barker v Gribble* [1990] 3 All ER 1 at 7. *In the Estate of Sherrington Deceased, Sherrington v Sherrington* [2005] EWCA Civ 326, [2005] WTLR 587. Where a will was validly executed in 1981 and alterations were made to it in 1984 which the witnesses signed, it was held that they did not attest the document as the 1984 will but merely as alterations to the 1981 will. Applying *Re Martin's Goods* (1849) 1 Rob Eccl 712 and *Re Shearn's Goods* (1880) 50 LJ P 15. See also *Olins v Walters* [2007] EWHC 3060 (Ch) where a question arose as to whether a will made in 1988 and a codicil made in 1998 had been properly witnessed. Norris J (at [32]–[40]) held that attestation was good despite one of the witnesses giving evidence to the contrary. For commentary as to the presumption of due execution where a witness has a recollection contrary to the attestation clause see **Chapter 13** below.

CHAPTER 13

Presumption of due execution

[Updated at footnote 2 for *Re Morgan, Griffin v Wood* [2008] WTLR 73.]

[13.1]

The presumption. If a will, on the face of it, appears to be duly executed, the presumption is in favour of due execution, applying the principle *omnia præsumuntur rite esse acta.*[1] The force of the presumption varies with the circumstances. If the will is entirely regular in form, it is very strong, but if the form is irregular and unusual the maxim does not apply with the same force.[2] If the witnesses are entirely ignorant of the details of the execution the presumption is the same.[3] If they profess to remember and state that the will was not duly executed, and this negative evidence is not rebutted by showing that the witnesses are not to be credited, or, taking their statement of the facts, that their memories are defective, the will must be pronounced against.[4] The court does not require direct affirmative evidence of due execution.[5]

1 *Re Musgrove's Estate, Davis v Mayhew* [1927] P 264, CA; *Byles v Cox* (1896) 74 LT 222; *Re Ferreira* [1927] VLR 90; *Re Denning, Harnett v Elliott* [1958] 2 All ER 1, [1958] 1 WLR 462; *Chester v Baston* (1980) 118 DLR (3d) 323. It is said in an Irish case that it is only where witnesses or persons present at the execution of the will are dead or cannot give evidence or their evidence is unreliable, that the doctrine can be called in: *Rolleston v Sinclair* [1924] 2 IR 157. When the deceased had lived alone leaving a will, wholly in the deceased's handwriting and witnessed apparently by two witnesses of whom nothing was known, the maxim was not applied to establish the will: *Re Robertson's Estate* [1964] NSWR 1087; *Re Sims, Sims v Faulkner* (1972) 116 Sol Jo 356.

2 *Re Bercovitz's Estate, Canning v Enever* [1962] 1 All ER 552, [1962] 1 WLR 321; *Re Lucas* [1966] VR 267; *Re Haverland* (1975) 55 DLR (3d) 122. This passage of the text was applied in *Re Young* [1969] NZLR 454 at 458. In *In the Estate of Sherrington Deceased, Sherrington v Sherrington* [2005] EWCA Civ 326, [2005] WTLR 587, the Court of Appeal held that where the testator's and witnesses' signatures appear in the right places and there is an attestation clause, very strong evidence indeed is needed before it is possible for the court to find that the will was not duly executed. Similarly *Briscoe v Green* [2006] All ER (D) 182 (Jul), where the presumption was applied and *Re Morgan, Griffin v Wood* [2008] WTLR 73 where summary judgment was granted on appeal on the strength of the presumption. But see *Re Papillon (decd), Murrin v Matthews* [2008] WTLR 269, [2006] All ER (D) 297 (Dec), where the will was pronounced against.

3 *Re Moriaty's Will* [1956] VLR 400.

4 *Burgoyne v Showler* (1844) 1 Rob Eccl 5; *Keating v Brooks* (1845) 4 Notes of Cases 253; *Brenchley v Still* (1850) 2 Rob Eccl 162; *Re Amos* [1954] 2 DLR 574 (where the will was found in irregular order of pages). For cases where the evidence of the two attesting witnesses was not accepted, see *Bailey v Frowan* (1871) 19 WR 511; *Dayman v Dayman* (1894) 71 LT 699; *Re Collins* [1955] OWN 603.

5 *Gregory v Queen's Proctor* (1846) 4 Notes of Cases 620; *Blake v Knight* (1843) 3 Curt 547; *Leech v Bates* (1849) 1 Rob Eccl 714. It has been suggested that a solicitor who has taken instructions for a will should furnish a statement of evidence to any one interested in challenging or upholding the will; 56 Law Society's Gazette 619.

[Updated at footnote 3 for *Olins v Walters* [2007] EWHC 3060 (Ch) and *Re Morgan, Griffin v Wood* [2008] WTLR 73.]

[13.2]

Attestation clause. Where there is a proper attestation clause, even though the witnesses have no recollection of having witnessed the will, the presumption applies.[1] In the absence of such a clause a will which on the face of it is duly executed is accepted, although no evidence is forthcoming.[2] Where there is such a clause, the court requires the strongest evidence before deciding that the will was not duly executed.[3]

1 *Lloyd v Roberts* (1858) 12 Moo PCC 158; *Wright v Sanderson* (1884) 9 PD 149; *Wright v Rogers* (1869) LR 1 P & D 678; *Woodhouse v Balfour* (1887) 13 PD 2 (witnesses having no recollection of having seen the paper before); *Vinnicombe v Butler* (1864) 3 Sw & Tr 580; *Harris v Knight* (1890) 15 PD 170, CA. Where the attestation does not say that the signature was made by the direction of the testator, the omission may be passed over in cases where everything is otherwise in order: *Re Cooper's Goods* (1847) 5 Notes of Cases 618.

2 *Re Peverett's Goods* [1902] P 205; *Clarke v Clarke* (1879) 5 LR Ir 47; *Re Malins' Goods* (1887) 19 LR Ir 231; *Vinnicombe v Butler* (1864) 3 Sw & Tr 580; *Re Rees' Goods* (1865) 34 LJPM & A 56; *Scarff v Scarff* [1927] 1 IR 13; *Re Griffiths* [1955] NZLR 127; *Re Laxer* (1963) 37 DLR (2d) 192; *Re Strong's Estate, Strong v Hadden* [1915] P 211. In *Re Denning, Harnett v Elliott* [1958] 2 All ER 1, [1958] 1 WLR 462, there were only two signatures on the back of a single sheet will.

3 See *Sherrington v Sherrington* [2005] EWCA Civ 326, [2005] WTLR 587; *Wright v Rogers* (1869) LR 1 P & D 678; *Whitting v Turner* (1903) 89 LT 71; *O'Meagher v O'Meagher* (1883) 11 LR Ir 117; *Goodisson v Goodisson* [1913] 1 IR 31, 218; *Dubourdieu v Patterson* (1919) 54 ILT 23. The decision in *Re Swinford's Goods* (1869) LR 1 P & D 630, seems out of line with the general run of the cases. Where it was suggested that the signature was a traced forgery the court accepted the positive evidence of the witnesses: *Re Kryskiw* [1954] OWN 717. In *Channon v Perkins (a firm)* [2006] WTLR 425, the Court of Appeal held, following *Sherrington v Sherrington,* that where a will had a regular attestation clause and appeared on its face to have been duly signed by the testator and the witnesses, the fact that the witnesses had, in one case, no recollection of signing the will and, in the other, no very precise recollection of signing the will was not, in the absence of any positive evidence of a specific failure to comply with the formalities, sufficient to rebut the presumption of due execution. See also *Briscoe v Green* [2006] All ER (D) 182 (Jul) in which it was held, following *Sherrington v Sherrington* and *Channon v Perkins*, that the strongest evidence would be required to show that a will had not been properly executed where it appeared on its face to have been properly executed and there was no question but that the will represented the testator's intentions. See also *Olins v Walters* [2007] EWHC 3060 (Ch) and *Re Morgan, Griffin v Wood* [2008] WTLR 73.

[Updated in the text to footnote 6 and at footnote 6 for *Channon v Perkins (a firm)* [2006] WTLR 425 and *Olins v Walters* [2007] EWHC 3060 (Ch).]

[13.3]

Evidence rebutting presumption. This must be positive and reliable[1] and the court must not give undue weight to the circumstances on which the presumption is founded and on the other hand must not lose sight of them.[2] The burden of proving due execution, whether by presumption or by positive evidence rests on the propounder.[3] The direct evidence of both attesting witnesses unless discounted rebuts the presumption[4] and the evidence of one of the witnesses has been held to do so[5] but even an apparently positive recollection of contradicting the attestation clause must be treated with caution.[6]

1 *Glover v Smith* (1886) 57 LT 60; *Wyatt v Berry* [1893] P 5; *Pilkington v Gray* [1899] AC 401, DC; *Re Moore's Goods* [1901] P 44.

2 *Cooper v Bockett* (1846) 4 Moo PCC 419 at 439; *Re Bladen* [1952] VLR 82 (presumption applied in spite of conflicting evidence); *Re Gramp* [1952] SASR 12 (presumption rebutted).

3 *Brenchley v Still* (1850) 2 Rob Eccl 162; *Clery v Barry* (1887) 21 LR Ir 152; *Loftus v Harris* (1914) 19 DLR 670.

4 *Croft v Croft* (1865) 4 Sw & Tr 10; *Glover v Smith* (1886) 57 LT 60; *Pennant v Kingscote* (1843) 3 Curt 642; *Re Michnik Estate* [1945] 4 DLR 521. See *Dayman v Dayman* (1894) 71 LT 699; *Neal v Denston* (1932) 147 LT 460, for cases where the evidence was discounted. Since the reason for the provisions of the Wills Act 1837, s 9, was the prevention of fraud, evidence is admissible to show that the two attesting witnesses are wrong: *Re Vere-Wardale* [1949] P 395, [1949] 2 All ER 250.

5 *Cregeen v Willoughby* (1860) 24 JP 408; *Noding v Alliston* (1850) 14 Jur 904. To the contrary: *Keating v Brooks* (1845) 4 Notes of Cases 253 (where the presumption prevailed although one witness said her signature was forged); *Re Thomas' Goods* (1859) 1 Sw & Tr 255 (incomplete recollection); *Wright v Rogers* (1869) LR 1 P & D 678 (perfect attestation clause rebutted only by strongest evidence). See also *Reeves v Grainger* (1908) 52 Sol Jo 355 (execution by illiterate testator: evidence of clerk writing testator's name as guide where signature should be, in ignorance of the fact that testator was too illiterate to sign); *Pattie v Fry* (1911) 30 NZLR 581; *Re Irwin* [1920] NZLR 440. The will was held good where one witness would not deny proper execution: *Re Johnson* [1953] 4 DLR 777.

6 See *Channon v Perkins (a firm)* [2006] WTLR 425 at [8]: 'Oral testimony as to the way in which a document was executed many years ago is not likely to be inherently particularly reliable on, one suspects, most occasions. As anyone who has been involved in contested factual disputes will know, people can, entirely honestly and doing their very best, completely misremember or wholly forget facts and events that took place not very long ago, and the longer ago something may have taken place, the less accurate their recollection is likely to be.' In *Olins v Walters* [2007] EWHC 3060 (Ch) Norris J found (at [32]–[40]) that a witness's express recollection contradicting the attestation clause was nonetheless unreliable.

PART E

Revocation, republication and revival of wills

CHAPTER 18

Voluntary revocation

IV. LATER WILL OR CODICIL

[Updated at footnote 2 for *Re Ciebrant* [2009] WTLR 69, [2008] EWHC 1268 (Ch).]

[18.12]

Lost will. Where a testamentary document has been lost or destroyed in such a way as not to effect a revocation[1] probate may be granted of the contents thereof upon proof of such contents and due execution and attestation of the instrument.[2] Where the person setting up an alleged will cannot produce any copy or draft of any written evidence of its contents, he must prove all these matters so as to remove all reasonable (but not all possible) doubt on these points.[3] The evidence of a solicitor that he had made the will and that it was not informal establishes due execution and attestation.[4] The contents may be proved from the instructions given to the solicitor[5] or by the evidence of a witness, although he is an interested party, but his evidence must be unimpeached.[6] An alleged draft will be considered side by side with the oral evidence.[7] There has been doubt about the admission of declarations made by the testator after the making of the will,[8] but almost certainly for the reason that evidence of such declarations would be hearsay[9] if that is the reason, such evidence will now be admissible under Civil Evidence Act 1968, s 1, or the replacement of it now going through Parliament. The fullest enquiries must be made in any such case.[10]

1 As to the position where the loss effects a revocation, see para **[18.28]** below.

2 *Brown v Brown* (1858) 8 E & B 876; *Sugden v Lord St Leonards* (1876) 1 PD 154, 238, CA; *Allan v Morrison* [1900] AC 604, PC; *Re Crandon's Goods* (1901) 84 LT 330; *Re Spain* (1915) 31 TLR 435 (where the testator, attesting witnesses and the will were lost in an explosion); *Re Phibbs' Estate* [1917] P 93; *Re Queen Marie of Roumania* (1950) 94 Sol Jo 673; *Re Davies, Panton v Jones* [1978] CLY 3095; *Re Ciebrant* [2008] EWHC 1268 (Ch), [2009] WTLR 69.

3 *Harris v Knight* (1890) 15 PD 170 at 179; *Re Wipperman's Estate* [1953] 1 All ER 764 at 766; *Re MacGillivray's Estate* [1946] 2 All ER 301. As to the contents of the affidavit to lead to probate of a lost will, see *Tristram and Coote's Probate Practice* (30th edn) LexisNexis Butterworths. For a case where the evidence was insufficient, see *Re Plunkett* [1965] VR 118.

4 *Re Hannah* [1954] NZLR 836.

5 *Fincham v Edwards* (1842) 3 Curt 63; on appeal 4 Moo PCC 198.

6 *Sugden v Lord St Leonards* (1876) 1 PD 154, 238, CA; applied in *Nicholls v Hudson* [2006] EWHC 3006 (Ch). See also *Jersey Society for the Prevention of Cruelty to Animals v Rees (2001–02)* 4 ITELR 294, where, notwithstanding the presumption that a will lost in the possession of the testator had been destroyed by him with an intention to revoke, there was held to be sufficient evidence on the facts of the case to rebut the presumption. For recent cases in which the presumption was held to have been rebutted, see *Rowe v Clarke* [2006] EWHC 1292 (Ch), [2006] WTLR 347 and *Nicholls v Hudson* [2006] EWHC 3006 (Ch). See also *Re Yelland, Broadbent v Francis* (1975) 119 Sol Jo 562 (will proved by daughter's recollection of contents).

7 *Burls v Burls* (1868) LR 1 P & D 472 at 474; *Re Webb Smith v Johnston* [1964] 2 All ER 91, [1964] 1 WLR 509 (a draft will was admitted because the inclusion of a proper attestation clause led to the presumption that the will had been duly executed).
8 *Atkinson v Morris* [1897] P 40; but they were admitted in *Sugden v Lord St Leonards* (1876) 1 PD 154, 238, CA.
9 This seems clear from *Atkinson v Morris* [1897] P 40, but *Barkwell v Barkwell* [1928] P 91 at 97 seems to suggest that the rule is based on the requirement of Wills Act 1837, s 9 that a will must be in writing.
10 See *Re Ferguson-Smith Estate* (1954) 13 WWR NS 387; on appeal (1955) 15 WWR 237, Sask CA.

V. BY DESTRUCTION

[Updated in the text to footnote 7 and at footnote 7 for *Nicholls v Hudson* [2006] EWHC 3006 (Ch), [2007] WTLR 341, [2006] All ER (D) 60 (Oct). Also updated in the text to footnote 8 and at footnote 8 for *Re Zielinski, Korab-Karpinski v Lucas-Gardiner* [2007] WTLR 1655. Also updated at footnote 2 for *Nicholls v Hudson* [2006] EWHC 3006 (Ch), [2007] WTLR 341, [2006] All ER (D) 60 (Oct); and at footnote 3 for *Wren v Wren* [2006] EWHC 2243 (Ch), [2007] WTLR 531, [2006] All ER (D) 30 (Sep).]

[18.29]

Rebuttal of presumption. The presumption may, however, be rebutted by evidence, but the evidence must be clear and satisfactory.[1] Recent declarations by a testator of satisfaction at having settled his affairs,[2] or of goodwill towards the persons benefited by the will, or of adherence to the will and to the contents of the will itself,[3] may be used for this purpose. A declaration by the testator of adherence to a will may be answered by his declarations to a contrary effect.[4] The presumption may, it seems, also be rebutted by a consideration of the contents of the will itself,[5] or by showing that the testator had no opportunity of destroying the will, or that it had been lost or destroyed without his privity or consent.[6] Other factors which might go towards rebutting the presumption would be the testator's lack of efficiency and methodology which may explain the loss of the will,[7] or the testator's inclination to instruct solicitors to carry out acts of legal significance making it unlikely a revocation would have been made without such intervention.[8]

1 *Eckersley v Platt* (1866) LR 1 P & D 281; *Battyll v Lyles and Phillips* (1858) 4 Jur NS 718; *Eaton (Norris Estate) v Heyman* [1946] 4 DLR 441.
2 *Whiteley v King* (1864) 17 CBNS 756; *Nicholls v Hudson* [2007] WTLR 341; [2006] EWHC 3006 (Ch), [2006] All ER (D) 60 (Oct).
3 *Keen v Keen* (1873) LR 3 P & D 105; *Patten v Poulton* (1858) 1 Sw & Tr 55; *Re Mackenzie's Estate* [1909] P 305. See also *Sugden v Lord St Leonards* (1876) 1 PD 154; *Unwin v Unwin* (1914) 20 BCR 77; *Public Trustee v Kells* (1904) 23 NZLR 605; *Re Matt Estate* (1954) 11 WWRNS 28; *Re Boyd's Will, ex p Whelan* [1959] SRNSW 369 (where the testator was asked shortly before his decease as to the whereabouts of the will and said it was in a bag beside his bed and there appeared to be no one who could benefit other than the named beneficiary); *Brown v Woolley* (1959) 27 WWR 425; *Re Keluga Estate* (1956) 64 Man R 138; *Wren v Wren* [2006] EWHC 2243 (Ch), [2007] WTLR 531, [2006] All ER (D) 30 (Sep).
4 *Keen v Keen* (1873) LR 3 P & D 105; *Re Sykes, Drake v Sykes* (1907) 23 TLR 747. But it seems that oral declarations of destruction are not admissible: *Atkinson v Morris* [1897] P 40.
5 *Sugden v Lord St Leonards* (1876) 1 PD 154, where the contents of a codicil and the testator's papers were also given weight. In *Re Witham* [1938] 3 DLR 142, the cutting out was so carefully done and an intelligible will left properly executed that the resulting will was admitted.
6 *Finch v Finch* (1867) LR 1 P & D 371.
7 *Nicholls v Hudson* [2006] EWHC 3006 (Ch), [2007] WTLR 341, [2006] All ER (D) 60 (Oct).
8 *Re Zielinski, Korab-Karpinski v Lucas-Gardiner* [2007] WTLR 1655.

PART F

Wills with foreign element

CHAPTER 24

Wills with a foreign element: essential validity and construction and exercise of powers of appointment

II. CONSTRUCTION

[Updated for new reference to *Dellar v Zivy* [2007] EWHC 2266, [2008] WTLR 17, [2007] All ER (D) 121.]

[24.6]

Law governing construction. As a general rule, wills of movables must be construed with reference to the law of the place which was the domicile of the testator at his death.[1] Where, however, there appears on the face of the will an intention that it should be construed by reference to some other law, that law will govern the construction.[2] For example, where technical expressions peculiar to a foreign law are used, that law and not the law of the domicile may determine the construction,[3] but the presence of a few such technical expressions may not by itself be a sufficient indication of the testator's intention to induce the court to construe the will with reference to the law to which such expressions belong,[4] and where it is shown that no technical rules of construction are applied to words by the law of the domicile, no reference to that law is necessary, and the will must be construed according to English rules of construction.[5] The construction of a will is not altered by reason of any change in the testator's domicile after the execution of the will.[6]

1 *Nisbett v Murray* (1799) 5 Ves 149; *Bradford v Young* (1884) 26 Ch D 656; on appeal (1885) 29 Ch D 617, CA; *Re Price, Tomlin v Latter* [1900] 1 Ch 442; *Re Lewal's Settlement Trusts, Gould v Lewal* [1918] 2 Ch 391; *Re Levick's Will Trusts, Ffennell v IRC* [1963] 1 All ER 95, [1963] 1 WLR 311; *Re Lord Cable, Garratt v Waters* [1976] 3 All ER 417, [1977] 1 WLR 7. Where a testator domiciled in Quebec made a will in English form it was to be construed according to the law of Quebec and the English rule that the later of two incompatible clauses is to prevail could not be applied: *Bayer v Montreal Trust Co* [1953] Que SC 89. In a gift of personalty to a person or his heirs, the persons taking under the words 'heirs' must be determined by the law of the domicle of the testator: *Re Collishaw* [1953] 3 DLR 829; *Re Cunnington, Healing v Webb* [1924] 1 Ch 68. But see *Dellar v Zivy* [2007] EWHC 2266, [2008] WTLR 17, [2007] All ER (D) 121, in which it was held that the will in English form of a Frenchman who had moved to England, but who the judge was not prepared to assume on a summary application had acquired a domicile of choice in England, was to be construed in accordance with English law.

2 *Re Price, Tomlin v Latter* [1900] 1 Ch 442.

3 *Studd v Cook* (1883) 8 App Cas 577; *Re Cliff's Trusts* [1892] 2 Ch 229; *Re Cunnington, Healing v Webb* [1924] 1 Ch 68 (where the rule was not applied); *Re Allen's Estate, Prescott v Allen and Beaumont* [1945] 2 All ER 264 (reference to English law).

4 *Bradford v Young* (1884) 26 Ch D 656.
5 *Bernal v Bernal* (1838) 3 My & Cr 559. As to translations of foreign will, see para **[57.7]** below.
6 Wills Act 1963, s 4; see Vol 2, Part G, para **[244.80]**.

PART G

Executors, trustees and guardians

CHAPTER 28

Appointment of guardians

I. APPOINTMENT OF GUARDIANS ON OR AFTER 14 OCTOBER 1991

[Updated in the text and footnotes 11–15 for Human Fertilisation and Embryology Act 2008.]

[28.2]

Who may appoint guardians—parental responsibility. The Children Act 1989, s 5 gives the power to appoint a guardian to the parent or parents with parental responsibility for a child, and to a guardian of a child.[1] Parental responsibility means all the rights, duties, powers, responsibilities and authority which by law a parent of a child has in relation to the child and his property, and includes the rights, powers and duties which a guardian of the child's estate appointed before the ChA 1989 came into force would have had in relation to the child.[2]

Both parents of a legitimate child[3] have equal parental responsibility for him.[4] In the case of an illegitimate child the mother has parental responsibility,[5] and in the case of a child whose birth is registered before 1 December 2003 the father only acquires it if there is an order of the relevant court that he shall have it or it is conferred by a parental responsibility agreement between him and the mother,[6] or he marries the mother. A parental responsibility agreement only has effect if it is in the form prescribed by regulations made by the Lord Chancellor,[7] and once made it can only be terminated by an order of the court,[8] ie the mother cannot revoke it at will. The Adoption and Children Act 2002, (ACA 2002), ss 111 and 112 have added to the possible ways of attaining parental responsibility for a child. Section 111 amends ChA 1989, s 4 so as to cause the father of an illegitimate child who is registered as the father on the birth certificate to have parental responsibility by virtue of the registration.[9] ACA 2002, s 112 adds a new s 4A to ChA 1989 which enables the parent or parents having parental responsibility for a child to confer by agreement parental responsibility for the child on a step-parent of the child, where the step-parent is the spouse or civil partner of the parent or of one of them. It also empowers the court to make an order conferring parental responsibility on a step-parent.[10]

The Human Fertilisation and Embryology Act 2008 (HFEA 2008) makes parallel provision for a child of a same sex female couple, where the child is born as a result of either artificial insemination or other form of treatment regulated under HFEA 1990 and 2008 and carried out on or after 6 April 2009.[11] If the couple are in a civil partnership[12] at any time between the treatment and the birth of the child, the one who is not the mother has parental responsibility for the child.[13] If not, but the one who is not the mother gave her consent to the treatment in such manner as to make her a parent of the child,[14] she will have parental responsibility for the child if her name appears on the birth certificate, there is a parental responsibility agreement with the mother, she and the mother form a civil partnership after the birth of the child, or there is a court order conferring parental responsibility on her.[15]

A guardian of a child whose appointment has taken effect also has parental responsibility for that child,[16] but power is expressly conferred on a guardian to appoint someone else to take his place in the event of his death, independently of the provisions about parental responsibility.[17] It is arguable that this power of a guardian to appoint his successor may be exercised by someone who has been appointed a guardian before that appointment has taken effect,[18] but on balance it is thought that such an argument is incorrect.[19] The court also has power to appoint a guardian.[20] There are no further categories of persons empowered to appoint guardians.[21]

1 ChA 1989, s 5(3) and (4).
2 ChA 1989, s 3(1) and (2).
3 This includes a child legitimated by the subsequent marriage of his parents, an adopted child, and a child otherwise treated in law as legitimate: see the Family Law Reform Act 1987, s 1(2) and (3) (Vol 2, Part G, para **[245.70]**) and ChA 1989, ss 2(1) and (3).
4 ChA 1989, s 2(1), (4) and (5).
5 ChA 1989, s 2(2)(a).
6 ChA 1989, s 4(1). Where an order made under Family Law Reform Act 1987, s 4(1) giving a father parental rights and duties in relation to a child was in force immediately before 14 October 1991 it has effect from then as an order under ChA 1989, s 4 giving the father parental responsibility, and an order in force immediately before that date under previous legislation giving the father custody or care and control has effect under the Children Act 1989 from then as an order conferring parental responsibility on him: ChA 1989, Sch 14, paras 4 and 6(2) and (4).
7 ChA 1989, s 4(2). For the prescribed form see the Parental Responsibility Agreement Regulations 1991, SI 1991/1478 as amended by SI 1994/3157. The ChA 1989, s 4(2) also requires such an agreement to be recorded in the prescribed manner if the relevant regulations so require; SI 1991/1478 requires recording of a parental responsibility agreement in the Principal Registry of the Family Division of the High Court as a precondition of it taking effect.
8 ChA 1989, s 4(3).
9 It came into force on 1 December 2003 (SI 2003/3079), and does not apply in relation to registrations which occurred before that date (see s 111(7)).
10 It came into force on 30 December 2005 (SI 2005/2213).
11 See HFEA 2008, ss 42 and 43, and paras **[74.5]**, **[74.6]** below.
12 Under the Civil Partnership Act 2004, in force from 5 December 2005.
13 HFEA 2008, ss 42, 43, FLRA 1987 s 1(2)(ba) and (bb) inserted by HFEA 2008, Sch 6, para 24, and Children Act 1989, s 2(1A) inserted by HFEA 2008, Sch 6, para 26.
14 See HFEA 2008, ss 43, 44.
15 Children Act 1989, s 4ZA inserted by HFEA 2008, Sch 6, para 27, Legitimacy Act 1976, s 2A inserted by HFEA 2008, Sch 6, para 16, FLRA 1987, s 1(2) and (3), and ChA 1989, s 2(1A) inserted by HFEA 2008, Sch 6, para 26.
16 ChA 1989, s 5(6).
17 See ChA 1989, s 5(4).
18 Because the reference in ChA 1989, s 5(8), to s 5(4) of that Act would appear to have no function if it is only a guardian whose appointment has taken effect who can appoint another guardian.
19 The wording of the power in ChA 1989, s 5(4) 'a guardian of a child may appoint … to take his place as the child's guardian in the event of his death' suggests it is a power only

exercisable after a guardian has taken up the office. Also a guardian is not really a guardian until his appointment has taken effect, and an appointment of a guardian is always revocable during the life of the appointor.

20 ChA 1989, s 5(1) and (2).

21 In particular, a person who is not the child's parent and in whose favour a residence order is made has parental responsibility but does not have power to appoint a guardian: see the ChA 1989, s 12(2) and (3)(c).

PART H

Contents of wills

CHAPTER 32

Interest and income on legacies

III. GENERAL AND DEMONSTRATIVE LEGACIES

[Updated in the text and at footnote 1 for a change in the rate of interest on general legacies with effect from 1 February 2009. Also updated at footnotes 1 and 2 for *Re Allen, Lewis v Vincent* [2008] WTLR 1691.]

[32.4]

When no time fixed for payment. Where no special time is fixed for the payment of a general legacy, it carries interest at the basic rate payable for the time being on funds in court, currently 2 per cent per annum with effect from 1 February 2009[1] from the expiration of one year after the testator's death,[2] although expressly made payable out of a particular fund which does not fall in until after a longer period.[3]

1 This rate of interest is that applicable where an account of legacies is directed by the court, and is set by the Civil Procedure Rules, Part 40, *Practice Direction– Accounts, Inquiries etc*, para 15 as the basic rate for funds in court. The rate was previously 4 per cent with effect from 1 February 2002. Prior to this it had been 6 per cent, RSC Ord 44, r 10; SI 1982/1111; see also CCR 1981 Ord 23, r 2; substituted for the previous 5 per cent with effect from 1 October 1983 by RSC (Amendment No 2) Order 1983, SI 1983/1181. Other relevant rates of interest are 6 per cent now payable on statutory legacies: (Intestate Succession (Interest and Capitalisation) Order 1983, SI 1983/1374); previously the rate was 7 per cent, after 1977; and 4 per cent, after 1952. All these rates of interest are liable to change by statutory instrument and should be checked to ascertain the prevailing rate at any particular time. CPR 40 PD 15 provides as an alternative to the court funds rate of interest 'such other rate as the court shall direct', so it may be that in a particular case executors could apply to the court for a different rate of interest to apply; see *Re Allen, Lewis v Vincent* [2008] WTLR 1691 where executors successfully applied to the High Court of New Zealand to pay interest on a legacy at a lower rate equivalent to the interest actually earned when the legatee had caused much of the delay in the administration and payment of her legacy.

2 *Re Lord's Estate, Lord v Lord* (1867) 2 Ch App 782 at 789; *Webster v Hale* (1803) 8 Ves 410 (direction in will to pay as soon as possible), but see para **[32.5]**, n 5, where legacy is immediately payable; *Bourke v Ricketts* (1804) 10 Ves 330 (legacy in currency of Jamaica where testator resided); *Wood v Penoyre* (1807) 13 Ves 325 (payment out of mortgage debt when recovered); *Marquis of Hertford v Lord Lowther* (1846) 9 Beav 266 (delay in payment); *Re Barr* [1947] 3 DLR 784. As to directions which do not amount to a direction for payment at a special time, see *Re Yates, Throckmorton v Pike* (1907) 96 LT 758; *Re Whiteley, Whiteley v Bishop of London* (1909) 101 LT 508; *Walford v Walford* [1912] AC 658. See, further, as to legacy payable at a future date, para **[32.10]** below. It has been held in New Zealand that there is no discretion in the court to change the period: *Re Allen, Lewis v Vincent* [2008] WTLR 1691.The interest is payable out of the residuary personal estate: *Greene v Flood* (1885) 15 LR Ir 450, and is subject to deduction of income tax at the current rate: *Hamilton v Linaker* [1923] 1 IR 104.

3 *Walford v Walford* [1912] AC 658.

VI. GENERAL POINTS

[Updated in the text and at footnote 2 for a change in the rate of interest on general legacies with effect from 1 February 2009.]

[32.31]

Rate of interest. The rate of interest set by the court is now governed by the Civil Procedure Rules.[1] It is the basic rate on funds in court unless the court orders otherwise. This rate is currently 2 per cent with effect from 1 February 2009.[2] Interest is not allowed at a higher rate, even though the residuary estate has been producing interest at a higher rate.[3]

1 CPR Part 40, *Practice Direction–Accounts, Inquiries etc*, para 15.

2 The rate had previously been 4 per cent which was substituted for the previous 6 per cent with effect from 1 February 2002; see para **[32.4]**, n 1 above.

3 *Re Campbell, Campbell v Campbell* [1893] 3 Ch 468.

CHAPTER 36

Secret trusts

I. GIFT IN WILL ABSOLUTE

[Updated in the text to footnotes 7 and 9 and at footnotes 6, 7 and 9 for *Kasperbauer v Griffith* [2000] WTLR 333 (CA). Also updated at footnote 7 for *Margulies v Margulies* [2008] WTLR 1871 (CA).]

[36.2]

Where gift in terms absolute. The law requires every testamentary disposition to be duly executed and attested as a will or codicil,[1] but this requirement of the law is not carried to the length at which it would enable an apparent donee to act fraudulently. Therefore, where a testator makes, or leaves unrevoked, a disposition on the faith of a promise, whether express or tacit, on the part of the donee that he will carry out the testator's intentions with respect thereto,[2] equity will admit evidence[3] as to the testator's intentions and the communication thereof to the donee and his acquiescence therein, and will compel the donee, as being a trustee, to carry out the testator's intentions,[4] unless they are such as are prohibited by law.[5] Thus the essential elements of a secret trust are: the intention of the testator to subject the primary donee to an obligation in favour of the secondary donee; the communication of that intention to the primary donee; and the acceptance of that obligation by the primary donee either expressly or by acquiescence.[6] The obligation must satisfy the traditional requirement of three certainties for a trust, namely language in imperative form, certainty of subject-matter and certainty of objects or beneficiaries.[7] The method by which the primary donee is to carry out the obligation, whether by making a will in favour of the secondary donee or by some form of inter vivos transfer, is immaterial.[8] It is open to the testator or the legatee accepting the gift to change his mind before the gift takes effect on the death.[9]

1 Wills Act 1837, s 9; as substituted by the Administration of Justice Act 1982, s 17; Vol 2, Part G, para **[244.7]**.

2 Though the language used sometimes seems to point to a basis of implied contract, this doctrine has always been explained as the prevention of an act of fraud on the part of the apparent beneficiary. The word 'fraud' in this connection must not be construed in the *Derry v Peek* (1889) 14 App Cas 337 sense, but as something which equity will prevent as being unconscionable. Cf the case of *Tharp v Tharp* [1916] 1 Ch 142, where a testator was induced to revoke a codicil and thus revive a power of appointment upon an undertaking that the power would be exercised in a certain way and the same equitable doctrine was applied to enforce the power being exercised in that way. The case, however, went to appeal and was settled on terms, [1916] 2 Ch 205.

3 If a will contains a gift which is in terms absolute, clear evidence is needed before the court will assume that the testator did not mean what he said but intended that the gift should be held by the beneficiary subject to a secret trust. The standard of proof is perhaps analogous

to that which the court requires before it will rectify a written instrument; per Brightman J in *Ottaway v Norman* [1972] Ch 698 at 712, [1971] 3 All ER 1325 at 1333.

4 *Wallgrave v Tebbs* (1855) 2 K & J 313; *McCormick v Grogan* (1869) LR 4 HL 82; *Moss v Cooper* (1861) 1 John & H 352; *Jones v Badley* (1868) 3 Ch App 362; *McDonald v Moran* (1938) 12 MPR 424; *MacMillan v Kennedy* [1942] 3 DLR 170; *Re Pugh's Will Trusts, Marten v Pugh* [1967] 3 All ER 337, [1967] 1 WLR 1262; it is easier to infer an intention that a sole trustee should take beneficially than that two or more trustees should do so, but that indication is not sufficient alone. Where a deceased spouse has bequeathed property to a surviving spouse and it is sought to prove a secret trust in favour of a particular person, the surviving spouse can be compelled to give evidence as to communications made between the spouses during the marriage: *Shenton v Tyler* [1939] Ch 620, [1939] 1 All ER 827, and see para **[36.13]** below.

5 Most of the cases turn upon gifts or charities being illegal under the Mortmain Acts: *Muckleston v Brown* (1801) 6 Ves 52; *Stickland v Aldridge* (1804) 9 Ves 516; *Russell v Jackson* (1852) 10 Hare 204; *Springett v Jenings* (1871) 6 Ch App 333; *Tee v Ferris* (1856) 2 K & J 357; *Rowbothan v Dunnett* (1878) 8 Ch D 430. As to the effect of a trust being illegal, see n 2, para **[36.4]** below, and text thereto. The Mortmain Acts have now been repealed by the Charities Act 1960, s 38.

6 *Ottaway v Norman* [1972] Ch 698, [1971] 3 All ER 1325; *Kasperbauer v Griffith* [2000] WTLR 333 (CA).

7 *Kasperbauer v Griffith* [2000] WTLR 333 (CA); *Margulies v Margulies* [2008] WTLR 1871 (CA). If there is any question as to what part of the property is affected by the trust, the onus is on the donee to show what part is not affected by it: *Russell v Jackson* (1852) 10 Hare 204.

8 *Ottaway v Norman* [1972] Ch 698, [1971] 3 All ER 1325 (primary donee's executor obliged to hold a bungalow on trust for secondary donee in accordance with the terms of a secret trust that the primary donee would, on his death, devise the bungalow to the secondary donee).

9 *Kasperbauer v Griffith* [2000] WTLR 333 (CA).

[Updated at footnote 7 for a change in the rate of interest on general legacies with effect from 1 February 2009.]

[36.5]

Effect of failure of trusts. If the secret trust is illegal, the apparent beneficiary holds the property on trust for those who would have taken if the gift had not been contained in the will.[1] Where, however, the trust is not illegal, but fails because, though not void in law, it cannot take effect,[2] or because it is not communicated to the donee,[3] or because it is not assented to by the donee during the lifetime of the testator,[4] the donee takes the gift absolutely and free from the trust.[5] If, therefore, in any such circumstances the donee does in fact apply the gift to the object indicated by the testator, he does so as a voluntary gift from himself.[6] Where the trusts fail as to part of the gift or where they relate in the first instance to part only of the gift the donee takes absolutely subject to the performance of the trusts, the benefits under the trusts being treated as legacies carrying interest after the expiration of one year from the testator's death.[7]

If there is any question as to what part of the property is affected by the trust, the onus is on the donee to show what part is not affected by it.[8]

1 That is to say it falls into residue or passes on intestacy according to the circumstances: see Chapter 48.

2 *Russell v Jackson* (1852) 10 Hare 204.

3 *Carter v Green* (1857) 3 K & J 591.

4 *Podmore v Gunning* (1836) 7 Sim 644; *Jones v Badley* (1868) 3 Ch App 362.

5 *Russell v Jackson* (1852) 10 Hare 204; *Re Gardom, Le Page v A-G* [1914] 1 Ch 662 at 672; revsd sub nom *Le Page v Gardom* (1915) 84 LJ Ch 749.

6 *Lomax v Ripley* (1855) 3 Sm & G 48 at 78; *Geddis v Semple* [1903] 1 IR 73.

7 *Irvine v Sullivan* (1869) LR 8 Eq 673; RSC Ord 44, r 10; SI 1982/1111; the current rate of interest set by the court is 2 per cent with effect from 1 February 2009, substituted for the previous rate of 4 per cent: Civil Procedure Rules, Part 40, *Practice Direction– Accounts, Inquiries etc*, para 15, see para **[32.4]**, n 1.

8 *Russell v Jackson* (1852) 10 Hare 204; *Re Huxtable, Huxtable v Crawfurd* [1902] 2 Ch 793.

PART I

Failure of gifts

CHAPTER 41

Ademption

I. GENERAL PRINCIPLES

[Updated at footnote 3 for *Re Clements Estate* [2007] WTLR 1717.]

[41.2]

Change in nature of property. Where a change has occurred in the nature of the specific property given, even though effected by Act of Parliament, ademption follows,[1] unless the change is a change in name or form only, and the property exists as substantially the same thing although in a different shape.[2] Whether the property exists substantially the same at the death of the testator is a question of fact.[3]

1 *Frewen v Frewen* (1875) 10 Ch App 610 (advowson affected by Irish Church Act 1869); *Re Slater, Slater v Slater* [1907] 1 Ch 665 (water company acquired by Metropolitan Water Board); *Re Lane, Luard v Lane* (1880) 14 Ch D 856 (debentures into debenture stock).

2 *Oakes v Oakes* (1852) 9 Hare 666; *Re Pilkington's Trusts* (1865) 6 New Rep 246; *Humphreys v Humphreys* (1789) 2 Cox Eq Cas 184; *Re Dorman* [1994] 1 All ER 804.

3 *Re Bridle* (1879) 4 CPD 336 at 341; *Re Slater, Slater v Slater* [1906] 2 Ch 480 at 484 (where the effect of the Wills Act 1837, s 24 (Vol 2, Part G, para **[244.26]**), which makes the will speak and take effect as if executed immediately before the death, is considered, and the description of a particular thing as 'my ring' is contrasted with a generic description of property, in this case 'the interest arising from money invested in the Lambeth Waterworks Co', the latter company having before the death of the testator been taken over by the Metropolitan Water Board: it was held that there was an ademption); *Re Jameson, King v Winn* [1908] 2 Ch 111 at 115 (where on an amalgamation of banks there was held to be no ademption). See also *Re Sikes, Moxon v Crossley* [1927] 1 Ch 364, and *Re Wilson* [1958] Qd R 559; and *Re Puczka Estate* (1970) 10 DLR (3d) 339. In *Re Clements Estate* [2007] WTLR 1717, the Supreme Court of Nova Scotia found that there was no ademption of a gift of a house when it was partly destroyed in a fire which killed the testator because the evidence showed that the substantial damage had occurred only after his death when title to the house had already passed to his personal representatives.

II. PARTICULAR CASES

[Updated in the text and at footnotes 1, 2, 3 and 6 for the Mental Capacity Act 2005.]

[41.12]

Disposals under the Mental Capacity Act 2005 or the Mental Health Act 1983. Where the property of a person lacking capacity ('P') has been disposed[1] of by a deputy or by the Court of Protection exercising its powers under the Mental Capacity Act 2005, and under P's will or intestacy[2] another person would have taken an interest in the property but for the disposal, and on P's death any property belonging to P's estate represents the property disposed of, the other person takes the same interest if and so far as circumstances allow in the property representing the property disposed of.[3] Similarly, where any property of a person of unsound mind has been disposed[4] of pursuant to the powers under the Mental Health Act 1983, and under that person's will or intestacy,[5] any other person would have taken an interest in the property but for the disposal, he shall take the same interest, if and so far as circumstances allow, in any property belonging to the estate of the deceased which represents the property disposed of.[6]

1 Disposal of property means sale, exchange, charging of or other dealing, otherwise than by will, with property other than money, the removal of property from one place to another; the application of money in acquiring property; or the transfer of money from one account to another, see the Mental Capacity Act 2005, Sch 2, para 8(5).
2 Or by any gift perfected or nomination taking effect on his death.
3 Mental Capacity Act 2005, Sch 2, para 8(1) iwith effect from 1 October 2007: see SI 2007/1897, art 2(1)(a), (d).
4 Disposal of property means sale, exchange, charging or other dealing, otherwise than by will.
5 Or by any gift perfected or nomination taking effect on his death.
6 Mental Health Act 1983, s 101 (reproducing the Mental Health Act 1959, s 107, which itself embodied previous legislation), repealed by the Mental Capacity Act 2005, s 66(1)(a) with effect from 1 October 2007: see SI 2007/1897, art 2(1)(c), (d); for transitional provisions see the Mental Capacity Act 2005, s 66(4), Sch 5, Pt I.

CHAPTER 42

Election

[Updated at footnote 5 for *Frear v Frear* [2008] EWCA Civ 1320, [2009] WTLR 221.]

[42.5]

Intention to dispose of particular property. To raise a case of election under a will upon the ground that the testator has attempted to dispose of property over which he had no disposing power, it must be clearly shown that the testator intended to dispose of the particular property;[1] and this intention must appear on the face of the will, either by express words or by necessary conclusion from the circumstances disclosed by the will.[2] The presumption is that a testator intends to dispose only of his own property;[3] and general words will not be construed so as to include other property,[4] nor will oral evidence be admitted to show that the testator believed such other property to be his own so as to allow it to be comprised in general words.[5] Similarly, where a testator has a limited interest in property, and purports to dispose of the property itself, the presumption is that he intends to dispose only of his limited interest;[6] and, if it is sought to carry the disposition further, it must be shown that he intended to dispose of more than that interest. But for this purpose positive declaration is not necessary. Regard may be had to the context of the will, and to the inaptitude of the testamentary limitations if applied to the testator's actual interest.[7] But a devise of an estate which is subject to incumbrances does not by itself import an intention to devise it free from incumbrances, so as to put incumbrancers who take under the will to their election.[8] Where it appears from a recital that a testator has disposed of his own property under an erroneous belief as to the interests in other property of certain beneficiaries under his will, giving less to some on the footing that they would be compensated by their interests in the other property, such a recital is not equivalent to a disposition of such other property, so as to raise a case of election against the persons who unduly benefit under the will.[9]

1 *Lord Rancliffe v Lady Parkyns* (1818) 6 Dow 149; *Wintour v Clifton* (1856) 8 De GM & G 641.

2 *Blake v Bunbury* (1792) 4 Bro CC 21; *Minchin v Gabbett* [1896] 1 IR 1; and see *Re Sullivan, Sullivan v Sullivan* [1917] 1 IR 38; *Re Goodwin* (1905) 5 SRNSW 576; *Re Dicey, Julian v Dicey* [1957] Ch 145, [1956] 3 All ER 696 (omission of numbers of houses but identity otherwise proved). In *Re Edwards, Macadam v Wright* [1958] Ch 168, [1957] 2 All ER 495, the property was specifically mentioned as part of the residue but here it was held that the doctrine of ademption applied and no case for election arose.

3 *Pickersgill v Rodger* (1876) 5 Ch D 163; *Cosby v Ashtown* (1859) 10 I Ch R 219; *Thornton v Thornton* (1861) 11 I Ch R 474.

4 *Miller v Thurgood* (1864) 33 Beav 496; *Re Bidwell's Settlement Trusts* (1862) 1 New Rep 176.

5 *Dummer v Pitcher* (1833) 2 My & K 262; *Clementson v Gandy* (1836) 1 Keen 309; *Galvin v Devereux* [1903] 1 IR 185. It has been said that evidence is admissible where the devise or bequest is specific: *Graham v Clark (Dorland Estate) and Dorland* [1949] 3 DLR 539. Parol evidence may be admissible under AJA 1982, s 21 to show what the testator intended to dispose of: see *Frear v Frear* [2008] EWCA Civ 1320, [2009] WTLR 221.

6 *Dummer v Pitcher* (1833) 2 My & K 262; *Howells v Jenkins* (1863) 1 De GJ & Sm 617; *Henry v Henry* (1872) 6 IR Eq 286. If the testator has only a life interest and the intention on the face of the will is to dispose of his interest (if any), there is no case of election; *Galvin v Devereux* [1903] 1 IR 185. Where a testator disposed of the residue of his property and the will was governed by English law, it was the residue according to English law, and as this included property of his wife to which community of goods applied, the wife must elect: *Re Allen's Estate, Prescott v Allen* [1945] 2 All ER 264.

7 *Wintour v Clifton* (1856) 8 De GM & G 641; *Usticke v Peters* (1858) 4 K & J 437. A bequest to a third person of stock standing in the joint names of the testator and his wife, where benefits are conferred on the wife by the will, puts the wife to her election (*Grosvenor v Durston* (1858) 25 Beav 97). Where a testator agreed to settle property on his niece and then left her a legacy on condition that she gave up her claim to a settlement, she was put to her election: *Central Trust and Safe Deposit Co v Snider* [1916] 1 AC 266.

8 *Stephens v Stephens* (1857) 1 De G & J 62; *Henry v Henry* (1872) 6 IR Eq 286. A devise inconsistent with the continuance of the incumbrance will put the incumbrancers to their election if they are beneficiaries under the will: *Blake v Bunbury* (1972) 1 Ves 514, and cf *Sadlier v Butler* (1867) IR 1 Eq 415; *Re Williams, Cunliffe v Williams* [1915] 1 Ch 450.

9 *Box v Barrett* (1866) LR 3 Eq 244. There is no case for election where a testator, erroneously reciting that a hotchpot clause will apply, refrains from appointing the unappointed residue of a fund: *Langslow v Langslow* (1856) 21 Beav 552.

CHAPTER 43

Estoppel

I. PROPRIETARY ESTOPPEL

[Updated in the text to footnotes 6 and 7 and at footnotes 1, 5, 6 and 7 for *Thorner v Major* [2009] UKHL 18. Also updated at footnote 3 for *Re Baker, Baker v Baker* [2008] WTLR 565.]

[43.1]

General principles. It is beyond the scope of this text to set out in detail the principles relating to proprietary estoppel as they have been developed in the modern law. But it can be noted that the doctrine can operate to affect a testamentary gift of property which is claimed by another relying on proprietary estoppel. The principles of proprietary estoppel are founded on representation, reliance and detriment[1] and can be stated in broad terms as follows. Where one person (A) has acted to his detriment on the faith of a belief which was known to and encouraged by another person (B) that he has or is going to be given a right in or over B's property, B cannot insist on his strict legal rights if to do so would be inconsistent with A' s belief.[2] This has been applied to a situation where a claimant worked on the testator's farm for forty years (for allegedly less than full remuneration) on the reliance of repeated assurances by the testator that he would leave the claimant the bulk of his estate including the farm, by his will on his death.[3] The testator made a new will excluding the claimant entirely from inheriting. The claimant succeeded in an action against the estate, claiming an equity in the testator's property under the doctrine of proprietary estoppel, arising from reliance in the testator's assurances causing him detriment.[4] The doctrine has also been applied in favour of claimants in cases of intestacy.[5] In a recent House of Lords decision, the claimant had worked at his father's cousin's farm without any remuneration for 29 years. Although the assurances relied upon in that case were somewhat oblique, the House of Lords said that what amounts to sufficient clarity is hugely dependent on context, and that in the context of two taciturn and undemonstrative countrymen, the assurances in question were sufficient.[6] It is a necessary element of proprietary estoppel that the assurances given to the claimant should relate to identified property owned (or, perhaps, about to be owned) by the deceased.[7]

1 See, for example, *Plimmer v Mayor of Wellington* (1884) 9 App Cas 699, at 714; *Crabb v Arun District Council* [1975] 3 All ER 865 at 880; *Greasley v Cooke* [1980] 3 All ER 710 and *Grant v Edwards* [1986] Ch 638, [1986] 2 All ER 426. For the application of these same principles in the case of testamentary dispositions, see *Thorner v Major* [2009] UKHL 18, para [29]. In this case, although four of the Law Lords applied the conventional proprietary estoppel analysis, Lord Scott expressed the view that in the case of testamentary dispositions a constructive trust analysis is more appropriate than the proprietary estoppel

analysis, with proprietary estoppel confined to cases where the representation is unconditional, and the principles of remedial constructive trusts applying to cases where the representations are of future benefits, and subject to qualification on account of unforeseen future events.

2 Per Balcombe LJ in *Wayling v Jones* (1993) 69 P & CR 170 at p 172, citing Mr Nugee's statement of principle in *Re Basham* [1987] 1 All ER 405 at 410.

3 *Gillett v Holt* [2001] Ch 210, [2000] 2 All ER 289, Court of Appeal reversing Carnwath J at first instance [1998] 3 All ER 917 who had rejected the claim. This was a case where the facts supporting an estoppel were strong; it is not every promise or assurance of inheritance which will give rise to a successful claim under this head. See also *Jennings v Rice* [2001] WTLR 871 affd; [2002] EWCA Civ 159, [2002] WTLR 367, a claim against a deceased estate based on inter vivos promises made by the deceased to the claimant, succeeded in part on the basis of proprietary estoppel. A claim based on proprietary estoppel failed in *Ottey v Grundy (Andreae's Executor)* [2002] EWCA Civ 1176, [2003] WTLR 1253, applying *Wayling v Jones* [1995] 2 FLR 1029 and *Re Baker, Baker v Baker* [2008] WTLR 565.

4 *Re Basham* [1987] 1 All ER 405, was applied and *Taylor v Dickens* [1998] 3 FCR 455 not followed. See also *Layton v Martin* [1986] 2 FLR 227 and *Jones v Watkins* [1987] CA Transcript 1200.

5 *Thorner v Major* [2009] UKHL 18; *Re Basham* [1987] 1 All ER 405 (the claimant worked for many years, without payment, for her stepfather in the expectation of inheriting his estate; the stepfather died intestate. It was held that since her expectation had been encouraged by the deceased and she had acted to her detriment in reliance on that belief, she was entitled to the estate).

6 *Thorner v Major* [2009] UKHL 18, para [56]. The relevant assurances included the deceased handing to the claimant a bonus notice, relating to two policies on the deceased's life with a then value of about £20,000, saying 'That's for my death duties'.

7 *Thorner v Major* [2009] UKHL 18, para [61]. In that case, it was found that the common understanding was that the deceased's assurance to the claimant related to whatever the farm consisted of at the deceased's death. No decided view was given as to whether *Re Basham* [1986] 1 WLR 1498 was correctly decided so far as it extended to the deceased's residuary estate, although it was pointed out that the deputy judge had there relied largely on authorities about mutual wills, which are arguably a special case.

PART J

Construction of wills: general principles

CHAPTER 57

Evidence admissible in a court of construction–extrinsic evidence

VI. THE ADMISSIBILITY OF EXTRINSIC EVIDENCE: POST-1982 DEATHS

[Updated in the text and footnote 4 for *Frear v Frear* [2009] WTLR 231.]

[57.26]

'Evidence, other than evidence of the testator's intention, shows that the language used in any part of it is ambiguous in the light of surrounding circumstances' (para (c)). There was already a rule permitting the admission of extrinsic evidence, including evidence of intention, in cases of latent ambiguities or equivocations before AJA 1982, s 21. The principle was expressed as follows: 'where the object of a testator's bounty, or the subject of disposition is described in terms which are applicable indifferently to more than one person or thing, evidence is admissible to prove which of the persons or things so described was intended by the testator'.[1] The case law illustrations of this principle are well known. Thus in *Re Jackson, Beattie v Murphy*,[2] the testator made a disposition to 'my nephew Arthur Murphy' and since this name was applicable to more than one legitimate nephew, evidence was admitted, which in fact established that it was an illegitimate nephew of that name who was intended. Similarly when the testator simply devises his house to a beneficiary and he owns more than one.

It is thought that para (c) has the effect of admitting evidence of the testator's intention in a wider class of cases than the latent ambiguity rule did. The conditions which had to be fulfilled for the latent ambiguity rule to apply[3] were more stringent. For example, it did not apply if the ambiguity could be resolved by the application of a rule of construction, or by the construction of the will as a whole, or from evidence of surrounding circumstances other than the testator's intention. It is thought that none of these restrictions would apply in relation to para (c), and that in general evidence of the testator's intention is no longer a last resort to be used only when all other methods of interpretation have failed (although it still cannot be admitted to show that there is an ambiguity if none is apparent from the will itself or the surrounding circumstances). Also, para (c) is not restricted, as the latent ambiguity rule apparently was, to ambiguity in descriptions (usually of persons or property), although other kinds of latent ambiguity in wills must be unusual. An indication that para (c) does permit evidence of intention to be admitted in a wider class of cases than under the traditional latent ambiguity rule, although in the absence of specific argument on the point, appears in *Frear v Frear*,[4] where evidence showing that the testatrix, who was the sole legal owner of a house, owned only a beneficial share of the same, was held admissible to show that the language disposing of her residuary estate was ambiguous.

It will be noticed that evidence of the testatrix's intention is not admissible to establish the ambiguity, but only to resolve an ambiguity that has been established by factual evidence.[5]

1 Wigram, *An Examination of the Rules of Law, Respecting the Admission of Extrinsic Evidence in Aid of the Interpretation of Wills*, 5th edn (1914), Proposition VII, p 110. See **[57.22]** above.
2 [1933] Ch 237.
3 See **[57.22]** above.
4 [2008] EWCA Civ 1320, [2009] WTLR 231, para [38].
5 Following the majority of the Law Reform Committee, 19th Report on the Interpretation of Wills (1973, Cmnd 5301).

PART L

Construction of wills: particular rules relating to persons

CHAPTER 72

Illegitimacy of donees

IV. LEGITIMATION

[Updated in the text and footnote 2 for Human Fertilisation and Embryology Act 2008.]

[72.18]

Human Fertilisation and Embryology Acts of 1990 and 2008 (HFEA 1990 and HFEA 2008). The HFEA 1990, ss 27–29 came into force on 1 August 1991 and make provision for who is treated as father and mother of a child produced by means (such as artificial insemination or in vitro fertilisation) regulated by the Act, and HFEA 2008 ss 33–53 replaced those sections of HFEA 1990 with effect from 6 April 2009.[1] The Legitimacy Act 1976 can apply where an unmarried couple have had fertility treatment which results in a child of which the man is by virtue of one or other HFEA treated as the father, and they marry each other after the birth of the child. Further, the Legitimacy Act 1976 is amended by HFEA 2008 so as to apply to cases where a child is born to a same sex female couple where the one who is not the mother is treated by HFEA 2008 as a parent of the child, and they are not civil partners at any time between the treatment and the birth but form a civil partnership after the birth.[2]

1 See **[74.3]** ff above.
2 See LA 1976, ss 2A and 3(2), inserted by HFEA 2008, Sch 6, paras 16, 17, and having effect in relation to assisted reproduction treatment carried out on or after 6 April 2009 (HFEA 2008, ss 43 and 57(1), SI 2009/479).

CHAPTER 74

Gifts to children

[Updated for Human Fertilisation and Embryology Act 2008.]

[74.3]

Child born as a result of fertilisation techniques. The Human Fertilisation and Embryology Act 2008 (HFEA 2008),[1] ss 33–53, replacing the narrower corresponding provisions of the Human Fertilisation and Embryology Act 1990 (HFEA 1990)[2] with effect from 6 April 2009,[3] contains provisions identifying the persons who are to be treated as the mother and the father of a child born as a result of *in vitro* fertilisation or artificial insemination and governing the status of any such child. The HFEA 1990 and HFEA 2008 contain consequential provisions modifying the intestacy rules and the rules governing the construction of written instruments, including wills. Where a parental order has been made under HFEA 1990, s 30[4] in favour of persons who provided gametes in relation to a child carried by a surrogate mother, the adoption legislation applies subject to amendments made for the purpose by statutory instrument.[5]

1 Vol 2, Part G, paras **[245.111]** ff.
2 Vol 2, Part G, paras **[245.82]** ff.
3 SI 2009/479, art 6.
4 Vol 2, Part G, paras **[245.88]**.
5 The power to do this is in HFEA 1990, ss 30(9) and 45(1) and (3), and has been exercised by the Parental Orders (Human Fertilisation and Embryology) Regulations 1994, SI 1994/2767, which came into force on 1 November 1994. HFEA 1990, s 30 is to be replaced by the wider provisions of HFEA 2008, ss 54 and 55, but no commencement order has yet been made for the latter provisions.

[Updated in the text and footnote 3 for Human Fertilisation and Embryology Act 2008.]

[74.4]

Child born as a result of artificial insemination. The Family Law Reform Act 1987 (FLRA 1987) anticipated these provisions with regard to a child born as a result of artificial insemination, on or after 4 April 1988. The FLRA 1987, s 27 provides that where after 1 April 1988 a child was born in England and Wales as the result of artificial insemination of a woman who was at the time of the insemination a party to a subsisting marriage and was artificially inseminated with the semen of some person other than the other party to that marriage, unless it is proved to the satisfaction of any court by which the matter has to be determined that the other party to that marriage did not consent to the insemination, the child should be treated in law as the child of the parties to that marriage and shall not be treated as the child of any person other than the parties to that marriage.[1] It has been held in

Tasmania that a child being the product of his father's semen and his mother's ovum, implanted in the mother's womb subsequent to the death of his father is upon birth entitled to a right of inheritance afforded by law.[2] This would not now be the case in England, as the relevant statutory provision is that the father is such a child's father for the purposes of the name of the father on the birth certificate and no other purpose.[3]

1 FLRA 1987, s 27(1); Vol 2, Part G, para **[245.74]**. The provision does not apply to unmarried couples, so that such a child would not be treated as the child of the male cohabitant.

2 *In the Estate of K* (1996) 5 Tas R 365.

3 See HFEA 1990, s 29(3A)–(3D) (inserted by the Human Fertilisation and Embryology (Deceased Fathers) Act 2003) and HFEA 2008, ss 39(3), 41(2). See para **[74.5]** below.

[Updated for Human Fertilisation and Embryology Act 2008.]

[74.5]

Human Fertilisation and Embryology Acts of 2008 and 1990. The relevant provisions are HFEA 2008, ss 33–53,[1] replacing HFEA 1990, ss 27–29.[2] HFEA 1990, ss 27–29 were brought into force on 1 August 1991 and have effect only in relation to children born as a consequence of in vitro fertilisation or artificial insemination carried out on or after that date and before 6 April 2009. HFEA 2008 ss 33–53 have effect in relation to children born as a consequence of in vitro fertilisation or artificial insemination carried out on or after 6 April 2009.[3]

HFEA 2008, s 33(1) and HFEA 1990, s 27(1), define the 'mother' of a child for the purposes of those Acts as follows: 'The woman who is carrying or has carried a child as a result of the placing in her of an embryo or of sperm and eggs, and no other woman, is to be treated as the mother of the child'.[4] This means that for the purposes of the HFEA 2008 and HFEA 1990 a woman may be treated as the mother of a child with whom she is not genetically connected.

The HFEA 2008, ss 35–37 (relating to treatment on or after 6 April 2009) and HFEA 1990, s 28 (treatment before 6 April 2009), define the 'father' for the purposes of these respective Acts. The provisions of these two Acts are for practical purposes the same where the woman is married at the time of the placing in her of an embryo or of sperm and eggs or of her artificial insemination. HFEA 2008, s 35(1) and HFEA 1990, s 28(2) provide that if (a) at the time of the placing in her of the sperm and eggs or of her insemination, the woman was a party to a marriage, and (b) the creation of the embryo carried by her was not brought about with the sperm of the other party to the marriage, then that other party is to be treated as the father of the child unless it is shown that he did not consent. In the case of an unmarried couple where the treatment does not use the man's sperm (and he is alive at the time of the treatment), there is parallel provision for the man to be treated as the father (HFEA 2008, ss 36 and 37, HFEA 1990, s 28(3)). There is a difference between the two sets of provisions in that under HFEA 1990, s 28(3) he is treated as the father if the treatment services were provided for the woman and the man together, whereas under HFEA 2008, ss 36 and 37 he is treated as the father if both he and the woman have given the person responsible for the treatment a written notice of their consent and not withdrawn or varied it before the treatment was carried out.

These provisions mean that for the purposes of the HFEA 1990 and HFEA 2008 a man may be treated as the father of a child with whom he is not genetically connected. Indeed the child might not be genetically connected with the woman either.

An innovation of HFEA 2008 is ss 42–45, relating to treatment occurring on or after 6 April 2009. These are provisions, parallel to the provisions outlined above, for any woman who at the time of having the treatment has a civil partner who has consented to the treatment, and for any woman who is not married and not in a civil partnership at the time of having the treatment where she and another woman have given the appropriate written notices of consent to the provider of the treatment. In these cases the civil partner of the mother or consenting other woman is treated as a parent of the child.

There are also provisions in HFEA 2008 and HFEA 1990 for fathers, civil partners, etc, who have died before the treatment was carried out to qualify for appearing on the birth certificate as the father or parent of the child,[5] but in such cases such a person is not treated as father or parent for any other purpose.[6]

The effect of these provisions for inheritance is set out in HFEA 1990, s 29 and HFEA 2008, s 48. Where by virtue of HFEA 1990, ss 27 or 28 or by virtue of HFEA 2008, ss 33, 35, 36, 42, or 43 a person is to be treated as the mother, father or (under HFEA 2008, ss 42 or 43) parent of a child, that person is to be treated in law as the mother, father or parent, as the case may be, of the child for all purposes.[7] Any provider of the genetic material for the treatment is expressly excluded from being the father, mother or parent.[8] Neither set of provisions says in terms that a child born to a married couple where the husband is treated as the father is to be treated as the legitimate child of that marriage, but this must surely follow from the principle established by the HFEA 1990 and 2008 that each party to the marriage is to be treated in law as the child's parent. This view is impliedly confirmed by the saving contained in HFEA 1990, s 27(5) and HFEA 2008, s 38(5) for any child who would be treated as the legitimate child of the parties at common law (eg a child born in wedlock as a consequence of the prescribed medical techniques carried out before the marriage with the consent of a man other than the husband), and by HFEA 2008, s 48(6). The latter provision is that where a child is born to a woman who is in a civil partnership at any point between the date of the treatment and the birth of the child, and the non-child bearing civil partner is treated as a parent of the child under HFEA 2008, s 42 or 43, the child is the legitimate child of his or her parents.

It also follows that where the person who is a child's father by virtue of HFEA 1990 or HFEA 2008 marries the child's mother after the birth of the child, the child will be legitimated under the Legitimacy Act 1976.[9] Where a child is born as a result of treatment under HFEA 2008 on or after 6 April 2009, and by virtue of HFEA 2008, s 43 a woman other than the mother is a parent of that child, and the mother and other parent form a civil partnership after the birth of the child, the child will become legitimate under the Legitimacy Act 1976.[10]

1 Vol 2, Part G, paras **[245.111]** ff.
2 Vol 2, Part G, paras **[245.82]** ff.
3 The commencement date fixed by SI 2009/479. See also HFEA 2008, s 57(1).

4 This includes cases where the procedure was carried out abroad (HFEA 1990, s 27(3), HFEA 2008, s 33(3)) and is subject to the possibility of adoption (HFEA 1990, s 27(2), HFEA 2008, s 33(2)).
5 HFEA 2008, ss 39, 40, 46; HFEA 1990, s 28(5A)–(5I) (inserted by the Human Fertilisation and Embryology (Deceased Fathers) Act 2003).
6 See HFEA 2008, ss 39(3), 41(2), 46(4), and HFEA 1990, s 29(3A)–(3D) (inserted by the Human Fertilisation and Embryology (Deceased Fathers) Act 2003).
7 HFEA 1990, s 29(1), HFEA 2008, s 48(1). An exception is made for devolution of dignities or titles of honour and property limited to devolve with them: HFEA 1990, s 29(4), HFEA 2008, s 48(7).
8 HFEA 1990, ss 27(1), 28(4), 29(2); HFEA 2008, ss 33(1), 38(1), 41, 45, 47, 48(2).
9 For legitimation under the Legitimacy Act 1976 see paras **[72.15]**, **[72.16]** and **[72.18]** above.
10 Legitimacy Act 1976, ss 2A and 3(2), inserted by HFEA 2008, Sch 6 paras 16, 17.

[Updated for Human Fertilisation and Embryology Act 2008.]

[74.6]

The construction of wills—retrospective effect of HFEAs. The HFEA 1990, s 29(3) provides that where s 29(1) of it applies, and HFEA 2008, s 48(5) provides that where (inter alia) s 48(1) of it applies, 'references to any relationship between two people in any enactment, deed or other instrument or document (*whenever passed or made*) are to be read accordingly' (emphasis supplied).[1] Further, HFEA 2008, s 53(1), (2) provide in cases where a child has by virtue of the Act a female parent in addition to his or her mother, references to the child's father in any enactment, deed or other instrument or document, whenever made, are to that additional parent. The retrospective effect of the HFEA 1990, s 29(3) and HFEA 2008, s 48(5) is thought to be unique. In the past a statutory provision modifying the rules of construction affecting references to children and issue have been limited in their operation to deaths occurring or instruments made after the commencement of the provision. HFEA 1990, s 29(3) and HFEA 2008, s 48(5) represent significant departures from this practice. The effect of this is that, for example, a child born to a married couple as a result of fertility treatment effected on or after 1 August 1991 could be a beneficiary under a settlement or will which came into force before 1970 which created continuing trusts for issue of an ancestor of one the persons treated as the child's parents, even though the will or settlement does not contain any provisions modifying the rules of construction affecting references to children and issue, and although an illegitimate child conceived naturally would not be.[2] Further, a child born to a woman in a civil partnership as a result of fertility treatment effected on or after 6 April 2009 could be a beneficiary under such a settlement or will.[3]

As regards the rules of intestacy the HFEA 1990, s 29(3) and HFEA 2008, s 48(5) will in practice operate only prospectively, as the next of kin of a deceased person are all identified at the date of his death.[4]

1 Vol 2, Part G, paras **[245.87]** and **[245.127]**. See also para **[74.5]** above.
2 Because the provisions of the FLRA 1969 are not retrospectively applied to wills executed before 1 January 1990, whereas the provisions of the HFEA 1990 and HFEA 2008 are. An example will illustrate the point. Suppose that in 1993 an illegitimate child is born to a granddaughter of a testator who died before 1970, such a child, though genetically connected with the settlor or testator, will not be eligible to benefit as a member of the class of issue of the testator benefited by his will. On the other hand if that granddaughter is married and in 1993 has a child with her husband's consent in consequence of the implantation of another woman's egg, that child would by force of the HFEA 1990 be

eligible to benefit as the granddaughter's legitimate child and so as the testator's issue, even though not genetically connected with the testator.

3 Such a child is treated as legitimate by virtue of HFEA 2008, s 48(6).

4 As does the Family Law Reform Act 1987, s 27 relating to children born as a result of artificial insemination.

[Updated for Human Fertilisation and Embryology Act 2008.]

[74.7]

Modifying or excluding the Acts. HFEA 1990 and HFEA 2008 do not expressly contain a provision stating that the effects of them can be excluded by a contrary intention expressed in the will. But it is thought that the provisions can be excluded by express wording in a will, if that is thought to be desirable, as a matter of the testamentary freedom of a testator to select his beneficiaries. A simple statement that the will should be construed as if the HFEA 1990 and HFEA 2008 had not been enacted should suffice.

CHAPTER 75

Adopted children

[Updated in the text and footnote 12 for Human Fertilisation and Embryology Acts 1990 and 2008.]

[75.1]

The position under previous Adoption Acts. Before 1 January 1950,[1] adoption, whether under an order of the court or otherwise, gave the adopted child no right to share in the property of the members of the adopting family, but, on the other hand, it did not deprive the child of any of its rights to share in the property of its original family to which it would have been entitled apart from the adoption.[2] This applied to all dispositions of property and to the rights upon intestacy.[3] This position was reversed by the Adoption of Children Act 1949 which provided that adopted persons were to be regarded as the children of the adopters, and of no other persons, for the purposes of intestacies[4]. However, an adopted person was only treated as a child of the adopter in relation to wills and settlements where the will or settlement was made *after* the adoption had taken place.[5] This basic provision was re-enacted in 1958, and again in 1975 with effect from 1 January 1976. The important change was made as from the latter date that an adopted person was treated as a child of the adopter, in relation to wills of persons dying and settlements made on or after 1 January 1976, even where the adoption was subsequent to the will or settlement. The earlier legislation continues to be printed in Vol 2, Part G, because it remains relevant to the devolution of property devolving under wills and settlements made at earlier dates. The failure until 1976 to legislate to give adopted children the same property rights as legitimate children may turn out to be a breach of the European Human Rights Convention.[6] The governing legislative provisions can be stated thus:

(i) deaths on or after 1 January 1950: Adoption Act 1950;[7]
(ii) deaths on or after 1 April 1959: Adoption Act 1958;[8]
(iii) deaths on or after 1 January 1976: Children Act 1975;[9]
(iv) deaths on or after 1 January 1988: Adoption Act 1976 (AA 1976).[10]
(v) deaths on or after 30 December 2005: Adoption and Children Act 2002 (ACA 2002).[11]

This discussion will refer to the ACA 2002[11] provisions which very largely, in so far as they are relevant to wills, reproduce the provisions of the previous CA 1975 and the AA 1976. Thus the current rules mostly date from 1 January 1976, and relate to settlements made and the wills of persons dying on or after that date. The position under the earlier Adoption Acts is described in more detail in previous editions of this text. AA 1976 also applies, subject to amendments made for the purpose by statutory instrument, where a parental order has been made under HFEA 1990, s 30 in favour of persons who provided gametes in relation to a child carried by a surrogate mother.[12]

1 The date when the Adoption of Children Act 1949 came into force.

2 Adoption of Children Act 1926, s 5(2), repealed by the Adoption of Children Act 1949; Vol 2, Part G, para **[245.4]**.

3 Adoption of Children Act 1926, s 5(2), repealed by the Adoption of Children Act 1949. Disposition includes assurance inter vivos as well as by will or codicil: Adoption of Children Act 1926, s 5(4); Vol 2, Part G, para **[245.4]**.

4 Adoption of Children Act 1949 s 9(2), re-enacted as Adoption Act 1950, s 13(1),vol 2, Part G, para **[245.18]**.

5 Adoption of Children Act 1949, ss 9, 10. See Adoption Act 1950, ss 13, 14, which re-enacted ss 9, 10 of the 1949 Act, in Vol 2, Part G, paras **[245.18]** and **[245.19]**.

6 See *Pla and Puncernau v Andorra* [2004] 2 FCR 630, ECtHR. The Human Rights Act 1998, however, does not apply to rights arising or failing to arise before it came into force.

7 Adoption Act 1950, ss 13, 14, Sch 5, para 4, proviso; see Vol 2, Part G, paras **[245.18]** and **[245.19]**; which replaced the Adoption of Children Act 1949 with effect from the same commencement date.

8 Adoption Act 1958, ss 16, 17; see Vol 2, Part G, paras **[245.26]** and **[245.27]**; which repealed the Adoption Act 1950.

9 The provisions were contained in the Children Act 1975, which were replaced by the Adoption Act 1976; Vol 2, Part G, paras **[245.43]** ff. The provisions of the Children Act 1975 applied from 1 January 1976 but were repealed with retrospective effect by the same provisions in the Adoption Act 1976, from 1 January 1976. See the Children Act 1975 and the Adoption Act 1976 (Commencement No 2) Order 1987, SI 1987/1242 which brought the latter Act into force on 1 January 1988.

10 See Vol 2, Part G, paras **[245.91]** ff, replacing the Children Act 1975.

11 See Vol 2, Part G, paras **[245.91]** ff. The Act restates and amends the law relating to adoption and makes further amendments to the law relating to children. It received the royal assent on 7 November 2002, and the provisions concerning the property and succession rights of adopted children came into force on 30 December 2005 (SI 2005/2213) in relation to adoptions occurring on or after that date. With effect from 30 December 2005, it also repeals the whole of AA 1976, apart from Part IV and para 6 of Sch 2 (which regulate the property and succession rights of adopted children), and replaces these provisions with the corresponding provisions of the 2002 Act.

12 For HFEA 1990, s 30 see Vol 2, Part G, para **[245.30]**. The power to apply the adoption legislation subject to amendments is in HFEA 1990, ss 30(9) and 45(1) and (3), and has been exercised by the Parental Orders (Human Fertilisation and Embryology) Regulations 1994, SI 1994/2767 which came into force on 1 November 1994. It applies AA 1976 subject to the amendments there set out, and has continued to do so since 30 December 2005 despite the replacement of AA 1976 by ACA 2002; the latter Act amended SI 1994/2767 so as to refer to AA 1976 as it stood immediately before the commencement of ACA 2002. HFEA 1990, s 30 is to be replaced by the wider provisions of HFEA 2008, ss 54 and 55, but no commencement order has yet been made for the latter provisions.

PART M

Construction of wills: particular rules relating to beneficial interests

CHAPTER 82

Quantity of interest given

I. IN GENERAL

[Updated at footnote 1.]

[82.3]

Intention of testator governs construction. The intention of the testator as shown by the context of the whole will must in every case govern the construction and may cut down an apparent absolute interest to a life interest[1] or make it subject to defeasance;[2] and a life interest may, on the other hand, be extended to an absolute interest[3] or may be reduced to an interest until marriage or remarriage or other event.[4] An absolute interest is not cut down to a life interest unless the contingency cutting it down happens,[5] and an absolute interest subject to an executory gift over on a contingency remains absolute if the contingency does not happen.[6]

1 *Sherratt v Bentley* (1834) 2 My & K 149 (where the latter part of the will was held to prevail). The following were gifts to one person without any words showing what interest he or she is to take followed by a gift over after his or her death: *Joslin v Hammond* (1834) 3 My & K 110; *Hayes v Hayes* (1836) 1 Keen 97; *Re Bagshaw's Trusts* (1877) 46 LJ Ch 567 (where the gift in question was of personalty, but was accompanied by a gift of realty to the same person (the wife) for life); *Re Russell* (1885) 52 LT 559; *Re Sanford, Sanford v Sanford* [1901] 1 Ch 939 (a complicated will and codicil, but held that there were no words of limitation in the gift to the wife); *In the Estate of Last* [1958] P 134.

The following were gifts either in terms absolute or with limitations which would normally give an absolute interest followed by a gift after the death of the donee: *Morrall v Sutton* (1842) 5 Beav 100; *Johnston v Antrobus* (1856) 21 Beav 556; *Re Lupton's Estate* [1905] P 321; *Re Houghton, Houghton v Brown* (1884) 53 LJ Ch 1018 (an unlimited gift of rents). Where there is a gift to A for life, with remainder to B with remainder to C, B takes only a life interest: *Earl of Lonsdale v Countess of Berchtoldt* (1854) Kay 646.

2 *Bird v Webster* (1853) 1 Drew 338 (gift of personalty to persons and 'their descendants'. This gave an estate tail, but, being personalty, that became an absolute interest).

3 A gift of personal estate for life and afterwards to the donee's executors and administrators gives an absolute interest: *Re Brooks, Public Trustee v White* [1928] Ch 214. As to gift with a superadded power, see para **[83.8]** below. As to unlimited gifts of income, see Chapter 62.

4 *Meeds v Wood* (1854) 19 Beav 215 (to A for life and if she should marry to B: B takes on marriage of A or on death of A, if she does not marry. B's interest is vested independently of A's marriage); *Lancaster v Varty* (1826) 5 LJOS Ch 41 (remarriage). On the other hand where there is a gift to a widow until remarriage with a gift over to A when he attains twenty-three, the widow, whether or not she re-marries, takes the property until A attains twenty-three: *Doe d Dean of Westminster v Freeman* (1786) 1 Term Rep 389; *Re Cabburn, Gage v Rutland* (1882) 46 LT 848.

5 *Re Watson, Clume-Seymour v Brand* [1930] 2 Ch 344.

6 *Watkins v Weston* (1863) 3 De GJ & Sm 434; *Re Bourke's Trusts* (1891) 27 LR Ir 573; *Parnell v Boyd* [1896] 2 IR 571; *Re Lady Monck's Will, Monck v Crocker* [1900] 1 IR 56; but see *Re Cohen's Will Trusts, Cullen v Westminster Bank Ltd* [1936] 1 All ER 103 (gift subject to the provisions and directions hereinafter contained).

CHAPTER 94

Perpetuities

II. APPLICATION OF THE RULE: THE COMMON LAW RULES

[Updated at footnote 1 for *Pengelly v Pengelly* [2008] Ch 375.]

[94.15]

'As far as the law admits'. These and similar words have no effect in a will except in the case of executory trusts.[1] Where the gift is direct and unambiguous these words have no effect whatever, but as stated above, where the will is ambiguous, and these words are present, they aid the court to choose a construction which will render the will operative rather than void.[2] In one case an appointment on the trusts of a previous instrument or such of them as were 'capable of taking effect' took effect with the trusts excluded which would have been void under the rule.[3] Executory trusts, though subject to the rule in common with other trusts,[4] are executed by the court in such a way as to preclude the objection arising from the rule and are moulded so as to carry out the intention of the testator so far as the rules of law admit.[5] Provisions which offend against the rule are omitted,[6] modified,[7] or confined within the rule,[8] unless the creator of the trust has specifically or by necessary implication directed the inclusion of such provisions,[9] or the trust is wholly incapable of being executed so as to avoid the objection arising from the rule.[10] It follows, therefore, that in the case of executory trusts the court will in the ordinary way be prepared to give effect to a direction by a testator that the provisions of his will are to take effect only so far as the law allows or will admit. Where property is settled or directed to be settled in a particular course of succession, so far as the rules of law will admit, or with other words to the same effect, then, according to the intention shown, the qualification may refer to the quality of the property, to which the course of succession may be inapt (as in the case of personal property settled to follow real estate)—this being the ordinary sense of the words in such a case[11]—or to the length of time that the property is to be tied up, having regard to the rule against perpetuities. In the first case, no executory trust is necessarily created, nor are the interests deemed to be settled to the limits of time allowed by the rule.[12] In the second case, if the intention is that the property is to be tied up as long as possible, then an executory trust may be created, but such trust must be executed by prolonging the settlement, not to the farthest limit possible in any event under the rules, but to that convenient limit which will enable the primary purpose of the instrument to be carried out.[13] In such a case the court inclines to give life interests only to all persons, becoming entitled under the limitations, who are in existence at the date of the death of the testator creating the limitations.[14]

1 *Christie v Gosling* (1866) LR 1 HL 279; *Re Viscount Exmouth, Viscount Exmouth v Praed* (1883) 23 Ch D 158; *Portman v Viscount Portman* [1922] 2 AC 473; *Pengelly v Pengelly* [2008] Ch 375.

2 See cases cited in n 1; and *Re Vaux, Nicholson v Vaux* [1939] Ch 465, [1938] 4 All ER 297 (power to trustees to deal with capital and income as they think best within limits prescribed by law); *Re Craig* [1955] VLR 196 (where land was not to be sold until such time or times as the law directs. Held to be a direction that the sale must take place at the end of the perpetuity period).

3 *Re Finch and Chew's Contract* [1903] 2 Ch 486.

4 *Duke of Marlborough v Earl Godolphin* (1759) 1 Eden 404; *Blackburn v Stables* (1814) 2 Ves & B 367.

5 *Christie v Gosling* (1866) LR 1 HL 279; *Re Beresford-Hope, Aldenham v Beresford-Hope* [1917] 1 Ch 287.

6 *Miles v Harford* (1879) 12 Ch D 691; distinguished in *Re Flavel's Will Trusts, Coleman v Flavel* [1969] 2 All ER 232, [1969] 1 WLR 444.

7 *Lord Dorchester v Earl Effingham* (1813) 10 Sim 587n: *Woolmore v Burrows* (1827) 1 Sim 512.

8 *Bankes v Le Despencer* (1840) 10 Sim 576; *Lyddon v Ellison* (1854) 19 Beav 565; *Shelley v Shelley* (1868) LR 6 Eq 540.

9 *Sackville-West v Viscount Holmesdale* (1870) LR 4 HL 543; compare *IRC v Williams* [1969] 3 All ER 614 ('upon such trusts as shall not impinge the rule against perpetuities'). See also *Re Earl of Coventry's Indentures, Smith v Earl of Coventry* [1974] Ch 77, [1973] 3 All ER 1, where the words 'due regard being had to the law relating to perpetuities' were ineffective to save a void appointment, since the purpose of the words was merely to remind the trustees to think carefully before exercising the powers conferred on them, rather than to cut down the period during which the power could be exercised.

10 *Tregonwell v Sydenham* (1815) 3 Dow 194.

11 *Countess of Lincoln v Duke of Newcastle* (1806) 12 Ves 218; *Christie v Gosling* (1866) LR 1 HL 279.

12 *Lord Deerhurst v Duke of St Albans* (1820) 5 Madd 232; *Re Hill, Hill v Hill* [1902] 1 Ch 807.

13 *Williams v Teale* (1847) 6 Hare 239; *Shelley v Shelley* (1868) LR 6 Eq 540; *Re Beresford-Hope, Aldenham v Beresford-Hope* [1917] 1 Ch 287; *Pole v Pole* [1924] 1 Ch 156.

14 *Woolmore v Burrows* (1827) 1 Sim 512 at 526; *Bankes v Le Despencer* (1840) 10 Sim 576; *Williams v Teale* (1847) 6 Hare 239.

PART N

Charities

CHAPTER 102

Charities: gifts for charitable purposes

I. CHARITABLE PURPOSES

[Updated for the Charities Act 2006.]

[102.2]

Charity. A charity is now defined as any institution, whether incorporated or not, including a trust or undertaking, which is established for charitable purposes only and falls to be subject to the control of the High Court[1] in the exercise of its jurisdiction with respect to charities.[2] There is provision for the registration of charities[3] and any registered charity is by the Charities Act 1993 (CA 1993), s 4(1) for all purposes other than rectification of the register, a charity.[4] Neither the Charities Act 1960 nor the CA 1993, defined charitable purposes. With effect from 1 April 2008, the Charities Act 2006 (CA 2006) now does so, although in a non-exhaustive way which remains dependent in various ways on the pre-existing law.[5]

1 Considered in *Construction Industry Training Board v A-G* [1973] Ch 173, [1972] 2 All ER 1339.

2 CA 2006, ss 1(1), 78(5), in force from 1 April 2008 (SI 2008/945), replacing the similarly-worded CA 1993, s 96(1). This definition of 'charity' does not apply for the purposes of an enactment if a different definition of that term applies for those purposes by virtue of that or any other enactment: CA 2006, s 1(2).

3 CA 1993, ss 3–3B, substituted by CA 2006, s 9 for CA 1993, s 3, with effect from 31 January 2009 (SI 2008/3267).

4 Previously Charities Act 1960, s 5(1). *Wynn v Skegness UDC* [1966] 3 All ER 336, [1967] 1 WLR 52; *Finch v Poplar Borough Council* (1967) 66 LGR 324. If an institution is registered under the Charities Act 1960, and so conclusively presumed to be a charity by virtue of s 5(1), and its purposes are shown to have been the same for a certain period prior to registration, it will be presumed to have been a charitable institution during that period also; *Re Murawski's Will Trusts, Lloyds Bank Ltd v Royal Society for the Prevention of Cruelty to Animals* [1971] 2 All ER 328, [1971] 1 WLR 707. See also *Construction Industry Training Board v A-G* [1973] Ch 173, [1972] 2 All ER 1339; and *Childs v A-G* [1973] 2 All ER 108, [1973] 1 WLR 497.

5 For the position under the CA 2006 see para **[102.3]**, below.

[Updated for the commencement of Charities Act 2006, ss 1–4.]

[102.3]

Meaning of 'Charitable Purposes' under the Charities Act 2006. CA 2006, ss 1–4 (which came into force in this respect on 1 April 2008)[1] includes for the first time a statutory definition of 'Charitable Purposes'.[2]

Under the 2006 Act a reference in any enactment or document to a charity within the meaning of the Charitable Uses Act 1601 or the preamble to it is to be construed as a reference to a charity as defined above.[3]

'Charitable purpose' is defined by the 2006 Act as a purpose which falls within any of 13 different descriptions and is for the public benefit.[4] The descriptions of purposes which, under the 2006 Act, are capable of being charitable purposes are:[5]

(a) the prevention or relief of poverty;
(b) the advancement of education;
(c) the advancement of religion (including a religion which involves a belief in more than one god and a religion which does not involve a belief in a god);[6]
(d) the advancement of health (including the prevention or relief of sickness, disease or human suffering) or the saving of lives;[7]
(e) the advancement of citizenship or community development (including rural or urban regeneration and the promotion of civic responsibility, volunteering, the voluntary sector or the effectiveness or efficiency of charities);[8]
(f) the advancement of the arts, culture, heritage or science;
(g) the advancement of amateur sport (meaning games which promote health by involving physical or mental skill or exertion);[9]
(h) the advancement of human rights, conflict resolution or reconciliation or the promotion of religious or racial harmony or equality and diversity;
(i) the advancement of environmental protection or improvement;
(j) the relief of those in need by reason of youth, age, ill-health, disability, financial hardship or other disadvantage (including the provision of accommodation or care to such persons);[10]
(k) the advancement of animal welfare;
(l) the promotion of the efficiency of the armed forces of the Crown, or of the efficiency of the police, fire and rescue services (under Part 2 of the Fire and Rescue Services Act 2004) or ambulance services;[11]
(m) any other purposes not within the previous categories but recognised as charitable under charity law as it was before this definition came into force or by virtue of Recreational Charities Act 1958, s 1; any purposes that may reasonably be regarded as analogous to, or within the spirit of, any purposes falling within any of the previous categories or the existing law; and any purposes that may reasonably be regarded as analogous to, or within the spirit of, any purposes which have been recognised under charity law as falling within the above.[12]

Any reference in any enactment or document (in whatever terms and whenever made) is to be construed in accordance with these definitions unless the context otherwise requires.[13]

A purpose must also be for the public benefit if it is to be a charitable purpose. Public benefit means the public benefit as that term is understood for the purposes of the law relating to charities in England and Wales.[14] A purpose is not presumed to be for the public benefit because it falls into one of the 13 categories set out above.[15]

The Act provides for guidance as to the operation of the public benefit requirement to beissued by the Charity Commission.[16]

It will be apparent from the above that the pre-existing law remains relevant, both to category (m) and to the general requirement of public benefit. The main differences made to the law by this definition is that a more detailed and up-to-date list of specific categories of charitable purposes is provided, and that the former presumption, that the advancement of education, advancement of religion or relief of poverty were ipso facto for the public benefit, is abolished.

1 SI 2008/945.
2 For the definition of 'charity' in CA 2006, s 1(1), which is much the same as that in CA 1993, s 96(1), see para **[102.2]** above.
3 CA 2006, s 1(3).
4 CA 2006, s 2(1).
5 CA 2006, s 2(2)
6 CA 2006, s 2(2)(c) and 2(3)(a).
7 CA 2006, s 2(2)(d) and 2(3)(b).
8 CA 2006, s 2(2)(e) and 2(3)(c).
9 CA 2006, s 2(2)(g) and 2(3)(d).
10 CA 2006, s 2(2)(j) and 2(3)(e).
11 CA 2006, s 2(2)(l) and 2(3)(f).
12 CA 2006, s 2(4).
13 CA 2006, s 2(6), (7).
14 CA 2006, s 3(3).
15 CA 2006, s 3(2).
16 CA 2006, s 4. See the Charity Commission's 'Charities and Public Benefit' (2008) and 'Analysis of the Law underpinning Charities and Public Benefit' (2008).

[Updated in footnotes 2 and 4 for the commencement of CA 2006, s 2, and in footnote 3 for *Re Harding, Gibbs v Harding* [2008] Ch 235.]

[102.10]

Purposes beneficial to the community. While all charitable gifts must be for the benefit of the public as distinct from private individuals,[1] the gifts now to be considered are essentially for the benefit of the general public. Under CA 2006 all charities must satisfy the public benefit test described here if their purposes are to be charitable purposes.[2] It is not enough that the trust should be for the public benefit, it must also be beneficial in a way which the law regards as a charitable trust.[3] Until CA 2006 came into force[4] the question whether the purposes were for the benefit of the general public did not need to be considered where the gift was exclusively for the relief of poverty, for educational or religious purposes or for purposes analogous to those purposes, but the ambit of the purposes must not have been so wide as to include purposes which the law considers as not charitable.[5] The question of the public nature of the trusts arises when the primary class of eligible persons is ascertained. If this primary class is sufficiently wide, the fact that the trustees are bound to give priority to a narrower class does not destroy the essential public and charitable nature of the trust,[6] but where the class is confined not only to a particular area but also to be selected from within it by reference to a particular creed it is not charitable.[7] The question whether or not the potential beneficiaries of a trust can fairly be said to constitute a section of the public is a question of degree and cannot be by itself decisive of the question whether the trust is a charity: much will depend on the purpose of the trust.[8] These gifts which are extremely various in their nature may for convenience be classified as follows: gifts encouraging patriotism or national feeling;[9] gifts for public works;[10] gifts for public instruction or recreation;[11] gifts promoting the efficiency of the Army;[12] gifts for the improvement of agriculture;[13] gifts for the protection of animals;[14] gifts for the care of the sick;[15] gifts for the spread of certain principles;[16] gifts to foster promote and increase public interest in dramatic art[17] or music.[18] The question whether the promulgation of a particular doctrine or principle is for the benefit of the public is to be answered by the court on the evidence before it.[19] A gift of this nature is none the less charitable if it benefits only a section of the public[20] or a particular locality or the inhabitants of a particular locality[21] but not members of a particular creed in a particular locality.[22]

1 *Peggs v Lamb* [1994] Ch 172, [1994] 2 All ER 15; citing *Williams' Trustees v IRC* [1947] AC 447, [1947] 1 All ER 513.

2 CA 2006, ss 2(1)(b) and 3, in force from 1 April 2008 (SI 2008/945). See also the Charity Commission's 'Charities and Public Benefit' (2008) and 'Analysis of the Law underpinning Charities and Public Benefit' (2008).

3 The importance of this aspect of charitable gifts came before the courts in *Re Compton, Powell v Compton* [1945] Ch 123, [1945] 1 All ER 198, and has been much discussed since that decision; see *Re Tree, Idle v Tree* [1945] Ch 325, [1945] 2 All ER 65; *Re Hobourn Aero Components Ltd's Air Raid Distress Fund, Ryan v Forrest* [1946] Ch 194, [1946] 1 All ER 501; *National Anti-Vivisection Society v IRC* [1948] AC 31, [1947] 2 All ER 217; *Gibson v South American Stores (Gath and Chaves) Ltd* [1950] Ch 177, [1949] 2 All ER 985; *Oppenheim v Tobacco Securities Trust Co Ltd* [1951] AC 297, [1951] 1 All ER 31; *Keren Kayemeth Le Jisroel Ltd v IRC* [1932] AC 650; *Williams' Trustees v IRC* [1947] AC 447, [1947] 1 All ER 513; *Re Scarisbrick* [1951] Ch 622, [1951] 1 All ER 822 (poor relations); *IRC v Glasgow City Police Athletic Association* [1953] AC 380, [1953] 1 All ER 747 (to encourage athletic sports connected with city police force not charitable); *Incorporated Council of Law Reporting for England and Wales v A-G* [1972] Ch 73, [1971] 3 All ER 1029; the publication of the Law Reports is a purpose beneficial to the community). See also *Scottish Burial Reform and Cremation Society Ltd v Glasgow City Corpn* [1968] AC 138, [1967] 3 All ER 215, HL. However, since the court leans in favour of making a testator's testamentary dispositions effective, it may lean in favour of finding a gift to the inhabitants of a locality, without a specified purpose, a valid charitable gift, see *Re Harding, Gibbs v Harding* [2008] Ch 235; [2007] 1 All ER 747.

4 CA 2006 places a public benefit requirement on all charitable purposes, including those which would have been charitable under the pre-existing law without the need to satisfy such a test: CA 2006, s 2(1)(b), in force from 1 April 2008 (SI 2008/945).

5 *IRC v Baddeley* [1955] AC 572, [1955] 1 All ER 525. The question whether a trust set up by a will was charitable because it was of public benefit stood or fell by the law and character of the objects of the trust at the date of the testator's death: *Re Bushnell, Lloyds Bank Ltd v Murray* [1975] 1 All ER 721, [1975] 1 WLR 1596, distinguishing *Scottish Burial Reform and Cremation Society Ltd v Glasgow City Corpn* [1968] AC 138, [1967] 3 All ER 215, HL.

6 *Re Koettgen's Will Trust, Westminster Bank Ltd v Family Welfare Association Trustees Ltd* [1954] Ch 252, [1954] 1 All ER 581 (trust for commercial education generally with a preference for employees of a company and members of their families).

7 *IRC v Baddeley* [1955] AC 572, [1955] 1 All ER 525.

8 Per Lord Cross in *Dingle v Turner* [1972] AC 601 at 624, [1972] 1 All ER 878 at p 889, 'sections of the public' include, for example, the ratepayers in the Royal Boroughs of Kensington and Chelsea, the blind; applied in *Re Denison* (1974) 42 DLR (3d) 652; the descendants of Gladstone and the employees of a small company are a private class: *Davies v Perpetual Trustee Co Ltd* [1959] AC 439, [1959] 2 All ER 128.

9 *Re Smith, Public Trustee v Smith* [1932] 1 Ch 153 (gift 'to my country England'); *Nightingale v Goulbourn* (1848) 2 Ph 594 (gift for benefit of country to be applied by the Chancellor of the Exchequer); *A-G v Bushby* (1857) 24 Beav 299 (for relief of taxes); *Thellusson v Woodford* (1805) 11 Ves 112 (for reduction of National Debt); *Newland v A-G* (1809) 3 Mer 684 (same); *Ashton v Lord Langdale* (1851) 4 De G & Sm 402 (same); *Re Bell, Ballarat Trustees, Executors and Agency Co Ltd* [1943] VLR 103 (person rendering in any year the greatest benefit to humanity); *Re Strakosch, Temperley v A-G* [1949] Ch 529, [1949] 2 All ER 6 (strengthen unity of mother country with South Africa: not charitable); *Re Spensley's Will Trusts, Barclays Bank Ltd v Staughton* [1954] Ch 233, [1954] 1 All ER 178 (residence of

High Commissioner: not charitable); *Re Elgar* [1957] NZLR 556 (patriotism); *Gray Estate v Yule* (1990) 73 DLR (4th) 162, gift to 'the German people' held charitable.

10 *A-G v Day* [1900] 1 Ch 31 (repair of highways); *Forbes v Forbes* (1854) 18 Beav 552 (building bridges); *Wilson v Barnes* (1886) 38 Ch D 507 (protection of coast); *Jones v Williams* (1767) Amb 651 (provision of water); *A-G v Eastlake* (1853) 11 Hare 205 (provision of public lighting); *Re Spence, Barclays Bank Ltd v Stockton-on-Tees Corpn* [1938] Ch 96, [1937] 3 All ER 684 (public hall for borough); *Re Bones, Goltz v Ballarat Trustees, Executors and Agency Co Ltd* [1930] VLR 346 (improvement of city); *Re Knowles* [1938] 3 DLR 178 (beautifying a street); *Re Bobier* [1949] 4 DLR 288 (hospital); *Re List, List v Prime* [1949] NZLR 78 (convalescent home for children); *Public Trustee v Nolan* (1943) 43 SRNSW 169 (to erect carillon: not charitable); *Re Wokingham Fire Brigade Trusts* [1951] Ch 373, [1951] 1 All ER 454 (provision of fire brigade); *Re Mair* [1964] VR 529 (gift of public park: charitable); *Scottish Burial Reform and Cremation Society Ltd v Glasgow City Corpn* [1968] AC 138, [1967] 3 All ER 215, HL (provision of crematorium and promotion of cremation).

11 *Re Scowcroft, Ormrod v Wilkinson* [1898] 2 Ch 638 (public library); *Re Holburne, Coates v Mackillop* (1885) 53 LT 212 (museum); *Re Scowcroft, Ormrod v Wilkinson* (reading-room); *Harrison v Southampton Corpn* (1854) 2 Sm & G 387 (botanical garden and observatory); *Re Jacobs, Westminster Bank v Chinn* (1970) 114 Sol Jo 515 (planting of a grove of trees in Israel); *Shillington v Portadown Urban Council* [1911] 1 IR 247 (recreation); *Re Hadden, Public Trustee v More* [1932] 1 Ch 133 (public recreation); *Taylor v Taylor* (1910) 10 CLR 218 (scientific research); *Re Vernon Estate, Boyle v Battye* [1948] 2 WWR 46 (community hall). A gift for the encouragement of mere sport is not charitable: *Re Jacques* (1967) 63 DLR (2d) 673 (residue to be distributed 'to finance some community project', possibly swimming pool: held, not charitable); *Re Gray, Todd v Taylor* [1925] Ch 362 (regimental sports: charitable); *Baddeley v IRC* [1953] 2 All ER 233 at 251; *Re Morgan, Cecil-Williams v A-G* [1955] 2 All ER 632 (public recreation ground); *Kearins v Kearins* [1957] SRNSW 286; *Alexandra Park Trustees v Haringey London Borough* (1967) 66 LGR 306 (public park and sports ground); *Royal College of Surgeons of England v National Provincial Bank Ltd* [1952] 1 All ER 984 (promotion of surgery); *Royal College of Nursing for England and Wales v St Marylebone Corpn* [1959] 3 All ER 663 (promotion of nursing); *General Nursing Council v St Marylebone Borough Council* [1959] 1 All ER 325 (regulation of nursing profession not charitable); *Re Lysaght, Hill v Royal College of Surgeons of England* [1966] Ch 191, [1965] 2 All ER 888 (gift for medical studentship: not void because Roman Catholics and Jews excluded there being a general charitable intent); *Re Pinion, Westminster Bank Ltd v Pinion* [1965] Ch 85 at 98, [1964] 1 All ER 890 (gift of studio paintings and old furniture to form exhibition not charitable where the few pieces of any educational value were not sufficient to make the whole charitable and the collection was directed by the will to be kept intact); *Incorporated Council of Law Reporting for England and Wales v A-G* [1972] Ch 73, [1971] 3 All ER 1029 (publication of Law Reports).

12 *Re Lord Stratheden and Campbell, Alt v Lord Stratheden and Campbell* [1894] 3 Ch 265 (volunteer corps); *Re Stephens, Giles v Stephens* (1892) 8 TLR 792 (teaching shooting); *Re Good, Harrington v Watts* [1905] 2 Ch 60, and *Re Donald, Moore v Somerset* [1909] 2 Ch 410 (officer's mess); *Re Gray, Todd v Taylor* [1925] Ch 362 (regimental fund for sport); *Re Barker, Sherrington v St Paul's Cathedral (Dean and Chapter)* (1909) 25 TLR 753 (prize for cadets); *Re Driffill, Harvey v Chamberlain* [1950] Ch 92, [1949] 2 All ER 933 (defence from air attack). A gift for training boys to become officers in the Navy or the mercantile marine is charitable: *Re Corbyn, Midland Bank Executor and Trustee Co Ltd v A-G* [1941] Ch 400, [1941] 2 All ER 160. See also *Whitmore v Regina Branch of Canadian Legion of British Empire Service League* [1940] 3 WWR 359 (returned soldiers); *Re Elgar* [1957] NZLR 556; *Re Gillespie* [1965] VR 402 (gift for any organisation for ex-members of forces, the choice is to be in the discretion of the trustee. Restriction to protestant members of British descent).

13 *IRC v Yorkshire Agricultural Society* [1928] 1 KB 611; *Re Pleasants, Pleasants v A-G* (1923) 39 TLR 675; *London University of Yarrow* (1857) 1 De G & J 72. As to gift to promote natural history, see *Re Benham* [1939] SASR 450. A gift of residue to found a bank for the purpose of granting loans to assist planters and agriculturalists at a low rate of interest, but compatible with the proper operation of the bank is not a valid charitable trust because the loans might not be applied by the planters or agriculturalists for agricultural purposes and restrictive words are not to be imported into a trust which without them is invalid: *Hadaway v Hadaway* [1955] 1 WLR 16.

14 See para **[102.13]** below.

15 *Re Resch's Will Trusts, Le Cras v Perpetual Trustee Co Ltd, Far West Children's Health Scheme v Perpetual Trustee Co Ltd* [1969] 1 AC 514, [1967] 3 All ER 915 (gift to a private hospital which charged fees, poor sometimes treated without payment). A gift for the purpose of a hospital is prima facie a good charitable trust; it is not a condition of validity of a trust for the relief of the sick that it should be limited to the poor sick; if a bequest is made on trusts requiring it to be applied for a particular purpose which is charitable, it is immaterial that some of the general purposes of the recipient body may not be charitable. See also *Re Adams, Gee v Barnet Group Hospital Management Committee* [1968] Ch 80, [1967] 3 All ER 285; *Re Smith's Will Trusts, Barclays Bank Ltd v Merchantile Bank Ltd* [1962] 2 All ER 563, [1962] 1 WLR 763.

16 *Re Scowcroft, Ormrod v Wilkinson* [1898] 2 Ch 638 (Conservative principles combined with mental and moral improvement); *Re Hood, Public Trustee v Hood* [1931] 1 Ch 240 (Christian principles); *Re Price, Midland Bank Exor and Trustee Co Ltd v Harwood* [1943] Ch 422, [1943] 2 All ER 505 (teaching of Steiner); and see *Barralet v A-G* [1980] 3 All ER 918, [1980] 1 WLR 1565 (whole of society's objects were for the mental and moral improvement of man and thus for purposes beneficial to the community). But the trust must not be political; see *McGovern v A-G* [1982] Ch 321, [1981] 3 All ER 493, and next section. *Re Trusts of Arthur McDougall Fund* [1956] 3 All ER 867 (advancement of education or other charitable purposes connected with the art and science of government is charitable and not invalidated by the fact that the trustees must be members of the Proportional Representation Society); *Re Shaw, Public Trustee v Day* [1957] 1 All ER 745 (reform of alphabet); *Re Davis, Watts v Davis and Westralian Farmers Co-operative Ltd* [1965] WAR 25 (a gift to the directors of the company to apply the income in perpetuity for the expansion of co-operation and the co-operative movement held invalid); *Re Shapiro* (1980) 107 DLR (3d) 133.

17 *Associated Artists Ltd v IRC* [1956] 2 All ER 583, [1956] 1 WLR 752.

18 *Royal Choral Society v IRC* [1943] 2 All ER 101; *Re Levien, Lloyds Bank Ltd v Worshipful of Musicians* [1955] 3 All ER 35; *Re Delius' Will Trusts, Emanuel v Rosen* [1957] Ch 299, [1957] 1 All ER 854.

19 *Re Hummeltenberg, Beatty v London Spiritualistic Alliance Ltd* [1923] 1 Ch 237; *Re Grove-Grady, Plowden v Lawrence* [1929] 1 Ch 557; *National Anti-Vivisection Society v IRC* [1948] AC 31, [1947] 2 All ER 217, disapproving *Re Foveaux, Cross v London Anti-Vivisection Society* [1895] 2 Ch 501, where it was stated that where the merits of a particular object are controversial the court stands neutral.

20 *Re Hummeltenberg, Beatty v London Spiritualistic Alliance Ltd* [1923] 1 Ch 237. The part of the public to be benefited must be substantial enough to give it a public character: *Shaw v Halifax Corpn* [1915] 2 KB 170; *Hall v Derby Borough Urban Sanitary Authority* (1885) 16 QBD 163, and may be a class of the inhabitants of a particular locality: *Mitford v Reynolds* (1842) 1 Ph 185 (native inhabitants of Dacca); *Re Norwich Town Close Estate Charity* (1888) 40 Ch D 298 (freemen of a borough); *Re Mellody, Brandwood v Haden* [1918] 1 Ch 228 (schoolchildren of a town); *Re Koetten's Will Trusts, Westminster Bank Ltd v Family Welfare Association Trustees Ltd* [1954] Ch 252, [1954] 1 All ER 581 (employees of a company). A gift to a parish council is not necessarily charitable and where the object was described as 'some useful memorial' of the testator it was held not charitable and too uncertain to be enforced: *Re Endacott, Corpe v Endacott* [1960] Ch 232, [1959] 3 All ER 562.

21 *A-G v Earl Lonsdale* (1827) 1 Sim 105 (county); *A-G v Dartmouth Corpn* (1883) 48 LT 933 (town); *Re St Nicholas Acons (Parish)* (1889) 60 LT 532 (parish); *Schellenberger v Trustees etc Co* (1952) 86 CLR 454 (gift to add to the beauty and advancement of a town); *Goodman v Saltash Corpn* (1882) 7 App Cas 633; *Peggs v Lamb* [1994] Ch 172, [1994] 2 All ER 15.

22 *IRC v Baddeley* [1955] AC 572, [1955] 1 All ER 525; *Re Lipinski's Will Trusts, Gosschalk v Levy* [1976] Ch 235, [1977] 1 All ER 33 (trust for the Hull Judeans (Maccabi) Association, founded as a cricket club and subsequently provided social, cultural and sporting activities for Jewish youths who were members, held not charitable because essentially a sports club for the benefit of its members).

CHAPTER 103

Charitable gifts; construction and cy-près

I. CONSTRUCTION OF CHARITABLE GIFTS

[Updated in footnote 2 for *Harwood v Harwood* [2005] EWHC 3019 (Ch).]

[103.1]

General charitable intention. Where a clear intention is expressed that a fund or other property shall be applied to charity, it is immaterial that the objects are not defined.[1] The general intention will be carried into effect, if necessary by means of a scheme, notwithstanding that the particular objects are not stated.[2] The principle is that the court treats charity as the substance and the particular disposition as the mode of the gift,[3] and draws a distinction between the charitable intention, which must be clear, and the mode of executing it, which, though vague and indefinite, does not affect the validity of the gift. The existence of such a general intention is a matter of construction, and is not dependent on the issue of any particular words,[4] but is deemed to exist wherever a testator intended the subject-matter of the gift to be applied in charity, notwithstanding the failure of the particular object or mode of application indicated.[5] The distinction to be drawn is between, on the one hand, the case where the scheme prescribed by the will can be regarded as the mode by which a general charitable purpose is to be effected, in which case the mode is not the substance of the gift, and, on the other, the case where no part of the scheme in the will can be disregarded as inessential without frustrating the testator's intention.[6] A declaration to give the whole estate to charity will prevail although only part is specifically given to charity,[7] and precatory recommendations in favour of particular charities do not prevent partial applications in other ways.[8] A charitable intention is not inferred from the fact that the trustees are a charitable society and given a wide discretion.[9] A gift to trustees to apply it in any manner in their absolute discretion in furtherance of the testator's 'general charitable intention' is not sufficient to validate an intention or purpose which is not in itself charitable in law.[10] A gift to a legatee 'for the charitable purposes agreed between us' does not imply a general charitable intention, but only an intention limited to the purposes agreed[11] and evidence is admissible to show that the purposes are, but not to limit the amount of the gift.[12] The rule of general charitable intention is applicable where the testator has neither specified the objects nor the particular way of carrying out his intention as in bequests for charitable purposes generally[13] or in relief of poverty[14] or for advancement of education[15] or religion[16] generally. It also applies where the testator states the class of objects to be benefited but does not prescribe the particular way in which his intention is to be carried out, as in gifts to the poor of a particular place,[17] or the clergy of a particular sect.[18] Effect is given to gifts where the testator omits the names of the charities he wishes to benefit,[19] or the gift is for the benefit of such charities as he shall direct and he makes no direction.[20]

1 *Moggridge v Thackwell* (1803) 7 Ves 36; *Re White, White v White* [1893] 2 Ch 41; *Re Forester, Jervis v Forester* (1897) 13 TLR 555; *Re Pyne, Lilley v A-G* [1903] 1 Ch 83; *Re Gott, Glazebrook v Leeds University* [1944] Ch 193, [1944] 1 All ER 293 (charitable trust cannot fail for uncertainty so long as there is a general or specific charitable intention).

2 *Re Gott, Glazebrook v Leeds University* [1944] Ch 193, [1944] 1 All ER 293; *Harwood v Harwood* [2005] EWHC 3019 (Ch) (on the failure of a testator's trust to establish a museum, the court found a general charitable intention to devote his residuary estate to educational purposes, probably in the field of museums, and so a scheme was directed).

3 *Lyons Corpn v Advocate General of Bengal* (1876) 1 App Cas 91 at 113; *Re Spence's Will Trusts, Ogden v Shackleton* [1979] Ch 483, [1978] 3 All ER 92, per Megarry V-C at 101,'... the court is nevertheless able to see a clear general charitable intention underlying the particular mode of carrying it out that the testator has laid down', applying *Biscoe v Jackson* (1887) 35 Ch D 460.

4 *Mills v Farmer* (1815) 1 Mer 55 at 95.

5 *Clark v Taylor* (1853) 1 Drew 642 at 644.

6 *Re Woodhams, Lloyds Bank Ltd v London College of Music* [1981] 1 All ER 202, [1981] 1 WLR 493; referring to *Mills v Farmer* (1815) 19 Ves 483; *Re Rymer, Rymer v Stanfield* [1895] 1 Ch 19; *Re Wilson, Twentyman v Simpson* [1913] 1 Ch 314; *Re Willis, Shaw v Willis* [1921] 1 Ch 44; *A-G for New South Wales v Perpetual Trustee Co Ltd* (1940) 63 CLR 209; and *Re Lysaght, Hill v Royal College of Surgeons of England* [1966] Ch 191, [1965] 2 All ER 888, applied. A useful test was formulated by Vinelott J in *Re Woodhams*, above (at pp 210 and 501), as follows: 'one way of approaching the question whether a prescribed scheme or project which has proved impracticable is the only way of furthering a desirable purpose that the testator or settlor contemplated or intended is to ask whether a modification of that scheme or project, which would enable it to be carried into effect at the relevant time, is one which would frustrate the intention of the testator or settlor as disclosed by the will or trust instrument interpreted in the light of any admissible evidence of surrounding circumstances'. In the case the testator had bequeathed gifts of residue to music colleges for music scholarships for orphans from named charitable homes. There were in fact adequate public grants available for the musical education of such orphans and thus the gift was regarded as impractical in its stated form. A *cy-près* scheme was directed. See also *Re Machin* (1980) 101 DLR (3d) 438; *Re Jung* (1980) 99 DLR (3d) 65.

7 *Beverley Corpn v A-G* (1857) 6 HL Cas 310 at 318.

8 *Moggridge v Thackwell* (1803) 7 Ves 36.

9 *Re Freeman, Shilton v Freeman* [1908] 1 Ch 720. A gift to a charitable society is construed as a gift for the purposes of the society: *Re White, White v White* [1893] 2 Ch 41.

10 *Re Sanders' Will Trusts, Public Trustee v McLaren* [1954] Ch 265, [1954] 1 All ER 667.

11 *Re Huxtable, Huxtable v Crawfurd* [1902] 2 Ch 793.

12 *Blackwell v Blackwell* [1929] AC 318.

13 *Miller v Rowan* (1837) 5 Cl & Fin 99 at 109.

14 *A-G v Rance* (1728) cited in (1762) Amb at 422.

15 *Whicker v Hume* (1858) 7 HL Cas 124.

16 *Re White, White v White* [1893] 2 Ch 41 at 52.

17 *A-G v Wilkinson* (1839) 1 Beav 370.

18 *A-G v Gladstone* (1842) 13 Sim 7.

19 *Re White, White v White* [1893] 2 Ch 41.

20 *Pocock v A-G* (1876) 3 Ch D 342; *Re Pyne, Lilley v A-G* [1903] 1 Ch 83.

[Updated in the text and footnote 5 for Charities Act 2006, s 44.]

[103.3]

Charity wrongly named or having ceased to exist. A charitable gift does not fail because the institution cannot be identified[1] or has never existed;[2] but it must be clear from the description of the institution that the testator intended to benefit a charitable purpose.[3] A gift to an institution which has ceased to exist in the testator's lifetime, whether before or after the date of the will, lapses[4], unless it is saved by the registered merger provisions of Charities Act 2006 (CA 2006),[5] or a general intention can be shown.[6] There is no lapse where the institution has not wholly ceased to exist;[7] nor where there has merely been a change of name,[8] nor where the institution is named merely as the channel for carrying out the charitable intention.[9] A gift to an institution carried on by the testator which ceased at his death is construed as a gift for the purposes of that institution[10] and similarly a gift to an institution properly described for purposes which have ceased to be exercised by that institution by reason of a profession ceasing to adopt a method of practice is good and possibly subject to a trust to apply to such purposes as far as possible.[11] If the charity ceases to exist after the death of the testator but before payment, the gift still takes effect.[12] Where the premises of the charity were before the execution of the will closed down on the expiration of the lease under which they were held but the charity was continued by a scheme, it was held that a gift by way of addition to the endowment of the charity and not merely for the upkeep of the particular premises of the charity did not fail.[13] Where the testator's intention was to benefit the charity generally the gift was not affected by the fact that he had referred to the address at which it was carried on at the date of his will, although the work at that address had been closed down before his death and transferred elsewhere.[14] A gift to a hospital does not lapse where its specified work is transferred to a general hospital and its funds are to be applied to such special work in the general hospital,[15] but where the hospital closed down and its work was carried on by the Australian Red Cross, the gift could not be treated as a gift to that society because the will said that the receipt of the treasurer of the hospital was to be a sufficient discharge.[16]

1 *Gibson v Coleman* (1868) 18 LT 236; *Re Kilvert's Trusts* (1871) 7 Ch App 170. As to the jurisdiction of the court to order a scheme in such a case, see para **[103.19]** below.

2 *Re Davis, Hannen v Hillyer* [1902] 1 Ch 876 at 884; *Re Clergy Society* (1856) 2 K & J 615; *Daly v A-G* (1860) 11 I Ch R 41; *Re Geary's Trusts* (1890) 25 LR Ir 171; *Re Mann, Hardy v A-G* [1903] 1 Ch 232; *Re Songest, Mayger v Forces Help Society and Lord Roberts Workshops* [1956] 2 All ER 765.

3 *Re Parkes, Cottrell v Parkes* (1909) 25 TLR 523. From *Re Bailey, Bailey v Working Ladies Guild* (1931) 75 Sol Jo 415, it might appear that the court requires only that there shall be no evidence to contradict the charitable intention shown by the name given by the testator to a society which has never existed. See also *Re Forshaw, Wallace v Middlesex Hospital* (1934) 51 TLR 97; *Re Nesbitt's Will Trusts* [1953] 1 All ER 936; *Re Kerr* [1957] QSR 292. In *Re Goldschmidt* [1957] 1 All ER 513, the gift was given to an institution not capable of identification and, the ultimate gift being to a charity, it passed under the ultimate gift. See also *Re Jacobsen* (1977) 80 DLR (3d) 122.

4 It is more difficult to find a general charitable intention where the gift is to a body which existed at the date of the will but ceased to exist before the testator died than it is to find the intention when the body never did exist: per Megarry V-C in *Re Spence's Will Trusts, Ogden v Shackleton* [1978] 3 All ER 92 at 100; *Re Ovey, Broadbent v Barrow* (1885) 29 Ch D 560 (ceasing to exist before date of will); *Re Rymer, Rymer v Stanfield* [1895] 1 Ch 19 (ceasing after date of will); *Re Joy, Purday v Johnson* (1888) 60 LT 175; *Makeown v Ardagh* (1876) IR 10 Eq 445; *Re Tharp, Longrigg v People's Dispensary for Sick Animals of the Poor Inc* [1942] 2 All ER 358; revsd on another point [1943] 1 All ER 257 (there is a lapse where the gift is to the particular society and not for the particular purpose); *Re Lucas, Sheard v Mellor* [1948] Ch 175 [1947] 2 All ER 773; *Re Stemson's Will Trusts, Carpenter v Treasury Solicitor* [1970] Ch 16, [1969] 2 All ER 517; *Re Rowell, Public Trustee v Bailey* (1982) 31 SASR 36.

5 CA 2006, s 44, inserting new CA 1993, ss 75C–75F with effect from 28 November 2007 (SI 2007/3286). See para **[103.9]** below.
6 *Clark v Taylor* (1853) 1 Drew 642; *Marsh v A-G* (1860) 2 John & H 61. It is difficult to find a general intention where the testator has taken care to identify the particular charity: *Re Harwood, Coleman v Innes* [1936] Ch 285; applied in *Re Spence, Ogden v Shackleton* [1979] Ch 483, [1978] 3 All ER 92 (a gift for the benefit of patients at a specified home; at the date of the will there were such patients but at the death of the testatrix there was no longer any home, or any patients there, or any possibility of them, held gift failed), distinguishing *Re Finger's Will Trusts, Turner v Ministry of Health* [1972] Ch 286, [1971] 3 All ER 1050. See also *Re Broadbent* [2001] 28 LS Gaz R 44.
7 *Re Waring, Hayward v A-G* [1907] 1 Ch 166 (school closed on weekdays, but used on Sundays); *Re Bradfield* (1892) 8 TLR 696 (closing of branch); *Re Faraker, Faraker v Durell* [1912] 2 Ch 488; *Re Scott Estate* (1957) 11 DLR (2d) 223 (cesser in named town but continuing elsewhere); applied in *Re Roberts, Stenton v Hardy* [1963] 1 All ER 674 (gift for the purposes of an institution not so correlated with the physical premises where the institution was located that it failed when those premises ceased to exist); *St Dunstan's University v Canada Permanent Trust Co* (1976) 67 DLR (3d) 480; *Re Bezpalko* (1980) 106 DLR (3d) 290; *Re Machin* (1980) 101 DLR (3d) 438.
8 *Re Donald, Moore v Somerset* [1909] 2 Ch 410; *Re Magrath, Histed v Queen's University of Belfast* [1913] 2 Ch 331; *Re Gray, Todd v Taylor* [1925] Ch 362; *Re Gordon* (1965) 52 DLR (2d) 197.
9 *Marsh v A-G* (1860) 2 John & H 61; *Re Ovey, Broadbent v Barrow* (1885) 29 Ch D 560 at 565; *Loscombe v Wintringham* (1850) 13 Beav 87; *Re Watt, Hicks v Hill* [1932] 2 Ch 243n.
10 *Re Mann, Hardy v A-G* [1903] 1 Ch 232; *Re Webster, Pearson v Webster* [1912] 1 Ch 106.
11 *Sydney Homoeopathic Hospital v Turner* [1959] ALR 782.
12 *Re Slevin, Slevin v Hepburn* [1891] 2 Ch 236; *Re Wright, Blizard v Lockhart* [1954] 2 All ER 98 (where the purpose became impracticable after the testator's death); *Re Morrison, Wakefield v Falmouth* (1967) 111 Sol Jo 758; *Re Hunter* (1973) 34 DLR (3d) 602.
13 *Re Lucas, Sheard v Mellor* [1948] Ch 424, [1948] 2 All ER 22; distinguished in *Re Spence's Will Trusts, Ogden v Shackleton* [1978] 3 All ER 92, where, having regard to the fact that the testatrix had provided for the gift to be for the benefit of the patients of a specified home, the gift could not be added to the association's general endowment but was to be restricted by way of the scheme, to being used for the benefit of the patients for the time being of the specified home.
14 *Re Hutchinson's Will Trusts, Gibbons v Nottingham Area No 1, Hospital Management Committee* [1953] Ch 387, [1953] 1 All ER 996; *Re Abbott* (1974) 45 DLR (3d) 478; *Re MacAulay* (1971) 18 DLR (3d) 726; and *Re Boyd* (1969) 6 DLR (3d) 110.
15 *Re Boyd* (1969) 6 DLR (3d) 110.
16 *Re Slatter's Will Trusts, Turner v Turner* [1964] Ch 512, [1964] 2 All ER 469.

[Updated in the text and footnote 2 for CA 2006, s 44.]

[103.5]

Unincorporated bodies. Every bequest to an unincorporated charity by name without more must take effect as a gift for a charitable purpose.[1] If the named charity ceases to exist in the testator's lifetime the gift will only fail if it is not preserved by the merger provisions of CA 2006[2] and the testator's intention is to make the gift dependent on the named charitable organisation being available at the time when the gift took effect to serve as the instrument for applying the subject matter of the gift to the charitable purposes for which it is by inference given.[3] But usually since the gift is per se a purpose trust, then if the work is still being carried on, effect will be given to it by way of a scheme, notwithstanding the disappearance of the donee in the lifetime of the testator.[4]

1 Per Buckley J in *Re Vernon's Will Trusts, Lloyds Bank Ltd v Group 20 Hospital Management Committee,* noted [1972] Ch 300n at 303, [1971] All ER 1061n at 1064; followed in *Re Finger's Will Trusts, Turner v Ministry of Health* [1972] Ch 286, [1971] 3 All ER 1050; and

in *Re Morrison, Wakefield v Falmouth* (1967) 111 Sol Jo 758. This is because no individual or aggregate of individuals would claim to take such a bequest beneficially.

2 CA 2006, s 44, inserting new CA 1993, ss 75C–75F with effect from 28 November 2007 (SI 2007/3286). See para **[103.9]** below.

3 Per Buckley J in *Re Vernon's Will Trusts*, see n 1 above; see also *Re Ovey, Broadbent v Barrow* (1885) 29 Ch D 560; *Re Meyers, London Life Association v St George's Hospital* [1951] Ch 534, [1951] 1 All ER 538. Thus, in *Re Finger's Will Trusts, Turner v Ministry of Health* [1972] Ch 286, [1971] 3 All ER 1050, a gift to an unincorporated charity was a purpose trust for the work of the body which did not fail because there was no indication in the will to make that body of the essence of the gift and the work of the body had, since its dissolution, been carried on by the Secretary of State for Social Services; the gift was therefore valid and a scheme for its administration was settled; distinguishing *Re Harwood, Coleman v Innes* [1936] Ch 285, [1935] All ER Rep 918.

4 Per Goff J in *Re Finger's Will Trusts, Turner v Ministry of Health* [1972] Ch 286 at 295, [1971] 3 All ER 1050 at 1057.

[Updated in the text and footnote 1 for CA 2006, s 44.]

[103.6]

Failure of particular intention. Where the intention is to benefit some particular charitable institution, or to accomplish some particular charitable purpose, then if circumstances render the carrying out impossible, and the gift is not preserved by the merger provisions of CA 2006,[1] then the gift fails and no *cy-près*[2] application is possible.[3] Where subscriptions are made and no intention can be inferred that the money should be returned on failure of the purpose, the funds are applied *cy-près*[4] but where return is possible such subscriptions must be returned though in some cases return is impossible.[5]

1 CA 2006, s 44, inserting new CA 1993, ss 75C–75F with effect from 28 November 2007 (SI 2007/3286). See para **[103.9]** below.

2 See para **[103.19]** below.

3 *Re Wilson, Twentyman v Simpson* [1913] 1 Ch 314; *Re Packe, Sanders v A-G* [1918] 1 Ch 437; *Re Stanford, Cambridge University v A-G* [1924] 1 Ch 73; *Re Blunt's Trusts, Wigan v Clinch* [1904] 2 Ch 767; *Re University of London Medical Sciences Institute Fund, Fowler v A-G* [1909] 2 Ch 1; *Re Good's Will Trusts, Oliver v Batten* [1950] 2 All ER 653; *Re Gwilym* [1952] VLR 282. But see *Re Hardy, Nelson v A-G* [1933] NI 150.

4 *Re Hillier, Hillier v A-G* [1954] 2 All ER 59.

5 *Re Ulverston and District New Hospital Building Trusts, Birkett v Barrow and Furness Hospital Management Committee* [1956] Ch 622, [1956] 3 All ER 164; *Re Gillingham Bus Disaster Fund, Bowman v Official Solicitor* [1958] Ch 300, [1958] 1 All ER 37. But see *Re West Sussex Constabulary's Widows, Children and Benevolent* (1930) *Fund Trusts, Barnett v Ketteringham* [1971] Ch 1, [1970] 1 All ER 544 (amalgamation of police force so that original purpose of benevolent fund could not be carried out. It was held that money contributed by members of the fund and money obtained through entertainments, raffles, sweepstakes and collecting boxes, was bona vacantia; money contributed by members of the public by donation and legacies, was held on resulting trusts for the donors and their estates).

[Updated in the text and footnotes 6–8 for CA 2006, s 44.]

[103.9]

Amalgamation of institutions. Before the commencement of CA 1993, ss 75C–75F, mentioned further below, amalgamation of institutions often did not affect the validity of a gift to one of them, which would be paid to the amalgamated institutions;[1] but the amalgamated institution might be put upon an undertaking to apply the gift for the purposes within the scope of the institution named in the will.[2] Where there were gifts to each of the amalgamated societies, the two legacies would be paid to the amalgamated institution[3] and where the gift was to the society and not expressed to be for its purposes, the gift could be applied by way of scheme or otherwise.[4] Although the objects of an amalgamated society are not identical with those of the named society yet if the general purposes of the named society were identifiable charitable purposes, then the bequest might be applied to those purposes by scheme or otherwise.[5] However, the problems which can be caused by charitable institutions merging with others or ceasing to operate and transferring funds to other charities are avoided where charities have merged and registered the merger in accordance with CA 1993, ss 75C–75F.[6] If this has been done, a gift which is expressed to be in favour of a charity which joined in the merger, and which takes effect after the date of the registration of the merger (typically this will be a gift in the will of someone dying after such registration), takes effect in favour of the resulting merged institution unless it is an 'excluded gift'.[7] It is an excluded gift for this purpose where the merged institution has not taken over the permanent endowment of a constituent charity, and the gift is intended to be held on the same trusts as some or all of that permanent endowment.[8]

1 *Re Adams, Harle v Adams* (1888) 4 TLR 757; *Re Faraker, Faraker v Durell* [1912] 2 Ch 488; *Re Pritt, Morton v National Church League* (1915) 85 LJ Ch 166; *Re Kappele* [1955] 1 DLR 29 (where the testator had executed several codicils after the amalgamation).
2 *Re Marchant, Weaver v Royal Society for the Prevention of Cruelty to Animals* (1910) 54 Sol Jo 425. It should be noted that in the case here cited the amalgamation took place 10 years before the date of the will. Most cases refer to amalgamations subsequent to the date of the will.
3 *Re Joy, Purday v Johnson* (1888) 60 LT 175. The fact that a dissolved society answers the testator's description better than an existing society does not prevent the latter taking so long as it sufficiently answers the description: *Coldwell v Holme* (1854) 2 Sm & G 31; *Re Magrath, Histed v Queen's University of Belfast* [1913] 2 Ch 331 (defunct institution reconstituted).
4 *Re Dawson's Will Trusts, National Provincial Bank Ltd v National Council of YMCA Inc* [1957] 1 All ER 177, [1957] 1 WLR 391.
5 *Re Roberts, Stenton v Hardy* [1963] 1 All ER 674, [1963] 1 WLR 406. See also *Re Bateman* 1972 SLT (Notes) 78.
6 Inserted by CA 2006, s 44 with effect from 28 November 2007 (SI 2007/3286).
7 CA 1993, s 75F(2), inserted by CA 2006, s 44 with effect from 28 November 2007 (SI 2007/3286).
8 CA 1993, ss 75C(5) and 75F(3), inserted by CA 2006, s 44 with effect from 28 November 2007 (SI 2007/3286).

[Updated in footnote 1 for *Christian Brothers in Western Australia Inc v AG of Western Australia* [2007] WTLR 1375.]

[103.11]

Illegality or impossibility of purpose. Where a general charitable intention is expressed but the mode of carrying it out is illegal or impracticable, the intention is executed *cy-près*,[1] but if some of the purposes or some of the modes of application are illegal or impossible, the trust must be carried out for the purposes or in the modes not open to objection.[2] An immediate gift to charity is good although its application may not of necessity take effect within any reasonable limit of time, or may never take effect at all except on the occurrence of events in their essence contingent and uncertain.[3] Thus, bequests for building when the necessary sites have been obtained,[4] to endow a bishopric in case a bishop should be appointed,[5] to endow a church if erected,[6] or a bequest postponed until a licence in mortmain is obtained,[7] have been upheld. Where a gift is void as illegal or impossible, a secondary bequest for endowment of the charity also fails[8] unless there is a direction for its alternative application.[9] A gift to establish a charity on property not devoted to charity and of which the testator has no power to dispose, is void ab initio.[10] A gift with a total prohibition of sale or mortgage is valid in the case of a charity.[11]

1 *A-G v Vint* (1850) 3 De G & Sm 704 (legacy to provide intoxicating liquor); *Chamberlayne v Brockett* (1872) 8 Ch App 206 (legacy dependent on land being provided for almshouses); *Biscoe v Jackson* (1887) 35 Ch D 460 (violation of Mortmain Acts); *Bunting v Marriott* (1854) 19 Beav 163 (reduction of debt on chapel which was already paid off); *Re Wright, Blizard v Lockhart* [1954] Ch 347, [1954] 2 All ER 98 (founding a convalescent home); *Re Woodhams, Lloyds Bank Ltd v London College of Music* [1981] 1 All ER 202, [1981] 1 WLR 493, (music scholarship for orphans from named charitable homes already adequately provided for, applied *cy-près* by deleting restriction); *Re J W Laing Trust, Stewards' Co Ltd v A-G* [1984] Ch 143, [1984] 1 All ER 50; *Christian Brothers in Western Australia Inc v AG of Western Australia* [2007] WTLR 1375 (land devised for young men to establish farms was insufficient to support even one family).

2 *Hunter v A-G* [1899] AC 309 at 324; *Sinnett v Herbert* (1872) 7 Ch App 232; *Re Douglas, Obert v Barrow* (1887) 35 Ch D 472. 'If at any time it proves impracticable' includes an initial failure of the purpose: *Re Adams, Gee v Barnet Group Hospital Management Committee* [1968] Ch 80, [1967] 3 All ER 285, CA. If, however, the gift is repugnant to the Mortmain Act, it fails entirely: *Girdlestone v Creed* (1853) 10 Hare 480.

3 *Wallis v New Zealand Solicitor-General* [1903] AC 173; *Re Monk, Giffen v Wedd* [1927] 2 Ch 197; *Re Swan, Monkton v Hands* [1905] 1 Ch 669; *Re Pearse, Genn v Pearse* [1955] 1 DLR 801.

4 *Chamberlayne v Brockett* (1872) 8 Ch App 206 (almshouses); *Henshaw v Atkinson* (1818) 3 Madd 306 (school).

5 *A-G v Bishop of Chester* (1785) 1 Bro CC 444; *Society for Propagation of the Gospel v A-G* (1826) 3 Russ 142.

6 *Sinnett v Herbert* (1872) 7 Ch App 232.

7 *Abbott v Fraser* (1874) LR 6 PC 96.

8 *Edwards v Hall* (1853) 11 Hare 1; *Cramp v Playfoot* (1858) 4 K & J 479; *Re Taylor, Martin v Freeman* (1888) 58 LT 538; *Re Packe, Sanders v A-G* [1918] 1 Ch 437. But, if the principal gift is good and the secondary gift is void, the former stands: *A-G v Stepney* (1804) 10 Ves 22; *Blandford v Thackerell* (1793) 2 Ves 238.

9 *Faversham Corpn v Ryder* (1854) 5 De GM & G 350; *Dunn v Bownas* (1855) 1 K & J 596.

10 *A-G v Earl of Lonsdale* (1827) 1 Sim 105; *Hoare v Hoare* (1886) 56 LT 147; *Thomson v Shakespear* (1860) 1 De GF & J 399.

11 *Re Clark, Horwell v Dent* [1961] NZLR 635 following *Caldell v Fleming* [1927] NZLR 145.

[Updated in footnote 6 for *Re Harding, Gibbs v Harding* [2008] Ch 235.]

[103.12]

Discrimination. Acts of discrimination against sections of the community[1] are now governed by the Race Relations Act 1976 (RRA 1976)[2] and the Sex Discrimination Act 1975 (SDA 1975). For the purposes of the RRA 1976 a person discriminates against another if on the ground of colour, race or ethnic or national origins he treats that other, in any situation to which the RRA 1976 applies, less favourably than he treats or would treat other persons (and it is expressly declared that if a person is segregated from other persons he is treated less favourably than they are treated).[3] The RRA 1976 expressly refers to charities[4] and to a 'charitable instrument', which means an enactment or other instrument passed or made for charitable purposes or an enactment or other instrument so far as it relates to charitable purposes, which are purposes which are exclusively charitable according to the law of England and Wales.[5] With reference to provisions taking effect after the coming into operation of the RRA 1976, the Act differentiates between discrimination on the grounds of colour and discrimination on other grounds. A provision which is contained in a charitable instrument which provides for conferring benefits on persons of a class defined by reference to colour has effect for all purposes as if it provided for conferring the like benefits, (a) on persons of the class which results if the restriction by reference to colour is disregarded or, (b) where the original class is defined by reference to colour only, on persons generally.[6] Where a charitable instrument provides for conferring benefits on persons of a class defined otherwise than by reference to colour (including a class resulting from the operation of the provision noted above) then the RRA 1976 is not to be construed as affecting the provision[7] or as rendering unlawful an act which is done in order to give effect to such a provision.[8] Thus charitable trusts which discriminate on the grounds of colour will be affected by the legislation but not trusts which discriminate in favour of a class defined otherwise than by reference to colour. The SDA 1975 likewise safeguards charities by providing that the Act does not affect provisions in a charitable instrument conferring benefits on persons of one sex only.[9]

1 For examples of discriminatory trusts before the anti-discriminatory legislation, see *Re Dominion Students' Hall Trusts* [1947] Ch 183 (colour bar); and *Re Lysaght, Hill v Royal College of Surgeons of England* [1966] Ch 191, [1965] 2 All ER 888 (exclusion of Roman Catholic or Jewish students from benefit).
2 This came into force on 13 June 1977 by virtue of SI 1977/840.
3 RRA 1976, s 1.
4 RRA 1976, s 34.
5 RRA 1976, s 34(4).
6 RRA 1976, s 34(1). In *Re Harding, Gibbs v Harding* [2008] Ch 235, [2007] 1 All ER 747, a gift to the Diocese of Westminster to hold in trust for the black community of Hackney, Haringey, Islington and Tower Hamlets took effect in accordance with RRA 1976, s 34(1) as a gift to the Roman Catholic Diocese of Westminster on charitable trusts.
7 RRA 1976, s 34(2)(a).
8 RRA 1976, s 34(2)(b).
9 SDA 1975, s 43. SI 1977/528 amends the Sex Discrimination Act 1975, s 43 in relation to 'charitable instrument' and redefines the phrase to correspond with that used in RRA 1976, s 34(4).

PART O

Intestacy

CHAPTER 104

Intestacy

I. TOTAL INTESTACY

[Updated for the increases in the fixed net sum from 1 February 2009.]

[104.2]

Entitlement: the spouse or civil partner. The succession to real and personal estate on intestacy is governed by the table of distribution in the Administration of Estates Act 1925 (AEA 1925), s 46.[1] The original wording of section 46 referred to 'a husband or wife', but with effect from 5 December 2005 the Civil Partnership Act 2004 has substituted the word 'spouse' and added 'or civil partner' throughout the section.[2] In the case of the death of a person intestate on or after 1 January 1996 all the rights of the intestate's spouse or civil partner are contingent on the spouse or civil partner surviving the intestate by 28 days.[3] There is no such contingency where the death occurs before that date. Where the intestate leaves a spouse or civil partner[4] and no issue, no parent or brother or sister of the whole blood or issue of a brother or sister of the whole blood, then the residuary estate is held in trust for the surviving spouse or civil partner absolutely.[5] Where the intestate leaves a spouse or civil partner and issue then the surviving spouse or civil partner takes the personal chattels absolutely;[6] a fixed net sum, currently (in relation to deaths on or after 1 February 2009) of £250,000,[7] and subject thereto the residuary estate is held as to one-half upon trust for the surviving spouse or civil partner and subject thereto on the statutory trusts for the issue of the intestate;[8]and as to the other half, on the statutory trusts for the issue of the intestate.[9] Where the intestate leaves a spouse or civil partner, no issue, but either a parent, or a brother or sister of the whole blood or issue of a brother or sister of the whole blood, then the surviving spouse or civil partner takes the personal chattels absolutely;[10] a fixed net sum, currently (in relation to deaths on or after 1 February 2009) of £450,000[11] and subject thereto the residuary estate is held as to one-half in trust for the surviving spouse or civil partner absolutely:[12] and as to the other half, where the intestate leaves one or both parents then in trust for the parent absolutely or, as the case may be, for the two parents in equal shares absolutely;[13]or where the intestate leaves no parent, on the statutory trusts for the brothers and sisters of the whole blood of the intestate.[14]

1 As amended in the case of deaths on or after 1 January 1953 by the Intestates' Estates Act 1952; in the case of deaths on or after 1 January 1967 by the Family Provision Act 1966; in the case of deaths on or after 1 January 1970 by the Family Law Reform Act 1969 and in the case of deaths on or after 1 January 1996 by the Law Reform (Succession) Act 1995. In the case of deaths on or after 5 December 2005, by the Civil Partnership Act 2004. See

Vol 2, Part G, paras **[244.62]** ff. The amount of the fixed net sum or statutory legacy has been progressively increased subsequent to 1967 by statutory instrument; see para **[104.5]** below.
2 Civil Partnership Act 2004, ss 71 and 263(2); Sch 4, para 7. See para **[104.3]** below.
3 AEA 1925, s 46(2A) inserted by Law Reform (Succession) Act 1995, s 1(1) and printed in Vol 2, Part G, para **[244.62]**.
4 Civil Partnership Act 2004, ss 71 and 263(2); Sch 4, para 7. The presumption in the Law of Property Act 1925, s 184 does not apply so that in a commorientes situation neither party is presumed to have survived the other; AEA 1925, s 46(3): see Vol 2, Part G, para **[244.62]**. In relation to deaths on or after 1 January 1996 this provision is largely superseded by the 28-day survivorship contingency (see above).
5 AEA 1925, s 46(1)(i)(1).
6 See para **[104.4]** below.
7 See para **[104.5]** below; see *Re Collens, Royal Bank of Canada (London) Ltd v Krogh* [1986] Ch 505, [1986] 1 All ER 611 concerning the entitlement of the spouse to the statutory legacy where he/she was also entitled to movable property in another jurisdiction.
8 See para **[104.5]** below.
9 AEA 1925, s 46(1)(i), (2).
10 See para **[104.4]** below.
11 See para **[104.5]** below.
12 AEA 1925, s 46(1)(i), (3)(a).
13 AEA 1925, s 46(1)(i), (3)(b)(i).
14 AEA 1925, s 46(1)(i), (3)(b)(ii).

[Updated for the increases in the fixed net sum from 1 February 2009.]

[104.5]

The fixed net sum. The amount to which the spouse or civil partner is entitled as a fixed net sum was initially fixed in 1925 as £1,000.[1] The Intestate's Estates Act 1952 increased the amount to £5,000, where there were issue surviving, and to £20,000, where there were no issue but specified relatives, with effect from 1 January 1953.[2] The Family Provision Act 1966 increased the amounts further, to £8,750 and to £30,000 respectively, with effect from 1 January 1967 and provided that henceforth the amounts should be increased by statutory instrument.[3] This has been done on six subsequent occasions of which the first five are: in the case of deaths on or after 1 July 1972 the entitlement was to £15,000 and £40,000 respectively;[4] in the case of deaths on or after 15 March 1977, the entitlement was to £25,000 and to £55,000 respectively;[5] in respect of deaths on or after 1 March 1981 the entitlement was to £40,000 and to £85,000 respectively;[6] in respect of deaths on or after 1 June 1987 to £75,000 and £125,000 respectively;[7] in respect of deaths on or after 1 December 1993, £125,000 and £200,000 respectively.[8] The current figures, in respect of deaths on or after 1 February 2009, are £250,000 and £450,000 respectively.[9] The absolute entitlement (in effect) to the statutory legacy (or the fixed net sum as it is more properly called) is often used to effect an appropriation of the matrimonial home under the Intestates' Estates Act 1952, Second Schedule, and the fixed net sum has been increased from time to time since 1981.[10] The sum carries interest at 6 per cent per annum from the date of death.[11]

1 AEA 1925, s 46(1)(i). In all cases, which was itself an increase on the £500 entitlement under the Intestates' Estates Act 1890.
2 AEA 1925, s 1(2).
3 Family Provision Act 1966, s 1.
4 Family Provision (Intestate Succession) Order 1972, SI 1972/96.
5 Family Provision (Intestate Succession) Order 1977, SI 1977/415.

6 Family Provision (Intestate Succession) Order 1981, SI 1981/255.
7 Family Provision (Intestate Succession) Order 1987, SI 1987/799.
8 Family Provision (Intestate Succession) Order 1993, SI 1993/2906.
9 Family Provision (Intestate Succession) Order 2009, SI 2009/135.
10 As to possible double entitlement where a foreign domicile is involved see *Re Collens, Royal Bank of Canada (London) v Krogh* [1986] Ch 505, [1986] 1 All ER 611 applying *Re Rea, Rea v Rea* [1902] 1 IR 451 and *Re Ralston* [1906] VLR 689.
11 Intestate Succession (Interest and Capitalisation) Order 1983 (Amendment) Order 1983, SI 1983/1374 with effect from 1 October 1983. The rate was previously 7 per cent with effect from 15 September 1977, SI 1977/1491; and before that date it was 4 per cent per annum, Intestate's Estates Act 1952, reducing the original rate of 5 per cent in the AEA 1925, in respect of deaths on or after 1 January 1953.

[Updated in footnote 1 for the new capitalisation tables effective on 1 February 2009.]

[104.6]

Redemption and appropriation. Where the surviving spouse or civil partner is entitled to a life interest in part of the residuary estate, he or she may elect to have the life interest purchased or redeemed by the personal representatives and thus receive the capitalised value instead.[1] The Intestates' Estates Act 1952[2] conferred a right on the surviving spouse to require the personal representatives to appropriate[3] the matrimonial home in or towards satisfaction of any absolute interest in the intestacy.[4] The right has now been extended to registered civil partners.[5]

1 AEA 1925, s 47A, added by the Intestates' Estates Act 1952, s 2(b) (see Vol 2, Part G, para **[244.64]**). For the method of ascertaining the capital value, see Intestate Succession (Interest and Capitalisation) Order 1977, SI 1977/1491, as amended, with effect from 1 February 2009, by Intestate Succession (Interest and Capitalisation) (Amendment) Order 2008. See Vol 2, Part G, para **[244.90]** ff. The amendments made by the latter Order, which allow for changes in government stocks, interest rates, and expectation of life since the previous Order was made, are not restricted to applying in relation to deaths on or after 1 February 2009, and apparently will apply to any redemption of a life interest which is elected for on or after that date.
2 See s 5 of and the Second Schedule to the Intestates' Estates Act 1952 as amended (see Vol 2, Part G, paras **[244.73]**, **[244.75]**).
3 In exercise of the power in the Administration of Estates Act 1925, s 41.
4 See *Re Phelps, Wells v Phelps* [1980] Ch 275, [1979] 3 All ER 373; *Robinson v Collins* [1975] 1 All ER 321, sub nom *Re Collins, Robinson v Collins* [1975] 1 WLR 309.
5 AEA 1952, s 5 and Sch 2 (rights of surviving spouse as respects the matrimonial home) have been amended by CPA 2004, Sch 4, para 13 (see Vol 2, Part G, paras **[244.73]**, **[244.75]**), to include civil partner (with spouse) and civil partnership (with marriage or matrimonial).

[Updated in the text and footnote 9 for Human Fertilisation and Embryology Act 2008.]

[104.7]

Entitlement of issue. Where the intestate leaves a surviving spouse or civil partner and issue then the spouse or civil partner has the primary entitlement as set out above.[1] Subject to the spouse's or civil partner's entitlement to the personal chattels, and to the fixed net sum, and to a life interest in one-half of the residuary estate, the estate is held on the statutory trusts for the issue.[2] In the case of one-half of the estate this is an interest in remainder after the spouse's or civil partner's life interest; in the case of the other half it is an immediate interest.[3] Where the intestate leaves issue but no spouse or civil partner, the residuary estate is held on the statutory trusts for the issue of the intestate.[4]

Leaving issue means leaving issue who attain an absolute vested interest.[5] Issue means children and grandchildren and more remote descendants,[6] and includes legitimated, adopted and illegitimate persons[7] and children en ventre sa mère at the death.[8] It also includes any person who counts as a descendant by having the deceased or a descendant of the deceased as a parent by virtue of the Human Fertilisation and Embryology Act 1990 or 2008.[9]

1 See para **[104.3]** above.
2 AEA 1925, s 46(1)(i), (2).
3 But possibly contingent, see para **[104.12]** below.
4 AEA 1925, s 46(1)(ii).
5 AEA 1925, s 47(2)(c).
6 See Chapter 76.
7 Legitimacy Act 1976, s 5(2); Adoption Act 1976, s 46(4); Adoption and Children Act 2002 ss 67, 68; and Family Law Reform Act 1987, ss 1 and 18 (replacing the more restricted provisions of Family Law Reform Act 1969, s 14), all of which are printed in Vol 2, Part G, para **[245.1]** ff. See Chapters 72 and 75.
8 AEA 1925, s 55(2), printed at Vol 2, Part G, para **[246.67]**. It is not possible in this section to discuss the meaning of issue for the purposes of intestate succession in any greater detail; see Chapter 76.
9 See paras **[74.3]**, **[74.5]** above.

[Updated in footnotes 2 and 3 for Human Fertilisation and Embryology Act 2008.]

[104.9]

Entitlement of other relatives. It has been seen above that a parent or parents, or brother or sister of the whole blood or issue of a brother or sister of the whole blood, have some entitlement where there is also a surviving spouse.[1] In other cases the entitlement of relatives other than the spouse and issue is set out in the order prescribed by the AEA 1925, s 46(1).[2]

If the intestate leaves no spouse or civil partner and no issue but both parents, then the residuary estate of the intestate is held in trust for the father[3] and mother in equal shares absolutely.

If the intestate leaves no spouse or civil partner no issue but one parent, then the residuary estate of the intestate is held in trust for the surviving father[4] or mother absolutely.

If the intestate leaves no spouse or civil partner and no issue and no parents, then the residuary estate of the intestate is held in trust for the following persons living at the death of the intestate, and in the following order and manner, namely:

First, on the statutory trusts for the brothers and sisters of the whole blood of the intestate; but if no person takes an absolutely vested interest under such trusts; then

Secondly, on the statutory trusts for the brothers and sisters of the half blood of the intestate; but if no person takes an absolutely vested interest under such trusts; then

Thirdly, for the grandparents of the intestate and, if more than one survive the intestate, in equal shares; but if there is no member of this class; then

Fourthly, on the statutory trusts for the uncles and aunts of the intestate (being brothers or sisters of the whole blood of a parent of the intestate[5] but if no person takes an absolutely vested interest under such trusts; then

Fifthly, on the statutory trusts for the uncles and aunts of the intestate (being brothers or sisters of the half blood of a parent of the intestate).

If the person or persons who are prima facie entitled in priority fails by reason of disclaimer,[6] or the public policy rule,[7] the persons entitled are the next class of qualifying relatives.

1 AEA 1925, s 46(1)(i), (3).

2 References to parents, brothers, sisters, etc have to be read subject to the adoption and legitimation legislation, the Family Law Reform Act 1987, ss 1, 18(1) in the case of deaths on or after 4 April 1988, and subject to HFEA 1990 and 2008 in relation to children born as a result of assisted reproduction techniques within either Act. See Chapters 72 and 75, and para **[74.3]** ff above.

3 There is a rebuttable presumption that the father of an illegitimate person (or any person claiming through the father) predeceased him: Family Law Reform Act 1987, s 18(2): see Vol 2, Part G, para **[245.71]**. The same applies to a female second parent of a child by virtue of HFEA 2008, s 43: see FLRA 1987, s 18(2A) inserted by HFEA 2008, Sch 6, para 25. For HFEA 2008, s 43 see para **[74.5]** above.

4 See n 3, above.

5 In *Re Patrick's Estate, Patrick v De Zeeuw* [2000] NI 506 a paternal uncle and a maternal aunt of the deceased intestate had married each other and had issue, and had not survived the intestate. It was held that the issue were entitled to claim shares under both stirpes.

6 See *Re Scott, Widdows v Friends of the Clergy Corpn* [1975] 2 All ER 1033. The Crown does not take as *bona vacantia* if there are qualified surviving relatives.

7 See *Re DWS, Re EHS, TWGS v JMG* [2000] 2 All ER 83; affd [2001] 1 All ER 97. The disqualified person is not regarded as having predeceased. But note that the reasoning supporting the conclusion in *Re DWS* is different from that in *Re Scott, Widdows v Friends of the Clergy Corpn* [1975] 2 All ER 1033, which could result in a different conclusion, ie the possibility of the Crown taking as *bona vacantia*, in certain situations; see para **[46.1]**, n 1, where the point is discussed. But see the Law Commission Report, No 295, 'The Forfeiture Rule and the Law of Succession', recommending that the law on this point should be changed to provide for the property to pass as if the disqualified person had predeceased the intestate. See para **[9.13]** above, where the recommendations are set out. The proposed Draft Bill has not yet been enacted.

PART P

Family provision

CHAPTER 105

Family provision

I. THE JURISDICTION

[Updated at footnote 6 for *Re Baker, Baker v Baker* [2008] WTLR 581.]

[105.5]

Time for application. Applications under the I(PFD)A 1975 should be made before the end of the period of six months from the date on which representation in regard to the estate of the deceased is first taken out.[1] The six-month period was also applicable under the Inheritance (Family Provision) Act 1938 and some of the decisions on that Act might still assist under the I(PFD)A 1975. Thus it was decided that the six-month period ran from the date of the grant of probate in common form and that no further period was initiated by a subsequent grant in solemn form.[2] If a grant of administration was revoked and a grant of probate made, the period ran from the date of the grant of probate.[3] Provided the originating summons was issued within six months, it was immaterial that it was not served within that time.[4] The court had power to order provision to be made as from a future date and could direct that the summons should stand over until a given date with liberty to all parties to apply in the meantime if circumstances should so require.[5]

An application should not be made before a grant of probate has been obtained and may be struck out as premature[6] but if a grant is obtained before the hearing and no objection on the ground of irregularity has been made before that time the application will be heard.[7]

The court has, however, power to permit applications to be made after six months.[8] The circumstances in which the court will permit an application for financial provision under the I(PFD)A 1975, to be made out of time, were considered in *Re Salmon*.[9] In that case permission to apply out of time under the I(PFD)A 1975, s 4 was refused for the following reasons; first, the delay was substantial and was wholly the applicant's fault; second, there had been no negotiations with, and no warning to, the executor during the six-month period;[10] third, almost all the estate had been distributed;[11] fourth, the applicant probably had a remedy in negligence against her solicitors;[12] fifth, it would in the circumstances have been unjust to the beneficiaries to grant the extension.

A similar application was also dismissed in *Re Dennis*,[13] where the court thought that a crucial factor in such cases was whether the applicant was able to satisfy the court that he had an arguable case that he was entitled to reasonable financial provision out of the estate.

1 I(PFD)A 1975, s 4; which must mean time begins to run from the date on which effective or valid representation was first taken out; *Re Freeman* [1984] 3 All ER 906, [1980] 1 WLR 1419 (probate revoked and letters of administration granted). In *Re Johnson* [1987] CLY 3882 it was held that time ran under the I(PFD)A 1975, s 4, not from the date of a limited grant, but from the date of the general grant.
2 *Re Miller, Miller v de Courcey* [1968] 3 All ER 844, [1969] 1 WLR 583.
3 *Re Bidie, Bidie v General Accident, Fire and Life Assurance Corpn Ltd* [1949] Ch 121, [1948] 2 All ER 995.
4 *Re Chittenden, Chittenden v Doe* [1970] 3 All ER 562, [1970] 1 WLR 1618.
5 *Re Franks, Franks v Franks* [1948] Ch 62, [1947] 2 All ER 638.
6 *Re McBroom* [1992] 2 FLR 49: the presence of some person entitled to administer the estate of the deceased was necessary. Cf. *Re Searle, Searle v Siems* [1949] Ch 73, [1948] 2 All ER 426, a decision under the Inheritance (Family Provision) Act 1938 (repealed): where a grant of representation had been obtained before trial, the objection was merely procedural and could not be taken at trial. The position is unsatisfactory: *Re Searle* was not cited in *Re McBroom* and see *Re Dawkins, Dawkins v Judd* [1986] 2 FLR 360: final order made before grant of representation taken out. In *Re Baker, Baker v Baker* [2008] WTLR 581 in which an I(PFD)A 1975 claim was made in conjunction with a probate claim, the judge, having found that the deceased died intestate so that the claimant had the right to apply for a grant of letters of administration, ruled, with the agreement of the parties, on the question of the I(PFD)A 1975 before the grant of representation had been obtained.
7 *Re Searle, Searle v Siems* [1949] Ch 73, [1948] 2 All ER 426.
8 Recognised as a power of the court in the I(PFD)A 1975, s 4.
9 *Re Salmon, Coard v National Westminster Bank Ltd* [1981] Ch 167, [1980] 3 All ER 532. For cases on the Inheritance (Family Provision) Act 1938, s 2(1A) see the seventh edition of this work.
10 See also *Re Ruttie, Ruttie v Saul* [1969] 3 All ER 1633, [1970] 1 WLR 89; *Re McNare, McNare v McNare* [1964] 3 All ER 373, [1964] 1 WLR 1255. An extension was granted where the delay was caused by the expectation that the executors would commence proceedings for the construction of the will and that the result of those proceedings might be materially to affect the provision to be made: *Re Bone, Bone v Midland Bank Ltd* [1955] 2 All ER 555, [1955] 1 WLR 703.
11 Distribution alone may not defeat an application if the beneficiaries have not changed their position: *Re Salmon* [1981] Ch 167 at 176C-D, [1980] 3 All ER 532 at 538a; *Re Longley, Longley and Longley v Longley* [1981] CLY 2885.
12 *See Re Gonin, Gonin v Garmeson* [1979] Ch 16, [1977] 2 All ER 720; *Re C* [1995] 2 FLR 24. A prospective claim in negligence against the claimant's own solicitors is not to be totally ignored but is not a factor of any great importance and does not counterbalance other important factors: *Adams v Adams* (12 November 1993, unreported), CA. A solicitor's ignorance of the limited time in which application might be made was not a circumstance which would justify an extension: *Re Greaves, Greaves v Greaves* [1954] 2 All ER 109, [1954] 1 WLR 760.
13 *Re Dennis, Dennis v Lloyds Bank Ltd* [1981] 2 All ER 140. See also *Re Longley* [1981] CLY 2885 and *Re Gonin, Gonin v Garmeson* [1979] Ch 16, sub nom *Re Gonin, Gonin v Garmeson* [1977] 2 All ER 720 (where the delay was 2.5 years and permission was refused since the vital dates were under the control of the plaintiff). Extensions were granted in *Stock v Brown* [1994] 2 FCR 1125 (delay of 5.5 years but applicant had no independent advice and there was no prejudice to other beneficiaries); *Re W (a minor)* [1995] 2 FCR 689 (child would otherwise suffer); *Re C* [1995] 2 FLR 24; (delay of 18 months, substantial estate and very strong claim); *Re W (a minor)* [1995] 2 FCR 689; *Re Abram* [1996] 2 FLR 379 (six months late) and in *Re B* [2000] 1 All ER 665 (court of appeal followed exercise of discretion by master and judge).

II. THE APPLICANTS

[Updated at the end of footnote 10. Also updated at footnote 12 for *P v E* [2007] WTLR 691. Also updated at footnote 13 for *Re Baker, Baker v Baker* [2008] 2 FLR 1956 and *Aston v Aston* [2007] WTLR 1349.]

[105.9]

The spouse. The specified class of persons who have locus standi to apply under the I(PFD)A 1975 includes the spouse of the deceased, formerly 'the wife or husband of the deceased'.[1] The applicant would thus have to prove that he or she was the deceased's spouse under a subsisting marriage at the date of the death. A judicially separated spouse can apply under this heading but provision is limited to maintenance.[2] Also included is a person who, in good faith, entered into a void marriage with the deceased, unless either the marriage of the deceased and that person was dissolved or annulled during the lifetime of the deceased, or that person has during the lifetime of the deceased entered into a later marriage.[3] Likewise, a party to a voidable marriage which has not been annulled before the death of the party is included.[4] In *Re Sehota, Surjit Kaur v Gian Kaur*,[5] the deceased had contracted two marriages at a time when all parties concerned had had Indian domiciles of origin and both marriages were valid under Indian law. The deceased had left the whole of his residuary estate to his second wife and it was held that the first wife was entitled to claim under the I(PFD)A 1975 despite the fact that the marriage was polygamous.

The I(PFD)A 1975 made an important change in the law so far as the standard of provision for a spouse is concerned. The Inheritance (Family Provision) Act 1938 set the standard of 'reasonable provision for the maintenance' of the applicant, whereas in divorce proceedings the court is not limited to any such standard.[6]

The Law Commission[7] recommended that the surviving spouse should have a claim upon the family assets at least equivalent to that of a divorced spouse. Accordingly, the I(PFD)A 1975, s 1(2)(a) provides:

> 'In this Act "reasonable financial provision"—
>
> (a) in the case of an application made by virtue of subsection (1)(a) above by the husband or wife of the deceased (except where the marriage with the deceased was the subject of a decree of judicial separation and at the date of death the decree was in force and the separation was continuing), means such financial provision as it would be reasonable in all the circumstances of the case for a husband or wife to receive, whether or not that provision is required for his or her maintenance.'

The court is instructed to have regard to what provision would have been awarded in divorce proceedings,[8] but this is not to be regarded as the sole criterion. The overriding consideration is what is reasonable in the circumstances.[9] Further it has been pointed out in a later case that the amount that might be awarded under the Matrimonial Causes Act 1973 is not analogous to the position on death, since an award under the former would have to take into account the husband's likely future needs.[10] Nevertheless this stated requirement of the Act in determining the level of provision for a surviving spouse, has been applied by the Court of Appeal. The intention of the Act was that the acceptable minimum posthumous provision for a surviving spouse should correspond as closely as possible to the inchoate rights enjoyed by that spouse during the deceased's lifetime under matrimonial law.[11] A successful application was made by a widow (competing against adult children) in *Singer v Isaac*.[12] The case raised several interesting points. In determining the amount of the award, the court had regard to the applicant's age, the length of the marriage and her contribution to it. An important factor was the divorce standard which was referred to, to determine the amount of the award.[13]

The Court of Appeal in *Cunliffe v Fielden*[14] has set out the approach to be adopted in relation to a claim for provision by a wife where the marriage had been very short.

In the case of stale marriages, if there is a principle to be derived from the cases it is that where the parties to the marriage have drawn a line under their financial relations there is little prospect of any significant award being made in favour of the surviving spouse.[15]

1 I(PFD)A 1975, s 1(1)(a). As amended by the Civil Partnership Act 2004, s 71, Sch 4, para 15.
2 I(PFD)A 1975, s 1(2)(a).
3 I(PFD)A 1975, s 25(4).
4 Law Com no 62, p 8.
5 *Re Sehota Surjit Kaur v Gian Kaur* [1978] 3 All ER 385, [1978] 1 WLR 1506.
6 Matrimonial Causes Act 1973, ss 23–25, and see *Wachtel v Wachtel* [1973] Fam 72, [1973] 1 All ER 829.
7 Law Com no 61, p 8.
8 I(PFD)A 1975, s 3(2). *White v White* [2001] 1 AC 596, [2001] 1 All ER 1, [2000] 2 FLR 981 has a significant impact on provision for spouses and may lead to more or less equal provision on death as in the case of divorce in the longer term.
9 *Re Besterman* [1984] Ch 458, [1984] 2 All ER 656 where, in the case of a very large estate where the testator's only obligation was to his widow who was wholly blameless and incapable of supporting herself, reasonable financial provision required that she should have access to a sufficient lump sum to ensure beyond any reasonable doubt that she was relieved of any anxiety for the future; capital sum of £378,000 awarded. But see now *Cunliffe v Fielden* [2005] EWCA Civ 1508, [2006] Ch 361, [2006] 2 All ER 115, where a different approach, based on the so-called divorce standard, was adopted.
10 *Re Bunning, Bunning v Salmon* [1984] Ch 480, [1984] 3 All ER 1, wife not limited to the amount she might have received under the Matrimonial Causes Act 1973 but given a lump sum award giving her roughly half the spouse's total assets; see now *White v White* [2001] 1 AC 596, [2001] 1 All ER 1, [2000] 2 FLR 981. See also *Re Rowlands* [1984] Fam Law 280 (small award); *Stead v Stead* [1985] Fam Law 154; *Rajabally v Rajabally* [1987] 2 FLR 390; *Davis v Davis* [1993] 1 FLR 54. See also *Re Krubert* [1997] Ch 97 where the approach in *Re Besterman* [1984] Ch 458, [1984] 2 All ER 656 which minimised the relevance of the 'divorce standard' was preferred to the approach in *Moody v Stevenson* [1992] Ch 486, sub nom *Re Moody, Moody v Stevenson* [1992] 2 All ER 524 which emphasised the relevance of the 'divorce standard'. See now the Court of Appeal decision in *Cunliffe v Fielden* [2005] EWCA Civ 1508, [2006] Ch 361, [2006] 2 All ER 115 that there is no presumption of equal division of assets. Since a deceased spouse who leaves a widow is entitled to bequeath his estate to whomsoever he pleases, and his only statutory obligation is to make reasonable financial provision for his widow, the concept of equality of division may bear little relation to such provision, depending on the value of the estate.
11 *Moody v Stevenson* [1992] Ch 486, sub nom *Re Moody, Moody v Stevenson* [1992] 2 All ER 524 (widower awarded a settlement of the matrimonial home to enable him to continue living in the house as long as he was willing and able to do so).
12 [2001] WTLR 1045. See also *P v E* [2007] WTLR 691.

13 Reasonable provision had to be determined objectively, see para **[105.23]** below. The two adult children had not established a particular need to be provided for to the detriment of the widow; considering *Re Krubert (decd)* [1997] Ch 97. A successful application was made by a widow in *Stephanides v Cohen* [2002] EWHC (Fam) 1869, [2002] WTLR 1373 for further provision out of her deceased husband's estate competing against a 37-year-old son. The estate was worth £643,500; the widow had been left £25,000; with the rest of the assets going to the son. The Court took into consideration the relative merits of the widow and the son based on the conduct of each in relation to the deceased, under s 3(1)(g) of the Act. The widow had been a good and loyal wife whereas the son, who had a history of drug dependency, had not been a good son. The Court awarded the widow some 55 per cent of the estate leaving the son with 45 per cent. A widow, competing against stepchildren, succeeded in a claim under the Act in *In the Estate of Grattan (Robin Francis), Grattan v McNaughton* [2001] WTLR 1305, as did a widow competing against her children in *Re Baker, Baker v Baker* [2008] 2 FLR 1956. The 'divorce fiction' was considered to play a large part in *Aston v Aston* [2007] WTLR 1349 because the marriage of the deceased and the claimant had effectively come to an end some years before the death.

14 [2005] EWCA Civ 1508, [2006] Ch 361, [2006] 2 All ER 115.

15 See *Re Rowlands* [1984] 5 FLR 813 (the applicant widow awarded only £3,000 out of an estate of £100,000 where there had been 43 years of separation in a marriage of 62 years). This can be contrasted with *Bheekun v Williams* [1999] 2 FLR 229 which involved a 37-year marriage for the second half of which the deceased had lived elsewhere. In that case divorce proceedings had begun and a decree nisi was obtained in 1990 (three years before the death) but never made absolute. The widow was awarded £70,000 out of an estate of £159,000 which award was upheld by the Court of Appeal. In *Parish v Sharman* [2001] WTLR 593 no award was made for a spouse of 33 years who had been separated for 11 years. A decree nisi was obtained in 1985 (at the time of the separation) but never made absolute. No award was made in part because Mrs Parish was probably better off than her late husband and, more particularly, because it was quite clear that the parties to the marriage had decided to let sleeping dogs lie at the time of the separation. It was also clear that the trial judge found Mrs Parish's evidence to be unreliable if not dishonest. *Barrass v Harding* [2001] 1 FLR 138 is another ostensibly harsh case concerning a couple who married in 1939 but who divorced in 1964. Agreement was reached as to the settlement of their financial affairs and Mrs Barrass' claim for Family Provision following her former husband's death failed. There was no ongoing relationship and no continuing moral claim even though the estate was of very substantial value.

[Updated at footnote 8 for *Negus v Bahouse* [2008] 1 FLR 381.]

[105.14]

Applications by cohabitees – different sex couples – deaths on or after 1 January 1996. A new category of applicant has been added, in relation to persons dying on or after 1 January 1996, by the Law Reform (Succession) Act 1995.[1] A person is within this category of claimant if he or she is not the spouse or un-remarried former spouse of the deceased and, during the whole of the period of two years preceding the deceased's death, he or she lived in the same household as the deceased and as the husband or wife of the deceased.[2]

The 'living as husband and wife' formula can be found in a number of other statutes,[3] and there is some case law on it.[4] A question which could arise in practice, particularly where the applicant and the deceased were elderly, is whether sexual intercourse must be proved (i) at some stage in the history of the relationship or (ii) during the two years preceding the deceased's death, for the applicant to qualify as falling in this category. It is submitted that the presence or absence of sexual relations will be an important but not decisive factor,[5] along with other factors.[6] It may be an unusual case (eg where there was physical incapacity) where an applicant is held to fall into this category and there is no history of a sexual relationship at all. That there should have been sexual intercourse during the two years before the deceased's death is probably not a requirement if there was a previous history of sexual relations. For example, if the applicant and the deceased had had a sexual relationship, but sexual intercourse had ceased more than two years before the deceased's death as a result of age or illness, they could still be regarded as living together as husband and wife during the two years preceding the deceased's death.[7] The standard of provision for persons falling into this category is 'maintenance' rather than 'what it is reasonable for a husband or wife to receive'.[8]

In assessing whether a claimant could satisfy the requirements of ss 1(1)(ba), (1A) and 3(2A) of I(PFD)A 1975 the court will have regard to the general arrangements for maintenance subsisting at the time of death. The words 'immediately before the death of the deceased' should not be construed literally but rather the settled state of affairs during the relationship should be regarded. Accordingly it was held in *Gully v Dix, Re Dix (decd)*,[9] that the claimant's three-month absence immediately before the death, in the context of a 27-year cohabitation, was, on the facts, an abnormal situation and should not prevent a successful claim. By contrast, in *Churchill v Roach*[10] the parties had started living in the same household less than two years before the deceased's death, and the claimant did not fall into this category.[11]

Where it is not certain that an applicant was living with the deceased as his or her wife or husband, the case may be put in the alternative that the applicant qualifies for an order for provision under the I(PFD)A 1975 as someone who was wholly or partly maintained by the deceased[12] (if there is evidence to support such a claim), and it will be necessary to rely on the latter ground where the applicant and the deceased were together for less than two years preceding the deceased's death (or the applicant is of the same sex as or a sibling of the deceased).

1 See the I(PFD)A 1975, ss 1(1)(ba), (1A) and 3(2A), as inserted by Law Reform (Succession) Act 1995, s 2, and printed in Vol 2, Part G, paras **[247.2]** and **[247.4]**. This new category of cohabitee applicants was introduced on the recommendations of the Law Commission, *Distribution on Intestacy* (Law Com no 187), to deal with the problems of proving dependence which sometimes arose in claims by cohabitees. For the problems which had arisen see para **[105.18]** below.

2 I(PFD)A 1975, s 1(1)(ba), (1A). See *Re Watson* [1999] 1 FLR 878, the test of living in the same household is objective. In *Witkowska v Kaminski* [2006] EWHC 1940 (Ch), [2006] 3 FCR 250 the claimant, a Polish national and an illegal overstayer in the United Kingdom, was awarded provision under s 1(1)(ba) and 1(1)(e) of the 1975 Act on the basis of her maintenance requirements in Poland rather than in the United Kingdom. Art 12 of the EC Treaty (Nice) had no application to the substantive law of succession, whether by will or on intestacy or by force of the jurisdiction conferred by the 1975 Act, and that the claimant _ s claim that the award discriminated against her under Art 12 failed.

3 Eg Fatal Accidents Act 1976, s 1(3)(b) (which was added to that Act for the first time by Administration of Justice Act 1982, s 3); Social Security Contributions and Benefits Act 1992, s 137, definition of 'unmarried couple'; Housing Act 1985, s 113; Domestic Violence and Matrimonial Proceedings Act 1976, s 1(2).

4 See the first case reported on the I(PFD)A 1975, s 1(1A), *Re Watson* [1999] 1 FLR 878; the correct approach is to ask whether a reasonable person with normal perceptions would regard them as having lived together as man and wife bearing in mind the multifarious nature of marital relations. For cases on other statutes see *Adeoso v Adeoso* [1981] 1 All ER 107 (a case on Domestic Violence and Matrimonial Proceedings Act 1976, s 1); *Crake v Supplementary Benefits Commission* [1982] 1 All ER 498; *Westminster City Council v Peart* (1991) 24 HLR 389 (a case on the Housing Act 1985, s 113(1)).

5 The test as to whether a person was living in the same household as the deceased as the husband or wife of the deceased is objective and should not ignore the multifarious nature of marital relationships: See *Re Watson* [1999] 1 FLR 878 *per* Neuberger J.
6 For a summary of the practice in social security cases see *Crake v Supplementary Benefits Commission* [1982] 1 All ER 498 at 505f–h. See also *Thomas v Thomas* [1948] 2 KB 294 at 297; *Re Watson* [1999] 1 FLR 878 and the Housing Act case of *Nutting v Southern Housing Group* [2004] EWHC 2982 (Ch), [2005] 1 FLR 1066.
7 See the remarks in *Crake v Supplementary Benefits Commission* [1982] 1 All ER 498 at 502g–h.
8 The I(PFD)A 1975, s 1(2)(b) applies. See para **[105.9]** above, and contrast the provision for spouses discussed in para **[105.9]** above. 'Maintenance' is maintenance in the context of the lifestyle of the claimant with the deceased, see *Negus v Bahouse* [2008] 1 FLR 381.
9 [2004] EWCA Civ 139, [2004] FCR 453. *Jelley v Iliffe* [1981] Fam 128 (discussed in paras **[105.18]**, **[105.19]**, **[105.22]** and **[105.29]**, below, applied.
10 [2002] EWHC 3230 (Ch), [2003] WTLR 779.
11 See *Kotke v Safferini* [2005] EWCA Civ 221, [2005] 1 FCR 642, on the same words in FAA 1976, where two people maintaining separate houses but planning to live together were held not to be living in the same household.
12 Ie that he or she falls within the I(PFD)A 1975, s 1(1)(e). See para **[105.19]** below.

[Updated in the text to footnote 3 and at footnote 3 for *Baynes v Hedger* [2008] 2 FLR 1805.]

[105.15]

Applications by cohabitees – same-sex couples. The Civil Partnership Act 2004[1] has added a new sub-s (1B) to s 1 I(PFD)A 1975 which is in similar terms to sub-s (1A) and which applies to a person who has cohabited with the deceased in the same household 'as a civil partner of the deceased', with effect from the commencement date of the Civil Partnership Act 2004, 5 December 2005.[2] It is not possible to establish that two persons have lived together as civil partners unless their relationship as a couple is an acknowledged one.[3]

1 Section 71, Sch 4, para 15.
2 See the House of Lords decision in the Housing Act case of *Ghaidan v Godin-Mendoza* [2004] UKHL 30, [2004] 2 AC 557 a same-sex couple can, since the coming into force of HRA 1998, be said to be living together as husband and wife, contrary to the decision in *Fitzpatrick v Stirling Housing Association* [2001] 1 AC 27. See also the decision of Master Bowles in *Saunders v Garrett* [2005] WTLR 749.
3 *Baynes v Hedger* [2008] 2 FLR 1805. (Lewison J's dismissal of the co-habitee's claim in this case was not appealed against, as was his dismissal of the dependent's claim, so the part of his judgement considering the co-habitation claim was not considered by the Court of Appeal in *Baynes v Hedger* [2009] EWCA Civ 374, [2009] All ER (D) 50 (May)).

[105.16]

Applications by children. Under the Inheritance (Family Provision) Act 1938 children of the deceased who could apply for provision were limited to unmarried and disabled daughters and minor and disabled sons. The definition of 'son' and 'daughter' included both adopted and illegitimate children as well as posthumous children of the deceased. The I(PFD)A 1975 refers simply to 'a child of the deceased'.[1] This removes the age limit and any distinction between married and unmarried children and the relevance of any disability, so far as locus standi is concerned. 'Child' includes an illegitimate child and a child en ventre sa mère at the time of the death of the deceased.[2] The standard of provision for children is limited to 'such financial provision as it would be reasonable in all the circumstances of the case for the applicant to receive for his maintenance'.[3] What is proper 'maintenance' depends on all the facts and circumstances of the case[4] but it has been said that it connotes only payments which would directly or indirectly enable the applicant to discharge the recurring costs of his living expenses.[5]

The element of mere obligation has been referred to as a criterion for determining whether a child should succeed in an application; however, whether the child is an adult or a minor,[6] in no case is there an invariable prerequisite that the child must show that the deceased had a moral obligation[7] to maintain him or that there is some other special circumstance which entitled him to seek provision.[8]

In the case of adult children whilst it is not necessary to show that the deceased had such a moral obligation to maintain the applicant, an adult child who is in employment, with an earning capacity for the foreseeable future is unlikely to succeed in his application without some special circumstance such as a moral obligation.[9]

Three further points[10] relevant to applications by children: first, a child who may have been qualified to apply for family provision ceases to be so qualified if he is subsequently adopted by another person before the application is made.[11] Second, in considering a claim under the I(PFD)A 1975 the court may take into account the wishes of the deceased expressed before death including any indications of his intentions in an invalid will. Third, any receipts of social security benefits by the applicant are to be disregarded in considering the applicant's financial resources.[12]

1 I(PFD)A 1975, s 1(1)(c).
2 I(PFD)A 1975, s 25(1).
3 I(PFD)A 1975, s 1(2)(b).
4 *Re Coventry,* [1980] Ch 461, [1979] 3 All ER 815 where an able-bodied 46-year-old son did not succeed in an application. The mere fact that it would have been reasonable for the deceased to make some provision was not sufficient; the applicant had to establish a moral claim to be maintained over and above the claim of a blood relationship. Not following *Re Christie, Christie v Keeble* [1979] Ch 168, [1979] 1 All ER 546. *Re Coventry* was followed in *Re Jennings* [1994] Ch 286, [1994] 3 All ER 27 in which the deceased's failure to support his son during his infancy was not of itself sufficient to justify an award. Likewise in *Garland v Morris* [2007] All ER (D) 11 where an adult daughter failed to prove that it had been unreasonable for the deceased to make no provision for her. See also *Harlow v National Westminster Bank* (3 January 1994, unreported), Fam D. But a successful claim was made by an adult son against his father's estate in *Re Goodchild* [1997] 3 All ER 63 where the award was justified on the basis of 'exceptional circumstances' arising from the fact that his parents had made similar (though not mutual) wills under which the son was the ultimate beneficiary of the joint estate, a consideration which was held to give rise to a 'moral obligation' to the son. For other successful applications by adult children see *Re Abram* [1996] 2 FLR 379; *Re Pearce* [1998] 2 FLR 705; *Myers v Myers* [2004] EWHC 1944 (Fam), [2005] WTLR 851 and *Re Gold deceased, Gold v Curtis* [2005] WTLR 673.
5 *Re Dennis, Dennis v Lloyds Bank Ltd* [1981] 2 All ER 140 where an adult son failed in an application for payment of tax out of the father's estate. The application was also out of time, see para **[105.5]** above.
6 Minor children have a strong claim for financial provision: *Re C* [1995] 2 FLR 24
7 *Re Coventry, Coventry v Coventry* [1980] Ch 461, [1979] 3 All ER 815, CA, (adult son failed to show moral obligation); *Re Dennis, Dennis v Lloyds Bank Ltd* [1981] 2 All ER 140, 124 Sol Jo 885 (desire for payment of capital sum to creditors was not an application for maintenance, application by adult son failed); *Re Callaghan* [1985] Fam 1, [1984] 3 All ER 790 (adult stepson awarded £15,000 out of estate of £31,000); *Re Leach, Leach v Lindeman* [1986] Ch 226, [1985] 2 All ER 754 (adult stepdaughter who never lived in the deceased's household and was never maintained by the deceased awarded half of the net estate); *Re Debenham* [1986] 1 FLR 404, adult epileptic daughter received an award of £3,000 capital plus a periodical payments order of £4,500; *Williams v Johns* [1988] 2 FLR 475 (a physically fit, 43 year-old adoptive daughter who was capable of maintaining herself was unable to

show that the deceased had any obligation to maintain her. The applicant had nor cared for and, in the past, had caused shame and distress to the deceased); *Re Jennings* [1994] Ch 286, [1994] 3 All ER 27, CA, (application by adult son failed: mere blood relationship did not give rise to an enduring moral obligation); *Re Goodchild* [1997] 3 All ER 63, [1997] 1 WLR 1216, CA, (adult son's application was successful because of moral obligation imposed on deceased by his former wife's mistaken belief that wills were mutually binding); *Re Hancock* [1998] 2 FLR 346, CA, (an adult daughter with no earning capacity who had left home at 19 to live with a man who now had no resources save his pension and disability benefits awarded periodical payments of £3000 per annum); *Re Pearce* [1998] 2 FLR 705, CA, (an adult son who worked on his father's farm between the ages of 6 and 16 and left only because the deceased could not afford to pay him was awarded a tax-free legacy of £85,000 out of an estate of £285,000); *Espinosa v Bourke* [1999] 1 FLR 747, CA, (55-year-old daughter, long out of employment, in financial need and with doubtful earning capacity did not have to show moral obligation. The deceased was under an obligation arising from his promise to leave his wife's portfolio of shares to the daughter).

8 See: *Re Pearce* [1998] 2 FLR 705 at 710 per Nourse LJ and the cases referred to above.; *Re Hancock* [1998] 2 FLR 346, CA; *Espinosa v Bourke* [1999] 1 FLR 747 at 755 per Butler-Sloss LJ; *Re Watson* [1999] 1 FLR 878; cf *Re Coventry, Coventry v Coventry* [1980] Ch 461, [1979] 3 All ER 815, CA; *Re Jennings* [1994] Ch 286, [1994] 3 All ER 27, CA.

9 *Re Hancock* [1998] 2 FLR 346 at 351F per Butler-Sloss LJ; *Re Pearce* [1998] 2 FLR 705 at 710 per Nourse LJ; *Espinosa v Bourke* [1999] 1 FLR 747 at 755 per Butler-Sloss LJ. Following the decision in *Re Hancock*, above, the moral obligation requirement derived from *Re Coventry, Coventry v Coventry* [1980] Ch 461, [1979] 3 All ER 815, CA, is of less rigid application but in many of the successful cases since *Re Coventry* the applicant has been able to rely on a moral obligation such as a promise made by the deceased to another. See, for example: *Re Goodchild; Espinosa v Bourke* (above). The older decisions are more eclectic and may not now be terribly reliable.

10 *Re Collins* [1990] Fam 56, [1990] 2 All ER 47.

11 This is consistent with the view taken in *Whyte v Ticehurst* [1986] Fam 64, [1986] 2 All ER 158, that the claim is neither an indefeasible right nor an interest expectant.

12 This is consistent with the view taken in *Re E, E v E* [1966] 2 All ER 44, [1966] 1 WLR 709, on a comparable point under the Inheritance (Family Provision) Act 1938.

[Updated for *Baynes v Hedger* [2009] EWCA Civ 374, [2009] All ER (D) 50 (May).]

[105.18]

Applications by other dependants. The most important extension made by the I(PFD)A 1975 to the categories of applicants who can make applications for provision is the class of applicants defined by s 1(1)(e) as follows 'any person (not being a person included in the foregoing paragraphs of this subsection) who immediately before the death of the deceased was being maintained, either wholly or partly, by the deceased'. The importance of this category is now much reduced following the introduction of a separate category of cohabitees (who need not prove dependence). This category is further defined in s 1(3) to the effect that 'a person shall be treated as being maintained by the deceased either wholly or partly as the case may be, if the deceased, otherwise than for full valuable consideration, was making a substantial contribution in money or money's worth towards the reasonable needs of that person'. The I(PFD)A 1975, s 3(4) provides that 'without prejudice to the generality of paragraph (g) of subsection (1) above, where an application for an order under s 2 of this Act is made by virtue of section 1(1)(e) of this Act, the court shall, in addition to the matters specifically mentioned in paragraphs (a) to (f) of that subsection, have regard to the extent to which and the basis upon which the deceased assumed responsibility for the maintenance of the applicant and to the length of time for which the deceased discharged that responsibility'. These provisions have been fully considered in a number of decisions which provide useful guidance on the applications under paragraph (e).

The first case is the decision of Sir Robert Megarry V-C in *Re Beaumont, Martin v Midland Bank Trust Co Ltd.*[1] The plaintiff, a man who had lived with the deceased as man and wife for 36 years, applied for financial provision out of her estate as a dependant under the I(PFD)A 1975. Sir Robert Megarry V-C, decided that s 1(1)(e) was qualified by both ss 1(3) and 3(4) and that the plaintiff could only claim under that paragraph if he satisfied three conditions. First, it was necessary to show that he was being maintained 'immediately before' the death of the deceased with reference to the degree of maintenance normally and habitually existing under the arrangement. Second, the substantial contributions made towards the reasonable needs of the applicant must have been 'otherwise than for full valuable consideration' which was not restricted to contributions supplied under a contract but extended to any contribution provided for full consideration.[2] Third, it had to be shown that the deceased had demonstrated an undertaking or assumption of responsibility for the applicant.[2a] This requirement was held not to have been satisfied on the facts of the case which indicated that the applicant was merely one of two people of independent means who had chosen to pool their individual resources to enable them to live together without either undertaking any responsibility for maintaining the other. The summons was accordingly struck out. The decision in *Re Beaumont*, was subsequently considered by the Court of Appeal in *Jelley v Iliffe*,[3] where a widower had been living with a widow in her house rent-free, for some eight years before her death. The parties had pooled their financial resources to pay living expenses and the widower had provided some furniture for the house, looked after the garden and done household jobs. The deceased widow, by her will, left all her property, including the house, to her children, which was consistent with an understanding she had had with them from whom he had acquired the house. The widower applied under the I(PFD)A 1975, s 1(1) for reasonable financial provision out of the deceased's estate on the ground that immediately before her death he was being maintained by her within s (1)(e) of the Act. The Court of Appeal held that the applicant satisfied the requirements of 'being maintained' in the I(PFD)A 1975, s 1(1)(e) as defined in s 1(3), applying *Re Beaumont*. Further that the fact of maintenance raised a presumption of 'assumed responsibility', and that it was not necessary to show a specific intention to this effect, not following *Re Beaumont*, on this point. In determining whether the deceased's contribution to the applicant's needs had been 'otherwise than for full valuable consideration' the court stated that a balance had to be struck between the benefits received, and those provided, by the applicant. On the facts of the case before them the Court of Appeal thought that the provision of rent-free accommodation was a significant contribution to a person's reasonable needs, particularly in the case of an old-age pensioner. Since it was not clear beyond doubt that the applicant's contribution had equalled or outweighed the benefit of the rent-free accommodation there was an arguable case and the issue was ordered to proceed to trial.

The Court of Appeal considered these cases in *Bishop v Plumley*[4] where the applicant was the cohabitee of the deceased, living with him as his wife and described as waiting on him 'hand and foot' and doing everything for him. She had enjoyed in return rent-free accommodation in a house that he had purchased with an inheritance. The court thought that there was no difficulty in finding that the deceased had made a substantial contribution towards her reasonable needs. The difficulty centred on whether she had provided full valuable consideration in return and thus disentitled herself from applying under paragraph (e). The court held that she had not, and this aspect of the case is more fully discussed in the next section.

In *Re B*[5] the Court of Appeal preferred the approach in *Jelley v Iliffe*[6] to the effect that the fact that one person has made a substantial contribution to another person's needs, in itself raised an inference of an assumption of responsibility for the latter.[7] On that basis a claim by a mother against the intestate estate of her deceased (disabled) daughter succeeded where the Court of Protection had made substantial inter vivos payments to her as her daughter's receiver for the maintenance of the daughter, out of which she also (as mother/carer) had benefited.[8]

1 [1980] Ch 444, [1980] 1 All ER 266.

2 On this requirement see also the confirmation of Sir Robert Megarry V-C's view by the Court of Appeal in *Jelley v Iliffe* [1981] Fam 128, [1981] 2 All ER 29. See also *Kourkgy v Lusher* (1981) 4 FLR 65 where the evidence established that the deceased had abandoned cohabitation and maintenance of the applicant some months before his death, and the claim failed. Likewise in *Layton v Martin* [1986] 2 FLR 227, [1986] Fam Law 212, a former mistress of the deceased whose five-year relationship with him ended two years before his death had no claim to any interest in his property, at law, equity, or under the 1975 Act.

2a That it is an essential ingredient in the qualification of a person entitled to make a claim as a dependant that the deceased assumed responsibility for his or her maintenance was approved by the Court of Appeal in *Jelley v Iliffe* [1981] Fam 128, [1981] 2 All ER 29, and more recently in *Baynes v Hedger* [2009] EWCA Civ 374, [2009] All ER (D) 50 (May). In *Jelley v Iliffe* and *Re B* [2000] 1 All ER 665 however, the Court of Appeal seem to have disagreed with Sir Robert Megarry V-C as to how such assumption might be demonstrated, and in both cases the mere fact of one person making a substantial contribution to another person's needs was said to raise an inference of an assumption by the former of responsibility for the latter. In *Baynes v Hedger* no assumption of responsibility was found in circumstances where the maintenance found was only partial, and where the facts showed that the deceased had sought to disclaim responsibility to the claimant in the last years of her life.

3 [1981] Fam 128, [1981] 1 All ER 29, provision of accommodation held to be a substantial benefit. Likewise in *Re Wilkinson, Neale v Newell* [1978] 1 All ER 221 (sister). See also *Graham v Murphy* [1997] 1 FLR 860; *Rees v Newbery and the Institute of Cancer Research* [1998] 1 FLR 1041 and *Wayling v Jones* [1995] 2 FLR 1029 (homosexual relationship). *Jelley v Iliffe* [1981] Fam 128, [1981] 2 All ER 29 has been considered in *Kourkgy v Lusher* (1981) 12 Fam Law 86 where a claim by a cohabitee failed, and applied in *Re Kirby* (1982) 11 Fam Law 210. See also *Malone v Harrison* [1979] 1 WLR 1353 on assumption of responsibility and computation of lump sum award; *Harrington v Gill* (1983) 4 FLR 265, cohabitant held entitled to a lump sum and also the deceased's house settled on her for life; *Williams v Roberts* [1984] Fam Law 210 and *Re Watson* [1999] 1 FLR 878 (ten years cohabitation).

4 [1991] 1 All ER 236, [1991] 1 WLR 582. It will be appreciated that this was a case, like many of those noted above, of an application by a cohabitee under the I(PFD)A 1975, s 1(1)(e), which would now be brought under s 1(1)(ba); See *Cyganik v Agulian* [2005] EWHC 444 (Ch), [2005] All ER (D) 400 (Mar), application by cohabitant, where the issue was whether the deceased was domiciled in England and Wales; see also *Witkowska v Kaminski* [2006] EWHC 1940 (Ch), [2006] 3 FCR 250.

5 [2000] 1 All ER 665; reversing Jonathan Parker J [1999] 2 All ER 425 who had dismissed the claim. The Court of Appeal emphasised that the 'assumption of responsibility' in the I(PFD)A 1975, s 3(4) was not part of the threshold requirements of s 1(1)(e) but was a factor to be taken into account, once the court was satisfied that the applicant had locus

standi, in determining the merits of the claim and thus the exercise of the court's discretion. *Jelley v Iliffe* [1981] Fam 128, [1981] 2 All ER 29, was applied; *Re Beaumont, Martin v Midland Bank Trust Co Ltd* [1980] Ch 444, [1980] 1 All ER 266 was doubted. See also *Rees v Newbery and the Institute of Cancer Research* [1998] 1 FLR 1041 (immaterial that the maintenance of the applicant arose through a tenancy agreement)

6 *Jelley v Iliffe* [1981] Fam 128, [1981] 2 All ER 29.

7 In *Baynes v Hedger* [2008] 2 FLR 1805, a one-off outright gift of a house and establishment of a trust fund made many years before death did not demonstrate an assumption of responsibility, and nor did it demonstrate a continuing action of maintaining.

8 The daughter had been severely disabled at birth owing to medical negligence and an award of £250,000 had been made to her. This money was controlled by the Court of Protection which applied it for the benefit and maintenance of the daughter which inevitably also benefited the mother who lived with and cared for the daughter. Thus the daughter had made a substantial provision in money or money's worth for the reasonable needs of the mother within the I(PFD)A 1975, s 1(1)(e) who could claim under that paragraph (as a dependant) against her daughter's estate.

III. THE DISCRETION

[Updated at footnote 2 for *Barron v Woodhead* [2008] WTLR 1675, [2008] Fam Law 844.]

[105.21]

All applicants. With reference to all applicants the court, under the I(PFD)A 1975, s 3(1), has regard to:

(a) the financial resources and financial needs which the applicant has or is likely to have in the foreseeable future;[1]

(b) the financial resources and financial needs which any other applicant for an order under the I(PFD)A 1975, s 2 has or is likely to have in the foreseeable future;

(c) the financial resources and financial needs which any beneficiary of the estate of the deceased has or is likely to have in the foreseeable future.

(d) any obligations and responsibilities which the deceased has towards any applicant or towards any beneficiary of the estate of the deceased;

(e) the size and nature of the net estate of the deceased;

(f) any physical or mental disability of any applicant or any beneficiary of the estate of the deceased;

(g) any other matter, including the conduct of the applicant or any other person, which in the circumstances of the case the court may consider relevant.[2]

1 For a case on valuation see *Re Estate of Quilter (decd), Quilter v Quilter* [2003] EWHC 2986 (Ch), [2004] 1 EGLR 79.

2 With respect to para (g), in *Stephanides v Cohen* [2002] EWHC 1869 (Fam), [2002] WTLR 1373, the relative conduct of a widow and a son was an important consideration in the making of an award under the 1975 Act. By contrast in *Re Waite (dec'd), Barron v Woodhead* [2008] WTLR 1675, [2008] Fam Law 844 a widower's alleged violence to the deceased was not relevant where he was likely to be homeless following the deceased's death and had been made bankrupt.

[Updated at footnote 3 for *Barron v Woodhead* [2008] WTLR 1675, [2008] Fam Law 844.]

[105.26]

Spouses or civil partners. Where the applicant is the spouse or the civil partner,[1] of the deceased the court will, under the I(PFD)A 1975, s 3(2), consider the following additional factors:

(a) the age of the applicant and the duration of the marriage or civil partnership;
(b) the contribution made by the applicant to the welfare of the family of the deceased, including any contribution made by looking after the home or caring for the family;

and, in the case of an application by a spouse or civil partner of the deceased, the court will also, unless at the date of the death a decree of judicial separation was in force and the separation was continuing, have regard to the provision which the applicant might reasonably have expected to receive if on the day on which the deceased died the marriage, instead of being terminated by death, had been terminated by a decree of divorce or by dissolution order of the civil partnership.

So far as matrimonial conduct is concerned the approach under the Act is analogous to that in the divorce court; Lord Denning MR in *Wachtel v Wachtel*[2] held that if the conduct of one spouse was 'both obvious and gross' so that it would be 'repugnant to anyone's sense of justice' to make an order against the other party, the court was free to decline an order. However, he went on, 'short of cases falling into this category, the court should not reduce its order for financial provision merely because of what was formerly regarded as guilt or blame'.[3]

1 As amended by the Civil Partnership Act 2004, s 71, Sch 4.
2 [1973] Fam 72; see also *Re Besterman* [1984] Ch 458, [1984] 2 All ER 656 where the fact that the wife was blameless was referred to: See also *Moody v Stevenson* [1992] Ch 486, sub nom *Re Moody, Moody v Stevenson* [1992] 2 All ER 524 and *Re Krubert* [1997] Ch 97.
3 *Wachtel v Wachtel* [1973] Fam 72 at 90. The Law Commission (Law Com no 61, p 11) expressed the hope that this standard would likewise apply for family provision. In *Re Waite (dec'd), Barron v Woodhead* [2008] WTLR 1675, [2008] Fam Law 844 a widower's alleged violence to the deceased was not relevant where he was likely to be homeless following the deceased's death and had been made bankrupt.

VOLUME 2

Precedents and statutes

PART A

Introductory note

Introductory note

I. GENERAL

(*a*) *Capacity and freedom from influence*

[Updated for the Law Society's April 2009 practice note.]

[200.4]
In any subsequent dispute the testator's solicitor may be called upon to give a statement as to the preparation of the will, and the circumstances in which it was executed, together with copies of any requested documents, to any interested party, and promptly when asked: see (1959) 56 Law Society's Gazette 619, *Re Moss, Larke v Nugus* [2000] WTLR 1033 (also reported sub nom *Larke v Nugus* in (1979) 123 Sol Jo 337), CA, and the Law Society's Disputed Wills practice note – 16 April 2009. If a solicitor, or indeed any other person, preparing a will takes any substantial interest under it he must see that the testator obtains independent advice (see *Re a Solicitor* [1975] QB 475, [1974] 3 All ER 853; *Tristram and Coote's Probate Practice* (30th edn) LexisNexis Butterworths, para 34.50; and the Solicitors Regulation Authority's 'Solicitors' Code of Conduct 2007', para 3.04).

(*c*) *Other points*

[Updated in para (d) for Human Fertilisation and Embryology Act 2008.]

[200.28]
Children, issue and other words descriptive of relationship. The rules of construction relating to references in wills and other instruments to children and issue and to any other terms used to denote a blood relationship have undergone major reform in recent years. For the development of the new statutory rules and the application of the former rules to existing instruments, reference should be made to Vol 1 (at paras **[72.1]**, **[74.1]** and **[75.1]** ff) and the statutes printed in Part G2 (at para **[245.1]** ff) and the notes thereto. The current position as regards the devolution of property on death, under a will made now, may be summarised as follows:

(a) ***Adoption.*** The governing statute is the Adoption and Children Act 2002 (ACA 2002), replacing with effect from 30 December 2005 the similar provisions of the Adoption Act 1976 (the relevant provisions of ACA 2002 are printed at paras **[245.92]–[245.101]** and discussed in Vol 1 at paras **[75.1]–[75.7]**). ACA 2002 provides that a child adopted under the Adoption Act 1976 or ACA 2002 or by any adoption recognised as valid by English law is to be treated for the purposes of the devolution of property, whether under a will or on an intestacy, as the legitimate child of his adoptive parent or parents (who can be same-sex couples). Effectively therefore any disability previously attaching to adopted status is removed. The one exception relates to property settled to devolve with a dignity or title of honour.

(b) ***Legitimation.*** The rights of persons who are legitimated by the subsequent marriage of their parents are governed by the Legitimacy Act 1976 (Part G, paras **[245.44]–[245.54]** and considered in Vol 1 at paras **[72.15]–[72.17]**) which provides that for succession purposes legitimated persons are to be treated as if born legitimate. There is a similar saving for property settled to devolve with a dignity or title of honour.

(c) ***Illegitimacy.*** The position is now governed by the Family Law Reform Act 1987 (FLRA 1987) (Part G, paras **[245.70]–[245.81]** and considered in Vol 1 at para **[72.14]**) which again effectively removes any disability to which persons who were either illegitimate or were claiming through illegitimate persons have in the past been subject, and in particular they are treated in the same way as legitimate children of the same parent when it comes to determining who is to benefit under a gift to, eg 'my children' or 'my nephews and nieces', unless a contrary intention is expressed. Again there is a saving for property settled to devolve with a dignity or title of honour. The FLRA 1987 replaces the FLRA 1969 and is wider in some respects than it (see para **[245.69]** for a summary of the main differences), although in the majority of cases where the meaning of a gift in a will is in issue the FLRA 1987 will have no different effect from that which the FLRA 1969 would have had.

(d) ***Artificial insemination and in vitro fertilisation.*** Recent medical developments have resulted in the enactment of special rules concerning the rights of succession of persons born in consequence of artificial insemination or other techniques designed to overcome infertility. These are now to be found in the Human Fertilisation and Embryology Acts of 1990 and 2008 (Part G, paras **[245.83]–[245.91]** and **[245.111]–[245.141]** and considered in Vol 1 at paras **[74.3]–[74.7]**). Where a woman carries a child as a result of the use of any of these techniques, the child is treated as her child in law and no other woman's; if she is married her husband will be treated as the father unless it is shown that he did not consent to the use of artificial insemination or other technique. The child will be treated as their legitimate offspring. If a woman who is not married has a child as a result of treatment regulated by these statutes, and with the consent of a man whose sperm has not been used to conceive the child and whom she has consented to have treated as the father, then he will be so treated (the rules for what constitutes consent for this purpose have been revised for treatment carried out on or after 6 April 2009). There is also, in relation to treatment carried out on or after 6 April 2009, parallel provision for same-sex female couples who have a child by means of treatment under the 1990 or 2008 Acts. The one who is not the mother is treated as a parent of the child if the couple have formed a civil partnership or the treatment is carried out with the appropriate consents. For the purposes of succession to property it is provided that any enactment, deed, instrument or other document (whenever made) is to be construed in accordance with the rules summarised above with the consequence that a child born as a result of one of the techniques in question will be eligible under a will or on an intestacy as if he were the legitimate or (as the case may be) the illegitimate child of his 'parent' or 'parents'. Again there is a saving for property settled to devolve with a dignity or title of honour.

(e) ***Gender change.*** Under GRA 2004 (Part G, paras **[245.102]** ff and considered in Vol 1 at para **[81.1]**) a change of gender in accordance with that Act has effect for all legal purposes (except under a will or other instrument made before 4 April 2005). This is capable of changing the effect of any gift by will where the designation of the donee or donees is gender specific.

[Updated for Human Fertilisation and Embryology Act 2008.]

[200.29]

The present position is thus that for all practical purposes children who are adopted, legitimated or illegitimate, and children who are born to 'parents' as a consequence of the medical techniques just mentioned, are treated for succession purposes on an equal footing with legitimate children. In the case of testamentary succession this is subject to any contrary intention being expressed in the particular will. The earlier law on the rights of adopted, legitimated or illegitimate children (Part G, para **[245.1]** ff) remains relevant to the administration of estates or will trusts where the testator died or, in cases involving succession by illegitimate persons, made his will before the law on one or more of the above topics was changed, and to making an appointment under a special power of appointment where the power was created by a will or other instrument to which the earlier law applied (see B13 at para **[213.1]** ff). Where illegitimate persons are involved, the earlier law remains relevant (irrespective of the date of death of the testator) to wills made before the FLRA 1987 came into force on 4 April 1988 (see FLRA 1987, s 19(7): Part G, para **[245.72]**), and, more importantly, to wills made before its predecessor the FLRA 1969 came into force on 1 January 1970 (see FLRA 1969, s 15(8): Part G, para **[245.39]**). It should be noted that a codicil which confirms a will made before one or both of these Family Law Reform Acts came into force does not by the fact of doing so cause the will to be treated as made after that or those Acts came into force (see the Preliminary Note to Part D at para **[237.8]**). By contrast, the rules in the Human Fertilisation and Embryology Acts 1990 and 2008, referred to at para **[200.28]**, sub-para (d) apply to any instrument, whenever made, and this includes all wills irrespective of their date or the date of death of the testator.

[Updated for Finance Act 2008.]

[200.40]

Capital gains tax rates. Until 5 April 2008, capital gains realised by individuals were charged to capital gains tax as if they were income, and capital gains realised by settlements and estates of deceased persons in the course of administration were charged to capital gains tax at the income tax trust rate, in 2007–08 40 per cent: TCGA 1992, s 4, ITA 2007, s 9. However, with effect from 6 April 2008 the rate of capital gains tax is 18 per cent for individuals, estates of deceased persons, and trusts alike, and the former difference between individual and trust rates of capital gains tax has disappeared. These tax rates are applied to the gains after deduction of annual exemption, which is more generous for individuals, and for estates in administration (until the end of the first two complete tax years after the deceased's death), than for settlements. Trust capital gains can obtain the more generous capital gains tax annual exemption attributable to a beneficiary where that beneficiary is a bereaved minor or disabled person and the trust is such that it qualifies for special treatment under FA 2005, ss 23–43 (see paras **[217.4]**, **[226.9]** ff).

[Updated for the reissue of Simon's Taxes and the 2009 Budget.]

[200.41]
Income tax. Different forms of disposition have different income tax consequences. Where a beneficiary is entitled to the income of an asset or a fund of assets, or to a fixed proportion or amount of such income (whether by virtue of an absolute or limited interest), that income will be taxed as his income (see *Simon's Taxes* C4.203, C4.501, C4.503), although income of a deceased person's residuary estate in the course of administration is only taxed as the beneficiary's when it is distributed to him, and what remains undistributed is taxed as his when the administration is completed (see *Simon's Taxes,* C4.116–127). Income which is accumulated or which is to be distributed under the exercise of a discretion is charged to income tax at the trust rate, currently (in 2009–10) 40 per cent, but can come to be treated for income tax purposes as the income of a beneficiary after it has been distributed to him: see B18 at paras **[218.29]** and **[218.30]** and *Simon's Taxes* C4.506. However, discretionary trusts have the income tax disadvantage as compared with interest in possession trusts that if there is dividend income which is then distributed to a beneficiary the tax credit on the dividend does not carry through to the beneficiary: see para **[218.31]**. Further, it was announced in the 2009 Budget that the trust rate will increase to 50 per cent from 6 April 2010. Undistributed trust income may be taxed at the personal income tax rate or rates of a beneficiary where that beneficiary is a bereaved minor or disabled person and the trust is such that it qualifies for special treatment under FA 2005, ss 23–43 (see paras **[217.4]**, **[226.9]** ff).

II. INHERITANCE TAX

(*a*) *Main characteristics*

[Updated for Finance Act 2008, s 10 and Sch 4.]

[200.75]
Nil-rate band transfer or carry-forward. This was announced by the Chancellor of the Exchequer in the Pre-Budget Report of 9 October 2007, to apply with effect from that date, and enacted by Finance Act 2008, s 10, Sch 4 inserting new IHTA 1984, ss 8A–8C. It allows the estate of anyone who dies

after 8 October 2007 who was the survivor of a marriage or civil partnership to make use of nil rate band which was not used on the death of the predeceasing spouse or civil partner, irrespective of when the predeceasing spouse or civil partner died. It will be unused where the chargeable amount of the first to die's estate is zero or less than the nil-rate band at the time of his or her death, whether because all or part was exempt or because his or her estate was worth less than the nil-rate band (for the exemptions see paras **[200.84]** ff). The carry-forward is calculated as follows, where A is the first to die of a married couple or civil partnership, and B is the second to die:

(1) Work out the maximum which could have been transferred on the death of A at a nil tax rate. This maximum is not reduced where the value of the assets owned by A at death was less than the then nil-rate band (see IHTA 1984, s 8A(2), definition of 'M'). This maximum is thus the amount of the nil-rate band under the rate table in force at the date of A's death, minus the aggregate of any lifetime chargeable transfers made or deemed to have been made by A in the seven years preceding his or her death, but increased by the previous application of these provisions if A died after 8 October 2007 and had had a previous spouse or civil partner who died without making full use of the nil-rate band. In the latter case the lack of a claim for nil-rate band transfer by A's personal representatives or anyone else within the permitted period (eg because A's estate was given to B or was too small for such a claim to make any difference) does not prevent a claim being made in respect of it as part of a claim for nil-rate band transfer on B's death, provided that it will not alter the amount of IHT payable on A's death (IHTA 1984, s 8B(2)).

(2) Then calculate the value actually transferred by the chargeable transfer taking effect on A's death, ie the value of the part of A's estate which has not on A's death gone to B, or a charity or other exempt recipient, or on IPDI trusts for B (for the exemptions see paras **[200.84]** ff). Where relevant this could include, for example, settled property in which A had an interest in possession or property subject to reservation in relation to A at death.

(3) Then deduct the amount arrived at under (2) above from the amount arrived at under (1) above. If the difference is a positive figure, there is available carry-forward. If the difference is zero or a negative quantity, there is no carry-forward and the calculation stops here (see IHTA 1984, s 8A(2)).

(4) If stage (3) above shows that there is carry-forward, arrive at the percentage of the nil-rate band not used. The amount arrived at under (3) above is divided by the nil-rate band in the rate table in force at the death of A, and the result is multiplied by a hundred (see IHTA 1984, s 8A(4)).

(5) Subject to (6)–(9) below, the nil-rate band in the rate table in force at the death of B is then increased by the percentage arrived at under (4) above when it comes to calculating the IHT on B's estate (see IHTA 1984, s 8A(3)).

(6) If the above calculations result in an increase in the nil-rate band in relation to B's estate on death of more than 100 per cent, the increase is

limited to 100 per cent. This could occur where B had had one or more predeceased spouses or civil partners other than A who failed to make full use of their nil-rate band, or where A died after 8 October 2007 and had an enhanced nil-rate band as a result of a previous application of these rules (see IHTA 1984, s 8A(5), (6)).

(7) A claim for carry-forward will have to be made (see IHTA 1984, s 8A(3) and s 8B). It may be made by B's personal representatives within two years from the end of the month in which B died, or, if it ends later, within three months of them first acting as B's personal representatives. HMRC has power in individual cases to allow a longer period. If the personal representatives do not make a claim, anyone else liable for the IHT on B's death may do so within a period allowed in individual cases by HMRC. The burden will be on the taxpayer to show that the dispositions on A's death did not make full use of the available nil-rate band. It will be important to retain relevant records, particularly where A died intestate, or was a joint tenant of property, or left a will which did not leave all A's estate to B, or had an interest in possession in settled property. Estate accounts, any IHT assessments, and any deeds of variation, disclaimers, or appointments within two years of A's death made out of discretionary trusts created by A's will, particularly need to be retained so as to be available to B's personal representatives.

(8) If in relation to A's death there were deferred tax charges, under the rules for heritage property, non-agricultural woodlands, or alternatively secured pensions, there are rules in IHTA 1984, s 8C, and in amendments to IHTA 1984, 151BA, to make sure that either the deferred tax charge is taken into account in determining carry-forward relief, or that any carry-forward relief is taken into account in determining the amount of the deferred tax charge.

(9) If A has died not only before 9 October 2007 but also before 18 March 1986, ie the date when IHT replaced capital transfer tax, the rules are subject to modification in Finance Act 2008, Sch 4, para 10 so as to refer to the relevant earlier taxes (ie capital transfer tax or estate duty).

These rules eliminate the need for nil-rate band discretionary trusts in the majority of cases. For discussion of circumstances where such trusts might still be useful see para **[200.130]**. They also make survivorship clauses undesirable in relation to gifts by will to spouses or civil partners (see paras **[224.7]**–**[224.9]**).

[Updated for Finance Act 2008 s 10 and Sch 4.]

[200.83]

Post-death rearrangement. It is often desired by the beneficiaries to alter the dispositions taking effect on the testator's death, sometimes to increase or alter the benefit taken by a particular beneficiary, sometimes to make better use of exemptions or reliefs, sometimes so as to pass assets on to the next generation. It is often possible to rearrange the devolution of the estate within two years of the testator's death so that the rearrangement is treated for IHT purposes as if done by the deceased, so that, for example, a rearrangement which gives more property to the deceased's surviving spouse obtains a corresponding increase in the amount of the estate which is exempt (see paras **[200.84]** ff below for the spouse exemption), or to increase the amount of nil-rate band carry-forward (see IHTA 1984, s 8A and para **[200.75]**). The main methods of making such rearrangements are disclaimers or instruments of variation under the IHTA 1984, s 142 (see F3 at paras **[241.1]** ff) and distributions out of discretionary trusts created by will in accordance with the IHTA 1984, s 144 (see C3 at paras **[225.83]** ff). There are also distribution in accordance with the deceased's wishes of personal property in accordance with the IHTA 1984, s 143 (see B4 at paras **[204.9]** and **[204.10]**) and court orders (including certain kinds of agreed order) under the I(PFD)A 1975 (see the I(PFD)A, s 19: Part G, para **[247.25]**; and the IHTA 1984, s 146; see also Vol 1, para **[105.51]**).

PART B

Clauses in wills

B2

Miscellaneous declarations and desires sometimes included in wills

GENERAL NOTE

Disposal of body

Updated in footnote 1 for *Lewisham Hospital NHS Trust v Hamuth* [2007] WTLR 309 and *Hartshorne v Gardner* [2008] 2 FLR 1681.

[202.4]

Form B2.2: Expressions of desire as to cremation

A. I desire that my body may be cremated [in the crematorium at ——] and my ashes deposited at —— [or scattered on consecrated ground at ——][1] *or*

B. [*If the testator desires a more elaborate form of words, the following may be suggested:*] I desire that my trustees shall dispose of my remains by the cleansing fires of cremation and that my ashes shall be spread upon the garden of remembrance at ——[2] *or*

C. I direct that my body shall not be cremated.[3]

1 As to the law relating to cremation, see Vol 1, para **[7.33]**. Cremation must take place in a recognised crematorium (and accordingly Hindu cremation on a funeral pyre in the open air has been held to be illegal: *Ghai v Newcastle City Council (Ramgharia Gurdwara, Hitchin and another intervening)* [2009] EWHC 978 (Admin), [2009] All ER (D) 68 (May)). Written directions for cremation are not essential, see also n 3 infra. The Cremation Society of Great Britain, Second Floor Brecon House, 16/16A Albion Place, Maidstone, Kent, ME14 5DZ; tel: (01622) 688 292, issue a printed form of this direction, which, when completed, they undertake to register in their records; and they endeavour to give effect to the expressed desire. The printed form is in duplicate, one part for registration with the society and the other to be handed to the executor or selected relative. The Cremation Society has a website at www.cremation.org.uk.

As to disposal of the body or ashes, disputes sometimes arise, as in *Fessi v Whitmore* [1999] 1 FLR 767, *Lewisham Hospital NHS Trust v Hamuth* [2007] WTLR 309 and *Hartshorne v Gardner* [2008] 2 FLR 1681 and *Burrows v HM Coroner for Preston* [2008] 2 FLR 1225.

2 This wording is based upon an actual will.

3 It is no longer unlawful to cremate a body where such a direction has been given, and whether cremation takes place is solely in the discretion of the deceased's executors or nearest relative, who are apparently free to disregard the deceased's wishes: see Vol 1, para **[7.33]**, n 4.

B3

Appointment of executors, trustees and guardians

PRELIMINARY NOTE ON EXECUTORS AND TRUSTEES

Guardians

[Updated for Human Fertilisation and Embryology Act 2008.]

[203.48]
(a) **Children with two parents with parental responsibility.** This category comprises children of a marriage, children whom the law deems to be the children of both the parties to a marriage or civil partnership, and children whose parents are not and have not been married to each other but whose fathers or other parents have acquired parental responsibility (for which see Vol 1, para **[28.2]**). Children deemed to be children of both parties to a marriage or civil partnership include children legitimated by the subsequent marriage or civil partnership of their parents, adopted by a married couple or civil partnership, or conceived by artificial insemination or in vitro fertilisation in circumstances that they are treated as the child of both parties to a marriage or civil partnership (ChA 1989, s 2(1) and (3): Part G, para **[244.113]**; HFEA 1990, ss 27 to 29, Part G, paras **[245.85]**–**[245.87]**, and HFEA 2008, ss 33–53, Part G, paras **[245.111]** ff).

[Updated for Human Fertilisation and Embryology Act 2008.]

[203.49]
An appointment of a guardian by the father of a child born out of wedlock will only be valid if it is made after he has acquired parental responsibility for the child, which he can do by agreement with the mother or a court order (see Vol 1, paras **[28.2]** and **[28.4]**), by having been registered as the father on the birth certificate where the registration was on or after 1 December 2003 (see para **[203.50]**), or by marrying the mother, which will have the effect that the child will be deemed to be the child of the marriage with both parents having parental responsibility (ChA 1989, s 2(1) and (3): Part G, para **[244.113]**; and FLRA 1987, s 1(2) and (3): Part G, para **[245.70]**). Where a same sex female couple who have not formed a civil partnership have a child by means of assisted reproduction where the treatment was on or after 6 April 2009, with the woman who is not the mother being treated as a parent of the child under HFEA 2008, s 43 (see Vol 1, para **[74.5]** and Part G, para **[245.122]**), the woman who is not the mother will acquire

parental responsibility in similar circumstances to those in which the father of a child born out of wedlock would. An appointment made by a father or parent before he or she has acquired parental responsibility will be of no effect even if he or she subsequently acquires it. It should be remembered that if he or she and the mother do decide to make a parental responsibility agreement the father or parent will not acquire parental responsibility unless and until the agreement has been made in the prescribed form and has been registered with the Principal Registry of the Family Division of the High Court (see Vol 1, para **[28.2]**).

[Updated for Human Fertilisation and Embryology Act 2008.]

[203.50]
In addition to agreement (a 'parental responsibility agreement') or the court (on his or her application) ordering that he or she shall have parental responsibility for a child, the father or parent of a child (not married to or a civil partner of the mother) may acquire parental responsibility for a child if he or she becomes registered as the child's father or parent. See ChA 1989, s 4, as amended by the Adoption and Children Act 2002 with effect from 1 December 2003 (opposite sex couples) and ChA 1989, s 4ZA inserted by HFEA 2008, Sch 6, para 27 with effect from 6 April 2009 (same sex couples). See Vol 1, para **[28.1]**. Under the ChA 1989, as amended by the Adoption and Children Act 2002, a person married to, or in a civil partnership with, a child's parent may acquire parental responsibility for a stepchild by agreement or by order declaring that he shall have parental responsibility for the child. See ChA 1989, s 4A, as inserted by the Adoption and Children Act 2002 with effect from 30 December 2005. However, ChA 1989 and Adoption and Children Act 2002 draw a distinction between a parent and a step-parent. The latter is not a parent and so cannot appoint a guardian under ChA 1989.

B5

Gifts and other provisions relating to business property

PRELIMINARY NOTE

Business assets and inheritance tax—general points

[Updated for *McCall (PRs of Maclean) v HMRC* [2009] STC 990.]

[205.8]

Types of business qualifying for business relief. Subject to the exceptions mentioned below, any trade or profession can qualify for inheritance tax business relief, either where it (or a partnership share of it) is directly owned by the testator, or where it is carried on by an unquoted company in which he has shares or a quoted company which he controls. The exceptions to this are for businesses of dealing in securities, stocks or shares, or land or buildings, or making or holding investments (IHTA 1984, s 105(3)), but that itself is subject to exceptions for UK discount houses, and market makers on the stock exchange or the London International Financial Futures and Options Exchange: IHTA 1984, s 105(4), (7) and SI 1992/3181. The Special Commissioners have held that ownership and management of land let to tenants is making or holding investments within the above exception and does not qualify for business relief, and this approach was approved by the High Court in *Weston v IRC* [2000] STC 1064 (see for the now numerous cases in this area *Foster's Inheritance Tax*, G1.12). In *McCall (PRs of Maclean) v HMRC* [2009] STC 990 the Northern Ireland Court of Appeal upheld the decision of the Special Commissioner that ownership and management of land let on seasonal grazing agreements was a business of holding investments and so not entitled to the relief. There is no territorial limit on the location of the business, and it can be anywhere in the world (whereas agricultural relief can apply only to land in the European Economic Area and in relation to events before 23 April 2003 was confined to land in the UK, Channel Islands, or Isle of Man—see para **[234.2]**). The assets of a farming business other than the agricultural land itself can only qualify for business relief not agricultural relief, as the latter relief is confined to land and buildings etc attached to land. See para **[205.15]** below and C12 at para **[234.8]** for what happens when both reliefs might apply to agricultural land.

Sole traders

[Updated for *Re Nelson Dance Family Settlement* [2009] STC 802.]

[205.23]

In relation to capital gains tax retirement relief, it was an established rule that an asset used in a business is not 'a business': see, e g *McGregor v Adcock*

[1977] STC 206, *Pepper v Daffurn* [1993] STC 466, and *Jarmin v Rawlings* [1994] STC 1005. It was generally thought that the same principle would apply to IHT business relief, but in *Re Nelson Dance Family Settlement* [2009] STC 802 the High Court, upholding the Special Commissioner, held that it does not (but there may be a further appeal). It was thus held that a lifetime gift by a sole trader of a single asset used in a business carried on immediately before the gift was made did qualify for business relief. This is a less significant point in relation to inheritance tax on death, because if a person is in business as a sole trader at his death the entire business will be included in his deemed transfer of value on death, and if he has already ceased to trade and retained an asset of the former business the relief clearly will not apply. However, there is a question whether, in relation to inheritance tax on death where the estate is partially exempt, the *Nelson Dance* decision (if not reversed on appeal) is relevant to the application of the IHTA 1984, s 39A (business or agricultural relief and partial exemption). In the absence of clarification on this point in litigation or an expression of opinion by HMRC, specific gifts by will of individual assets of the business should be avoided where there are exempt gifts: see the Preliminary Note to C11 at para **[233.6]**.

B12

Charitable gifts

PRELIMINARY NOTE

[Updated for Charities Act 2006 commencement.]

[212.1]
For a statement of the general law relating to charities see Vol 1, paras **[102.1]**–**[103.21]**. And see the Note in B2 at para **[202.28]** ff for charitable gifts for the maintenance of graves. The Charities Act 2006 received Royal Assent on 8 November 2006 and important parts of it are now in force: see paras **[102.2]**, **[102.3]**, **[103.9]**. Although the charitable status of some entities which are presently charities may be affected, Charities Act 2006 is unlikely to affect the making of testamentary gifts to charities described in this Chapter, except in one (helpful) respect: see para **[212.2]**.

[Updated for Charities Act 2006, s 44.]

[212.2]
Charitable gifts are wholly exempt from inheritance tax: Inheritance Tax Act 1984 (IHTA 1984), s 23. It is thought that, like the exemption for charities from income tax, the inheritance tax exemption is confined to charities established in the UK (see the income tax case of *Camille and Henry Dreyfus Foundation v IRC* [1956] AC 39, [1955] 3 All ER 97). Gifts to certain institutions, eg the British Museum, the National Gallery and the National Trust are wholly exempt: IHTA 1984, s 25 and Sch 3. Gifts to political parties may in certain circumstances enjoy a similar exemption: IHTA 1984, s 24. Gifts to housing associations may also be exempt: IHTA 1984, s 24A. For HMRC's treatment of charitable gifts for inheritance tax purposes, see the Inheritance Tax Manual at IHTM11101.

Many charitable gifts are concerned with quite small charities in which the testator has taken an active interest. It is with such charities that practical difficulties may occur: that is, that they have very little organisation and it may be difficult to find someone who can give a proper receipt for the legacy. It is wise in such cases to provide not only that the receipt of the treasurer or other proper officer shall be a full discharge, but to go further and say that the receipt of the person who professes to be the proper officer shall be such a discharge. In all cases it is important for those drawing the will to ascertain the precise name of the charity which the testator intends to benefit, for, on the one hand, there are many with very similar names and, on the other hand, testators commonly speak of a charity by a name which is quite different from its proper name. Failure to give the charity's correct name may result in the gift going to the wrong charity or even failing altogether. At the very least a misdescription of a charity can lead to delay and expense in the administration of the estate, and often greater expense than the value of the gift itself. Now that most charities can be registered the name should be checked with the Charity Commission and there is no excuse for failing to do so. The Charity Commission's Register of Charities can be consulted online at www.charity-commission.gov.uk (England and Wales) and www.oscr.org.uk (Scotland) to find the correct name and address of any registered charity which a testator wishes to benefit (but some charities are of course exempt from registration).

Where a charitable institution, to which a gift is made by will, merges with one or more other charities before the death of the testator, the problems this often used to cause will in most cases be avoided where the charities have registered the merger in accordance with Charities Act 1993, ss 75C–75F (inserted by Charities Act 2006, s 44 with effect from 28 November 2007). The gift will in most cases take effect in favour of the post-merger entity: see para **[103.9]**.

B18

Discretionary trusts and powers

DISCRETIONARY TRUSTS

[Updated for Finance Act 2008.]

[218.27]
Capital gains tax and discretionary trusts. Prior to 6 April 2008, the rates of capital gains tax for an individual were arrived at by adding the capital gains made in a tax year to his or her income and charging them in effect to income tax. By contrast, capital gains tax on the gains of a settlement prior to 6 April 2008 was charged at the income tax trust rate under the Income Tax Act 2007, s 9(1) (formerly known as the rate applicable to trusts under Income and Corporation Taxes Act 1988 (ICTA 1988), s 686), 40 per cent in the tax year 2007–08 (see the Taxation of Chargeable Gains Act 1992 (TCGA 1992), s 4(1AA)(a)). The realisation of a chargeable gain on the sale of assets held in a discretionary trust before 6 April 2008 thus involved paying more capital gains tax than would be paid if the assets were owned absolutely by an individual who, after taking into the account the chargeable gain, was not a higher rate tax payer. However, on and from 6 April 2008 there is a flat rate of capital gains tax applicable across the board, including individuals and trusts, of 18 per cent (without indexation relief or taper relief): TCGA 1992, s 4 as substituted by Finance Act 2008, s 8. Therefore, on and after 6 April 2008 a discretionary trust does not pay significantly more capital gains tax than an individual would, although it pays a little more since a trust only has the benefit of up to one-half (maximum) of an individual's annual exempt amount.

[Updated for *HMRC v Peter Clay Trust* [2009] STC 469 and the 2009 Budget.]

[218.30]
The Income Tax Act 2007, s 479(4) (formerly ICTA 1988, s 686(1)) provides that income which is not UK company dividend income is to be taxed on the trustees at 'the trust rate' (currently 40 per cent). The income caught by the section includes inter alia income which falls to be accumulated and income which is payable to a beneficiary under a discretion (whether or not there is power to accumulate) (see the Income Tax Act 2007, s 480(1), (2)). Income applicable under the TA 1925, s 31 (Part G, para **[246.29]**) during the minority of a beneficiary would fall within this definition. Various categories of income are excluded from the operation of s 479(4), of which it is sufficient to mention income applied in defraying trust expenses which are properly chargeable to income (or would be so chargeable but for some

express provision of the trust): a restrictive interpretation of these words was adopted by the House of Lords in *Carver v Duncan* [1985] 2 All ER 645. What is so chargeable to income is expenditure exclusively for the benefit of the income beneficiaries, though this can be an apportioned part of a fee, even a fixed fee, in respect of work some of which was exclusively for income beneficiaries and some of which also benefited capital: see *HMRC v Peter Clay Trust* [2009] STC 469. The Income Tax Act 2007, ss 493–494 (formerly ICTA 1988, s 687) provide that income paid to a beneficiary as income is to be treated as income net of the trust rate. The trustees are responsible for the payment of the amount of such tax subject to set off of the 'tax pool' which will include the income tax already paid to HMRC. A beneficiary who receives income under a discretion and who pays tax at a rate below the trust rate or who has unused personal reliefs available to him may be able to recover some part of the tax paid by the trustees in respect of such income. The ultimate burden of tax on income to which these sections apply is thus unaffected as long as such income is distributed as income, but if, for example, income is accumulated and subsequently distributed in the form of capital there can be no recovery of any part of the tax paid in respect of such accumulations. Thus accumulation of discretionary trust income (excluding UK company dividends), as opposed to distributing it, is often fiscally unattractive. An impending change is that it has been announced in the 2009 Budget that the trust rate (currently 40 per cent) will increase to 50 per cent from 6 April 2010.

[Updated for the 2009 Budget.]

[218.31]

If the trust includes UK company dividend income, however, the rules which came into force from 1999–2000 mean that accumulation of such income will generally be preferable to distribution of it, where it is subject to a discretionary trust, and that a beneficiary having an interest in possession is preferable to it being subject to a discretionary or accumulation trust. A dividend from a UK company comes with a tax credit (currently 1/9 of the amount distributed), and under the Income Tax Act 2007, ss 9(2), 479(3) (formerly ICTA 1988, s 686), tax on such income is charged on the trustees at the dividend trust rate (formerly the Schedule F trust rate) (currently 37.5 per cent). It was announced in the 2009 Budget that the Schedule F trust rate is to be increased to 42.5 per cent from 6 April 2010. If the trustees distribute the dividend income, they are deemed to make a payment grossed up at the normal trust rate (currently 40 per cent, 50 per cent from 6 April 2010), and are liable under Income Tax Act 2007, ss 493–494 (formerly ICTA 1988, s 687) to tax on this grossed up amount. The tax credit on the dividends does not, however, go into the 'tax pool' to reduce this liability, so the trustees are only able to set off the tax actually paid by them under Income Tax Act 2007, s 479. The beneficiary who receives the dividend income is liable for tax on that payment at his own income tax rate, but with the benefit of a credit for the amount paid by the trustees, so he is entitled to a tax repayment or liable for further tax, as appropriate. The overall effect of the rules is that if a discretionary trust is to invest in UK company shares it will probably be better for the income produced thereby to be accumulated, rather than distributed, and for capital payments or loans to be made to the beneficiaries rather than income distributions. Another possibility is to appoint an interest in possession, so that the income and the tax credit is the beneficiary's. The 2006 changes to IHT on trusts means that it is possible to have an interest in possession for income tax purposes while retaining 'relevant property' IHT status, provided, in the case of a will trust, that the interest in possession commences more than two years after the testator's death (see, further, para **[200.126]** sub-para (2)).

B21

Trustees and executors

CONDUCT OF TRUSTEESHIP

[Updated for Human Fertilisation and Embryology Act 2008.]

[221.34]

Form B21.30: Power to distribute on assumption that no further children

My trustees shall have power at their absolute discretion to distribute income or capital of my estate or of any fund deriving from it on the assumption that a woman who has attained the age of 55 years will have no further children and if they exercise this power my trustees shall not be liable for the assumption turning out to be incorrect (without prejudice to any beneficiary's right to trace trust assets against any other beneficiary).[1]

1 Existing authority that trustees can distribute on the assumption that a woman of 55 is past the age of childbearing (see Vol 1, paras **[66.3]** and **[216.29]**) can no longer be relied on, because advances in medical science mean that a woman who has passed the menopause could still have a child by means of in vitro fertilisation using donated eggs, and because if this were to happen she would be treated as the mother of the child for all purposes, including gifts by will, by virtue of the HFEA 1990, ss 27 and 29 (Part G, paras **[245.85]** and **[245.87]**) or, in relation to treatment on or after 6 April 2009, HFEA 2008, ss 33–53 (Part G, paras **[245.112]** ff.) It is still possible to apply to the court for liberty to distribute on the basis of evidence that a particular person having another child is impossible or very unlikely (see *Re Levy Estate Trust* [2000] CLY, para 5263 and *Re Cassidy* [1979] VR 369). There is a statutory presumption that a woman over 55 will not adopt a child: see the AA 1976, s 42(5) (Part G, para **[245.60]**). Provision as in this clause is not usually needed if the beneficial trusts, powers and provisions themselves confer powers, such as a wide power of appointment or powers of advancement over the whole of a presumptive share, which would enable a trust fund to be appointed absolutely or distributed absolutely without waiting to see if more members of a class are born.

PART C

Complete wills

C2

Wills for married couples (or civil partners) with young children

PRELIMINARY NOTE

[Updated for Human Fertilisation and Embryology Act 2008.]

[224.14]
One method of excluding *illegitimate* children of one or other party to the marriage from taking under a gift is to exclude the statutory rules of construction which include illegitimate persons in words descriptive of relationship (see Part A, paras **[200.28]**–**[200.33]** and Vol 1, para **[72.14]**). This will not be sufficient where there are children who are intended to be excluded from the gift who are children of another marriage of one of the spouses. In Forms C2.1 (at para **[224.27]**) and C2.2 (at para **[224.42]**) where the primary gift of residue is an absolute gift to the surviving spouse, optional words are included in the alternative gift which restrict the donees of the gift to the children of the marriage (see paras **[224.35]** and **[224.50]**). If such words are included, any illegitimate children of the testator or testatrix, or children by some other marriage, will be excluded, but the gift will include legitimated children of the marriage (see the Legitimacy Act 1976, s 5(3): Part G, para **[245.48]**), adopted children of the marriage (see the Adoption Act 1976, s 39(1), Part G, para **[245.58]**, and the Adoption and Children Act 2002, s 67, Part G, para **[245.93]**) and children of the marriage born as a result of in vitro fertilisation or artificial insemination with the husband's consent (see the Human Fertilisation and Embryology Act 1990, s 28(2) and 29(1), (3): Part G, paras **[245.86]** and **[245.87]**; Human Fertilisation and Embryology Act 2008, ss 35 and 48(1) and (5): Part G, paras **[245.114]** and **[245.127]**). On these topics see also Vol 1, paras **[72.15]**–**[72.18]**, **[74.5]**–**[74.7]**, and **[75.1]**–**[75.9]** respectively.

C11

Wills disposing of business property

PRELIMINARY NOTE

Allocation of business and agricultural relief between the exempt and non-exempt parts of an estate

[Updated in sub-para (1) for *Re Nelson Dance Family Settlement* [2009] STC 802.]

[233.6]
What is a specific gift for the purposes of the Inheritance Tax Act 1984, s 39A. As stated above, a testator's estate will get maximum benefit from business relief or agricultural relief if there is a specific gift to a non-exempt beneficiary *of* 'relevant business property' (ie property qualifying for business relief) or *of* 'agricultural property' (see para **[234.2]** for the meaning of this expression). 'Specific gift' is defined in IHTA 1984, s 42(1) (which applies to s 39A, among other sections of the Act) to mean any gift other than a gift of residue or a share of residue, but this does not determine what is a specific gift *of* a particular kind of property. The only other provision with any relevance to its meaning is s 39A(6) mentioned at para **[233.4]**— gifts payable out of business or agricultural property are not for the purposes of s 39A specific gifts of that property.

It is our view that a specific gift will only qualify as a specific gift of relevant business property or agricultural property for the purposes of IHTA 1984, s 39A(2) if the property comprised in the gift and going to the beneficiary, considered in isolation from the rest of the estate, is relevant business property or agricultural property. If this is correct, the following points should be noted—

(1) When a business is carried on by the testator as sole proprietor and the business as a whole qualifies for business relief on his death as 'a business' (see B5 at para **[205.22]**), a specific gift of an individual asset of that business by itself will on this view not be a specific gift of relevant business property (see B5 at para **[205.23]** for the distinction between a business and individual business assets). Whether business relief is available in respect of a business on a testator's death depends on the circumstances immediately before his death, not on the dispositions made by his will, and so it is thought that the business relief attributable to this individual asset comprised in a specific gift will not be lost completely in a case such as this, but will be divided rateably between the exempt and non-exempt parts of the estate instead of being concentrated on the specific gift. There is a question whether the

decision of the High Court in *Re Nelson Dance Family Settlement* [2009] STC 802, that a lifetime gift of an individual asset used in a business carried on immediately before the gift was made could qualify for business relief, has any relevance to the interpretation of IHTA 1984, s 39A(2). The reasoning in *Nelson Dance* is based very much on the definition of a transfer of value as being the diminution in the value of the transferor's estate, and there is considerable doubt as to whether it has any relevance to the meaning of 'specific gifts of relevant business property' in s 39A(2). In the absence of encouragement from the courts or HMRC to believe otherwise, it should be assumed that a specific gift by will of an individual asset of a business will not be a specific gift of relevant business property.

(2) A similar point would arise in relation to a specific gift of a farm building or farm house, where the farm land itself was the subject of another gift. As stated in the Preliminary Note to C12 at paras **[234.2]** and **[234.3]**, buildings and farmhouses only qualify as agricultural property if they are combined with agricultural land and are of a character appropriate to it: IHTA 1984, s 115(2). Again, it is thought that a farm house or building given by a specific gift which did not also include the farm land would still qualify for agricultural relief on the testator's death, but that the relief attributable to the farmhouse would be apportioned rateably between the non-exempt and exempt parts of the estate because the house by itself is not 'agricultural property' for the purposes of IHTA 1984, s 39A(2).

(3) In the rare cases of controlling holdings of unquoted voting securities qualifying for 100 per cent business relief or controlling holdings of quoted shares or securities qualifying for 50 per cent business relief (IHTA 1984, ss 104(1) and 105(1)(b) and (cc)), the type of problem described above does not seem to arise where, for example, a testator makes a specific gift of part only of his holding. Shares or securities in either category qualify for the relief even if they do not by themselves give control, provided that they contribute to the testator's control of the company together with other shares or securities owned by him: see IHTA 1984, s 105(1)(b) and (cc).

(4) There is also a question as to whether a gift of relevant business property or agricultural property to one person, subject to a testamentary option for another to purchase it, is a specific gift of that property for the purposes of IHTA 1984, s 39A. It might be argued that it is not a gift of such property to the person to whom the primary gift is made, because he may end up with cash instead of the property, and that the option holder is not the recipient of a *gift* of such property (or not wholly—it depends on the price) and anyway might not exercise the option and receive the business (or agricultural) property. Such an arrangement is at its most provocative to HMRC where the property entitled to relief is given to a non-exempt beneficiary subject to an option given to the testator's spouse or civil partner to purchase it. However, whether or not it is an exempt beneficiary who is given the option is not strictly relevant to the legal merits of the argument. The attitude of HMRC to this point is not known, and in the absence of a clear indication that HMRC accept such arrangements as specific gifts

of the business or agricultural property within IHTA 1984, s 39A(2) they are better avoided if possible; see para **[233.7]** for alternatives.

C12

Wills disposing of farms and farming businesses

PRELIMINARY NOTE

IHT agricultural relief

[Updated for the 2009 Budget.]

[234.2]
Meaning of agricultural property. This is defined by IHTA 1984, s 115(2) as agricultural land or pasture and as including woodland and any building used in connection with the intensive rearing of livestock or fish if such woodland or building is occupied with agricultural land or pasture and such occupation is ancillary to that of the land or pasture; the definition also includes such cottages, farm buildings and farmhouses and land occupied with them as are of a character appropriate to the property. Other assets which are included expressly or as a matter of Revenue practice are stud farms (IHTA 1984, s 115(4)), milk quota when given or devolving on death with the land, ponds, land used for short-rotation coppice (IHTA 1984, as amended by Finance Act 1995, s 145), set aside land, and land in a wildlife habitat scheme (IHTA 1984, as amended by the Finance Act 1997, s 124C). It used to be the case that in order to qualify for relief, agricultural property must be situated in the UK, the Channel Islands or the Isle of Man (IHTA 1984, s 115(5)). However, this restriction has turned out to be a breach of EU, EEC, and EEA law, and in the 2009 Budget it was announced that the relief will be extended to agricultural land anywhere in the EEA, and with retrospective effect back to 23 April 2003.

Other aspects

[Updated for the 2009 Budget.]

[234.14]
Woodlands. Woodlands which are not ancillary to agricultural land and which do not therefore qualify for agricultural relief may qualify for the separate relief which is available under the IHTA 1984, Part V, Chapter III for woodlands which have been beneficially owned for five years or acquired by gift: see generally *Foster's Inheritance Tax*, G4. The relief takes the form of a deferment of the charge to IHT on death until the woodlands are sold or given away by inter vivos transfer other than to the donor's spouse. This

relief resembles the conditional exemption for works of art etc under the IHTA 1984, ss 30–34 but it is not strictly an exemption within the meaning of the Act, but a right to elect to have the woodlands left out of account in determining the chargeable transfer made on death: see ss 126(1)(a) and 130(1)(a). Since anyone who inherits woodlands which qualify for this relief will himself be qualified for the relief on his death however soon it may occur (see s 125(1)), there are less strong reasons than in the case of business assets or agricultural property for testators avoiding gifts of woodlands which qualify for relief to their spouses. It is advisable for specific gifts of woodlands to be made subject to IHT attributable thereto and payable on the testator's death for the reasons given in B14 at para **[214.67]**. It used to be the case that in order to qualify for the relief, woodlands must be situated in the UK (IHTA 1984, s 125(1)(a)). However, this restriction has turned out to be a breach of EU, EEC, and EEA law, and in the 2009 Budget it was announced that the relief will be extended to woodlands anywhere in the EEA, and with some retrospective effect.

PART D

Codicils

D

Codicils

PRELIMINARY NOTE

[Updated for Human Fertilisation and Embryology Act 2008.]

[237.10]
The statutory rules of construction relating to adopted persons which have had effect from 1 January 1976 (they were introduced by the Children Act 1975, consolidated into the Adoption Act 1976 as from 1 January 1988, and re-enacted in the Adoption of Children Act 2002, Pt 1, Ch 4, which came into force on 30 December 2005 (see Part H, Additional Statutes, para **[245.96]**, below), apply to the will of a person dying on or after 1 January 1976 regardless of the date of execution of the will, so that a confirmation of a codicil can make no difference (see Vol 1, para **[75.4]** and, see ACA 2002, s 73(4), Sch 4, para 18, Part H, Additional Statutes, paras **[245.100]** and **[245.102]**, below. See also Chapter 75, above). The position is the same as regards the rules of construction relating to legitimated children contained in the Legitimacy Act 1976 (see Vol 1, para **[72.16]** and the Legitimacy Act 1976, s 10(3): Part G, para **[245.51]**). The Human Fertilisation and Embryology Act 1990 (HFEA 1990), ss 27 to 29, which came into force on 1 August 1991, and HFEA 2008, ss 33 to 53 which replaced the 1990 Act provisions from 6 April 2009, and make provision for who is to be treated as father, mother or parent of a child produced by means (such as artificial insemination or in vitro fertilisation) regulated by the Act, seems to apply to dispositions made before or after the Act so that a post-Act confirmation of a pre-Act instrument will not bring these provisions into play; they will already apply (see Vol 1, para **[74.6]** and the HFEA 1990, s 29(3): Part G, para **[245.87]**). For the law relating to codicils generally, see Vol 1, para **[20.1]** ff.

PART F

Non-testamentary instruments

F3

Disclaimers and variations of beneficial interests

PRELIMINARY NOTE

[Updated for *Wills v Gibbs* [2008] STC 808.]

[241.3]

Notice of intention for IHTA 1984, s 142 to apply. Since the effect of the IHTA 1984, s 142 is to treat a disposition made by a beneficiary as one made by the deceased, it can result in additional IHT becoming payable where an exempt beneficiary, such as the deceased's wife, assigns her interest. The personal representatives might not have enough assets left in their possession with which to pay the extra tax, and anyway s 142 not applying could be more advantageous in some circumstances (such as where the deceased has fully utilised his available nil-rate IHT band and the wife makes a substantial gift out of the deceased's assets). Section 142(2), (2A) therefore provides that for the section to apply to an instrument varying the deceased's dispositions, the instrument of variation must contain a statement, made by all the 'relevant persons', to the effect that they intend s 142(1) to apply to the variation. The 'relevant persons' are defined as the person or persons making the instrument, and where the variation results in additional tax being payable, the personal representatives. Personal representatives may, however, decline to join in such a statement if they have no or insufficient assets to discharge the additional tax. These requirements for a statement of intention were introduced for variations made after 31 July 2002 and replace the former requirement for an election to be made within six months of execution of the instrument of variation. If additional tax is payable as a result of the variation, there is an obligation on the relevant persons to deliver a copy of the instrument of variation to HMRC, and notify them of the amount of additional tax within six months: see IHTA 1984, s 218A, inserted by FA 2002, s 120(2), (4). Otherwise there is no obligation, as previously, to report the instrument.

If it is desired that some dispositions should be made to which s 142 applies, and some to which it does not, they could be made by separate instruments, with the one containing the appropriate statement, and the other not. It should also be noted that s 142(2) does not apply to *disclaimers* within s 142(1), and that the application of s 142 to disclaimers is thus automatic (unless they are made orally—in which case s 142 does not apply at all), so a statement within s 142(2) is not required, although it may be desirable for the sake of clarity. Where the deceased's surviving spouse makes an instrument of variation under which he or she assigns (to a non-exempt beneficiary) a specific gift or legacy which does not bear its own IHT, the persons interested in residue, out of which any extra tax will be paid, cannot, it seems, prevent a statement of intention under s 142(2) being made. A statement of intention under s 142(2), once made, cannot be revoked.

If it is intended that TCGA 1992, s 62(6) should apply to an instrument of variation (see para **[241.17]**), it must similarly contain a statement by the persons making the instrument that they intend s 62(6) to apply: see TCGA 1992, s 62(7) as substituted by FA 2002, s 52 with effect for instruments made after 31 July 2002. Note that there is no requirement for the personal representatives to join in this statement if they are not making the instrument.

For an example of a statement of intention within IHTA 1984, s 142(2) and TCGA 1992, s 62(7), see para **[241.25]**, below.

If the statement of intention is omitted, once the deed has been made it is too late to get the deed within s 142 unless rectification can be obtained. For a case where the statement of intention for the purposes of s 142(2) was omitted accidentally from a deed of variation, and the omission remedied by way of rectification, see *Wills v Gibbs* [2008] STC 808. It was held, following *Jervis v Howle and Talke Colliery* [1937] Ch 67, to be sufficient evidence of intention that the maker of the deed intended the deed to come within s 142, though he was not aware of the specific need for a statement of that intention in the deed.

[Updated for *Wells (PRs of Glowacki) v HMRC* [2008] STC (SCD) 188.]

[241.5]

Meaning of 'estate' for the purposes of section 142. Section 142(1) is expressly confined to variations or disclaimers relating to the property comprised in a deceased person's estate immediately before his death, which at first glance means the aggregate of all property to which that person was beneficially entitled other than excluded property (see IHTA 1984, s 5(1)). However, s 142(5) gives a special meaning to 'estate' for the purposes of s 142(1), by providing that it includes excluded property. It also provides that it does not include property in which the deceased had an interest in possession immediately before his death. This means that the only relieving provision where someone wishes not to receive an interest in settled property which falls into possession on the death of a life tenant is s 93 of the IHTA 1984, which applies only to a disclaimer made otherwise than for a consideration in money or money's worth. Section 142(5) also provides that 'estate' for s 142(1) purposes does not include property which was treated as comprised in the deceased's estate at death because it was property subject to a reservation within FA 1986, s 102 (see para **[200.76]**).

It should also be noted that s 142 can apply to assets passing on a person's death, other than property which was settled property immediately before the death, which do not pass under that person's will, such as nominated savings bank accounts and interests in joint tenancies. For a form of variation of the disposition of a deceased's interest under a joint tenancy, see Form F3.5 at para **[241.26]**.

A deed of variation within IHTA 1984, s 142 cannot take assets out of the death estate, and in particular cannot give rise to a deemed lifetime gift, treated as made by the deceased before his death, of an asset of the deceased's estate at his death, but can only substitute, for the dispositions taking effect on death, other dispositions deemed to take effect on death of the assets which were comprised in the deceased's estate for the purposes of s 142(1): see *Wells (PRs of Glowacki) v HMRC* [2008] STC (SCD) 188.

[Updated for *Lau v HMRC*.]

[241.7]

Consideration. Section 142(3) of the IHTA 1984 provides that s 142(1) does not apply to a variation or disclaimer made for any consideration in money or money's worth, other than consideration consisting of the making in respect of another of the deceased's dispositions of a variation or disclaimer to which s 142(1) applies. One particular point to watch in relation to this provision is that if the donee under an instrument of variation agrees to pay the costs of the instrument that could be consideration which takes the instrument outside s 142(1). For further points relating to this provision see paras **[241.13]** and **[241.14]**. For an example of a disclaimer failing to fall within s 142 because done for a consideration see the Special Commissioner case of *Lau v HMRC* [2009] STC (SCD) 352. It was a disclaimer by the testator's son of a non-exempt specific gift so as to fall into exempt residue (given to the testator's widow), where the disclaimer was done on the basis of an assurance that the widow would make an equivalent lifetime gift back to the son.

[Updated for Finance Act 2008, ss 99, 100, Sch 32.]

[241.18]

Stamp duty and stamp duty land tax. Stamp duty on deeds of variation is now a muddle; it has almost been superseded but not quite in all circumstances. The subject is best approached historically. An instrument within the IHTA 1984, s 142, other than a disclaimer, used to attract ad valorem stamp duty as a voluntary disposition to the extent of the bounty passing thereunder: cf *Thorn v IRC* [1976] 2 All ER 622, [1976] 1 WLR 915. The charge to ad valorem stamp duty on voluntary dispositions was abolished as was the charge to ad valorem duty on instruments varying the dispositions of the estate of a deceased person where such instruments would formerly have attracted duty as conveyances on sale, provided that such instruments were executed within two years of the death: Finance Act 1985, ss 82(1) and 84(1). There remained the fixed duties (50p until 30 September 1999, then £5) but the fixed duty and the need for adjudication was avoided if the instrument was certified to be an instrument falling within category L or category M of the Schedule to the Stamp Duty (Exempt Instruments) Regulations 1987. Then, from 1 December 2003, stamp duty was largely replaced by stamp duty land tax (SDLT). FA 2003, s 125 provided that stamp duty under FA 1999, Sch 13 was, from the commencement of SDLT only, to be charged in respect of instruments relating to stock or marketable securities. However, in addition to the fixed duties on such instruments, the £5 duty on deeds of variation which would otherwise be chargeable as conveyances on sale remained (FA 1985, s 84(8)), as did the requirements of adjudication for deeds of variation and gifts (FA 1985, ss 82(5) and 84(9)), unless there was a certificate under the 1987 Regulations. A certificate that an instrument falls within category L or category M of the Schedule to the Stamp Duty (Exempt Instruments) Regulations 1987 should no longer have been necessary in order to avoid paying a fixed stamp duty, apart from the case of an instrument varying the disposition of stock or marketable securities, or an instrument which would be a conveyance or transfer on sale (ie a variation made in consideration of another variation in relation to the same estate where the latter constituted dutiable consideration). The requirement of adjudication apparently remained. In response to the introduction of stamp duty land tax, HMRC specifically amended its Inheritance Tax Manual IHTM 35060 on 10 April 2006, but to instruct its staff that where an instrument has not been duly stamped, or does not contain the appropriate exemption certificate within categories L or M in the schedule to the Regulations, they should apply the following procedure:

(a) any communication to the effect that IHTA 1984, s 142 applies must contain a caveat in such terms as 'provided the document is duly stamped and adjudicated, or the appropriate exemption certificate under the Stamp Duty/Exempt Instruments Regulations 1987 is attached';
(b) if the parties are relying on the instrument to reduce the liability to IHT, they must insist that the document is stamped, or the exemption certificate is attached, before giving effect to the terms of the instrument; but
(c) in other cases, having raised the caveat above, the matter need not be pursued further.

This guidance does not appear limited to variations affecting stock or marketable securities, although previously in their Customer Newsletters of April 2004 and August 2004, HMRC had indicated that an exemption certificate would only be required where both the deed effected a variation of stocks or shares, and unusually the deed acted as the transfer. This guidance also dates from before FA 2008, for which see below.

FA 2008 then abolished, for instruments executed on or after 13 March 2008, the remaining fixed duties and adjudication requirements, in particular in relation to gifts and deeds of variation relating to stock or marketable securities, except in relation to instruments effecting 'land transactions' (FA 2008, ss 99, 100, Sch 32, paras 1, 2, 3, and 10). Land transactions here are any acquisition of an estate, interest, right or power in or over land in the UK other than a security interest, licence, tenancy at will, franchise advowson or manor (FA 2008, s 99, Sch 32, para 22(2), FA 2003, ss 43 and 48(1)–(3)). Accordingly, it apparently remains the case that a deed of variation needs still to be certified under the Stamp Duty (Exempt Instruments) Regulations 1987 to avoid the need for adjudication and, in the case of one involving stampable consideration, the £5 duty, where it involves the acquisition of an estate, interest etc in or over land. However, it may be that deeds of variation relating to unadministered residuary estate will not fall into this category, even where there is land in the residuary estate, because of the nature of an interest in unadministered residue: see Vol 1, para **[38.16]**.

Stamp duty land tax is essentially a tax on land transactions, charging ad valorem tax on the consideration given for the acquisition of an interest in land (see para **[220.72]**, above). Generally, s 142 variations in respect of land or interests in land will not give rise to a liability because they will not be made for consideration. But where they are so made (ie in consideration of the variation of other dispositions in the same estate) they will be exempt from stamp duty land tax by reason of FA 2003, Sch 3, para 4(1), (2), which provides that a transaction following a person's death that varies a disposition (whether effected by will, under the law relating to intestacy or otherwise) of property of which the deceased was competent to dispose is exempt from charge if:

(1) the transaction is carried out within the period of two years after a person's death; and
(2) no consideration in money or money's worth other than the making of a variation of another such disposition is given for it.

This exemption applies whether or not the administration of the estate is complete or the property has been distributed in accordance with the original dispositions (FA 2003, Sch 3, para 4(3)). It is not clear though, whether this exemption covers a variation involving a deceased's severable share of assets held on a joint tenancy since the same is not generally property *of which the deceased was competent to dispose*. The exemption from SDLT means that no SDLT return is required (FA 2003, ss 76, 77).

PART G

Statutes

Contents

SECTION 1

Wills and intestacy

ADMINISTRATION OF ESTATES ACT 1925

(15 & 16 Geo 5 c 23)

[9 April 1925]

[244.59]

Note. This Act came into force on 1 January 1926 (s 58(2) (repealed)).

PART IV
DISTRIBUTION OF RESIDUARY ESTATE

* * * * *

[244.61]

Note to sections 46 to 49. Sections 46 to 49 of this Act were extensively amended in relation to deaths occurring on or after 1 January 1953 by the Intestates' Estates Act 1952.

They were further amended in relation to deaths on or after 1 January 1967 by the Family Provision Act 1966 (FPA 1966), s 1, and further minor amendments were made by the Administration of Justice Act 1977 (AJA 1977), s 28.

Further amendments as respects intestates dying on or after 1 January 1996 were effected by the Law Reform (Succession) Act 1995, s 1 and are noted to the provisions concerned.

In relation to the estates of persons dying on or after 1 January 1970 and before 4 April 1988 Part IV of the AEA 1925 takes effect subject to the FLRA 1969, s 14 (para **[245.38]** below) and in relation to deaths on or after 4 April 1988 subject to the FLRA 1987, ss 1 and 18 (paras **[245.70]–[245.71]** below).

With effect from 5 December 2005 extensive amendments are made to Pt IV of AEA 1925, particularly ss 46 and 47, by CPA 2004, ss 71 and 263(2), Sch 4, paras 7–12 and Civil Partnership Act 2004 (Commencement No 2) Order 2005, SI 2005/3175.

Two recent amendments should be noted. First, in relation to the spouses or civil partners of persons dying intestate on or after 1 February 2009 the amounts of the fixed net sums payable under paras (2) and (3) of the Table in AEA 1925, s 46(1)(i) are increased from £125,000 to £250,000 and from £200,000 to £450,000 respectively: Family Provision (Intestate Succession) Order 2009, SI 2009/135. Secondly, the basis on which the life interest of a surviving spouse or civil partner is capitalised under s 47A is adjusted in cases where the election to do so is made on or after 1 February 2009 to take account of changed social and economic circumstances by the substitution of new tables to the Intestate Succession (Interest and Capitalisation) Order 1977: Intestate Succession (Interest and Capitalisation) (Amendment) Order 2008, SI 2008/3162: see paras **[244.90]** ff below.

[244.62]

46 Succession to real and personal estate on intestacy (1) The residuary estate of an intestate shall be distributed in the manner or be held on the trusts mentioned in this section, namely:—

[(i) If the intestate leaves a [spouse or civil partner][1], then in accordance with the following Table:

TABLE

If the intestate—

(1) leaves— (a) no issue, and (b) no parent, or brother or sister of the whole blood, or issue of a brother or sister of the whole blood	the residuary estate shall be held in trust for the surviving [spouse or civil partner][1] absolutely.
(2) leaves issue (whether or not persons mentioned in sub-paragraph (b) above also survive)	the surviving [spouse or civil partner][1] shall take the personal chattels absolutely and, in addition, the residuary estate of the intestate (other than the personal chattels) shall stand charged with the payment of a [fixed net sum][2], free of death duties and costs, to the surviving [spouse or civil partner][1] with interest thereon from the date of the death ... [at such rate as the Lord Chancellor may specify by order][3] until paid or appropriated, and, subject to providing for that sum and the interest thereon, the residuary estate (other than the personal chattels) shall be held— (a) as to one half upon trust for the surviving [spouse or civil partner][1] during his or her life, and, subject to such life interest, on the statutory trusts for the issue of the intestate, and (b) as to the other half, on the statutory trusts for the issue of the intestate.
(3) leaves one or more of the following, that is to say, a parent, a brother or sister of the whole blood, or issue of a brother or sister of the whole blood, but leaves no issue	the surviving [spouse or civil partner][1] shall take the personal chattels absolutely and, in addition, the residuary estate of the intestate (other than the personal chattels) shall stand charged with the payment of a [fixed net sum][4], free of death duties and costs, to the surviving [spouse or civil partner][1] with interest thereon from the date of the death ... [at such rate as the Lord Chancellor may specify by order][5] until paid or appropriated, and, subject to providing for that sum and the interest thereon, the residuary estate (other than the personal chattels) shall be held— (a) as to one half in trust for the surviving [spouse or civil partner][1] absolutely, and (b) as to the other half—

(i) where the intestate leaves one parent or both parents (whether or not brothers or sisters of the intestate or their issue also survive) in trust for the parent absolutely or, as the case may be, for the two parents in equal shares absolutely

(ii) where the intestate leaves no parent, on the statutory trusts for the brothers and sisters of the whole blood of the intestate.]

[The fixed net sums referred to in paragraphs (2) and (3) of this Table shall be of the amounts provided by or under section 1 of the Family Provision Act 1966]

(ii) If the intestate leaves issue but no [spouse or civil partner][1], the residuary estate of the intestate shall be held on the statutory trusts for the issue of the intestate;

(iii) If the intestate leaves no [spouse or civil partner][1] and no issue but both parents, then ... the residuary estate of the intestate shall be held in trust for the father and mother in equal shares absolutely;

(iv) If the intestate leaves no [spouse or civil partner][1] and no issue but one parent, then ... the residuary estate of the intestate shall be held in trust for the surviving father or mother absolutely;

(v) If the intestate leaves no [spouse or civil partner][1] and no issue and no] parent, then ... the residuary estate of the intestate shall be held in trust for the following persons living at the death of the intestate, and in the following order and manner, namely:—

First, on the statutory trusts for the brothers and sisters of the whole blood of the intestate; but if no person takes an absolutely vested interest under such trusts; then

Second, on the statutory trusts for the brothers and sisters of the half blood of the intestate; but if no person takes an absolutely vested interest under such trusts; then

Third, for the grandparents of the intestate and, if more than one survive the intestate, in equal shares; but if there is no member of this class; then

Fourth, on the statutory trusts for the uncles and aunts of the intestate (being brothers or sisters of the whole blood of a parent of the intestate); but if no person takes an absolutely vested interest under such trusts; then

Fifth, on the statutory trusts for the uncles and aunts of the intestate (being brothers or sisters of the half blood of a parent of the intestate) ...

(vi) In default of any person taking an absolute interest under the foregoing provisions, the residuary estate of the intestate shall belong to the Crown or to the Duchy of Lancaster or to the Duke of Cornwall for the time being, as the case may be, as bona vacantia, and in lieu of any right to escheat.
The Crown or the said Duchy or the said Duke may (without prejudice to the powers reserved by section 9 of the Civil List Act 1910, or any other powers), out of the whole or any part of the property devolving on them respectively, provide, in accordance with the existing practice, for dependents, whether kindred or not, of the intestate, and other persons for whom the intestate might reasonably have been expected to make provision.

[(1A) The power to make orders under subsection (1) above shall be exercisable by statutory instrument subject to annulment in pursuance of a resolution of either House of Parliament; and any such order may be varied or revoked by a subsequent order made under the power.][6]
(2) A husband and wife shall for all purposes of distribution or division under the foregoing provisions of this section be treated as two persons.
[(2A) Where the intestate's [spouse or civil partner][1] survived the intestate but died before the end of the period of 28 days beginning with the day on which the intestate died, this section shall have effect as respects the intestate as if the [spouse or civil partner][1] had not survived the intestate.][7]
[(3) Where the intestate and the intestate's [spouse or civil partner][1] have died in circumstances rendering it uncertain which of them survived the other and the intestate's [spouse or civil partner][1] is by virtue of section one hundred and eighty-four of the Law of Property Act 1925, deemed to have survived the intestate, this section shall, nevertheless, have effect as respects the intestate as if the [spouse or civil partner][1] had not survived the intestate.
(4) The interest payable on [the fixed net sum][8] payable to a surviving [spouse or civil partner][1] shall be primarily payable out of income.][9]

1 The words 'spouse or civil partner' are substituted throughout s 46 for the words 'husband or wife' by CPA 2004, ss 71 and 263(2). Sch 4, para 7.
2 Words in square brackets substituted by the Family Provisions Act 1966, s 1(2), in relation to persons dying on or after 1 January 1967, for the words 'net sum of five thousand pounds'. The Lord Chancellor has power under s 1(3), (4) of that Act to vary this fixed net sum by statutory instrument. This 'fixed net sum' was £8,750 where the date of death was prior to 1 July 1972 (FPA 1966, s 1(1)) but is £15,000 where the death occurred on or after that date and before 15 March 1977 (Family Provision (Intestate Succession) Order 1977, SI 1977/415); £40,000 where the death occurred on or after 1 March 1981 (the Family Provision (Intestate Succession) Order 1981, SI 1981/255); £75,000 where the death occurred on or after 1 June 1987 (the Family Provision (Intestate Succession) Order 1987, SI 1987/799); £125,000 where the death occurred on or after 1 December 1993 (the Family Provision (Intestate Succession) Order 1993, SI 1993/2906); and £250,000 where the death occurred on or after 1 February 2009 (the Family Provision (Intestate Succession) Order 2009, SI 2009/135).
3 Words omitted were repealed by SL(R)A 1981. Words in square brackets substituted by AJA 1977, s 28(1) for the rate of per cent per annum. The rate of interest was 7 per cent per annum from 15 September 1977 to 30 September 1983 and from 1 October 1983 is 6 per cent per annum: see the Intestate Succession (Interest and Capitalisation) Order 1977 (SI 1977/1491), art 2, as amended by SI 1983/1374 (see para **[244.92]** below).
4 Words in square brackets substituted by FPA 1966, s 1(2), in relation to persons dying on or after 1 January 1967, for the words 'net sum of twenty thousand pounds'. The Lord Chancellor has power under s 1(3), (4) to vary this fixed net sum by statutory instrument. This

fixed net sum was £30,000 where the death occurred before 1 July 1972, £40,000 for deaths on or after that date and before 15 March 1977, £55,000 for deaths on or after the latter date and before 1 March 1981, and is £85,000 for deaths on or after 1 March 1981 and before 1 June 1987, £125,000 for deaths on or after 1 June 1987 and before 1 December 1993, and is £200,000 for deaths on or after 1 December 1993 and before 1 February 2009; and is £450,000 for deaths on or after 1 February 2009. The relevant statutory instruments are the same as those relating to the fixed net sum under para (2) of the Table; see n 2.

5 The words omitted were repealed by SL(R)A 1981. See n 2 for the rates of interest.

6 Sub-s (1A): inserted by AJA 1977, s 28(1).

7 Sub-s (2A): inserted by LR(S)A 1995, s 1(1), as respects an intestate dying on or after 1 January 1996.

8 Words in square brackets substituted by FPA 1966, s 1(2), in relation to persons dying on or after 1 January 1967, for the words 'net sum of five thousand pounds or, as the case may be, twenty thousand pounds'. As to the fixed net sum, see n 2 above.

9 Sub-ss (3) and (4) inserted by the Intestates' Estates Act 1952, s 1(4) and subsequently amended: see nn 1 and 8 above.

INTESTATE SUCCESSION (INTEREST AND CAPITALISATION) ORDER 1977

SI 1977/1491

[244.90]

Note. This Order was made on 4 September 1977 by the Lord Chancellor under the AEA 1925, s 46(1)(i) (as substituted by the Intestates' Estates Act 1952, s 1, and as amended by the AJA 1977, s 28(1)) and s 47A(3A) of the 1925 Act (as inserted by the AJA 1977, s 28(3)). The Order came into force on 15 September 1977: see article 1(1). Article 2 of the Order originally increased the rate of interest payable on the statutory legacy until paid or appropriated from 4 per cent pa to 7 per cent pa or, in the case of persons dying before 1 January 1953, to 8 per cent, pa). Article 2 was amended by the Intestate Succession (Interest and Capitalisation) Order 1983, SI 1983/1374 so as to reduce the rate to 6 per cent per annum with effect from 1 October 1983. This last rate of interest has not since been altered.

Article 3 and the Schedule sets out the formula for calculating the value of the life interest of the surviving spouse of an intestate who elects to capitalise his or her life interest. With effect from 1 February 2009 the Schedule and its tables have been replaced with a new schedule and new tables designed to take account of increases in life expectancy and decreases in the yields on Government Stocks.

The 1977 Order is printed below as amended by the Intestate Succession (Interest and Capitalisation) Order 1983, SI 1983/1374, the Civil Partnership Act 2004 (Amendments to Subordinate Legislation) Order 2005, SI 2005/2114 and the Intestate Succession (Interest and Capitalisation) (Amendment) Order 2009, SI 2009/3162.

The Schedule to the 1977 Order and the replacement Schedule together with their respective tables are printed at paras **[244.129B]** ff below.

[244.91]

1. Citation and Interpretation.— (1) This Order may be cited as the Intestate Succession (Interest and Capitalisation) Order 1977 and shall come into operation on 15th September 1977.

(2) The Interpretation Act 1889 shall apply to the interpretation of this Order as it applies to the interpretation of an Act of Parliament.

[244.92]

2. Interest on Statutory Legacy. For the purposes of section 46(1)(i) of the Administration of Estates Act 1925, as it applies both in respect of persons dying before 1953 and in respect of persons dying after 1952, the specified rate of interest shall be [6] per cent per annum.[1]

1 The figure in square brackets was substituted by SI 1983/1374 with effect from 1 October 1983: see para **[244.90]** above.

[244.93]

3. Capitalisation of Life Interests.— (1) Where after the coming into operation of this Order an election is exercised in accordance with subsection (6) or (7) of section 47A of the Administration of Estates Act 1925, the capital value of the life interest of the surviving spouse [or civil partner][1] shall be reckoned in accordance with the following provisions of this article.
(2) There shall be ascertained, by reference to the index compiled by the Financial Times, The Institute of Actuaries and the Faculty of Actuaries, the gross redemption yield[1] on fifteen-year Government Stocks[1] at the date on which the election was exercised or, if the index was not compiled on that date, by reference to the index on the last date before that date on which it was compiled; and the column which corresponds to that yield in whichever of the Tables set out in the Schedule hereto is applicable to the sex of the surviving spouse [or civil partner][1] shall be the appropriate column for the purposes of paragraph (3) of this article.[2]
(3) The capital value for the purposes of paragraph (1) of this article is the produce of the part of the residuary estate (whether or not yielding income) in respect of which the election was exercised and the multiplier shown in the appropriate column opposite the age which the surviving spouse [or civil partner][1] had attained at the date on which the election was exercised.[1]

1 Words in square brackets in sub-ss (1), (2) and (3) inserted with effect from 5 December 2005 by Civil Partnership Act 2004, s 259 and Civil Partnership Act 2004 (Amendments to Subordinate Legislation) Order 2005, SI 2005/2114, arts 1, 2(6), Sch 6, para1(1), (2).
2 As originally in force art 3(2) referred to 'the *average* gross redemption yield on *medium coupon* fifteen-year Government Stocks'. With effect from 1 February 2009 article 3(2) is amended by the Intestate Succession (Interest and Capitalisation) Order 2008, SI 2008/3162, arts 1, 2(1) by omitting the words 'average' and 'medium coupon' to reflect changes since 1977 in the way that the yields on United Kingdom Government stocks are calculated. 'Medium coupon' yields are no longer produced; however, the yield figures for 15-year United Kingdom Government Stocks are published as 'FTSE UK Gilt Indices' on the website of the Financial Times.

[244.93A]

SCHEDULE

[The schedule and replacement schedule to this Order which contain the tables referred to in article 3 are printed at paras **[244.129B]** ff below.]

CHILDREN ACT 1989

(1989 c 41)

[16 November 1989]

[244.112]

Note. The Children Act 1989 (ChA 1989) was brought into force on 14 October 1991 (SI 1991/828). The Act as amended contains comprehensive provisions or the welfare of children, including their guardianship. The powers to appoint guardians are now contained in s 5. A parent with 'parental responsibility' (a term defined by s 3) has power under s 5(3) to appoint an individual to be the child's guardian after his or her death and a guardian is given the like power by s 5(4). The power may be exercised by will or any other writing, subject to the requirement that it be dated and either signed by the person making the appointment or signed at his direction before witnesses; see s 5(5). Sections 2 to 4 prescribe the circumstances in which a parent is deemed to have the parental responsibility which is a prerequisite to the exercise of the power to appoint guardians. Section 4 has been amended with effect from 1 December 2003 by the Adoption and Children Act 2002, s 111. The amendments extend parental responsibility for illegitimate children to fathers registered on the birth certificate, where registration occurs on or after the commencement day. Adoption and children Act 2002, s 112 added with effect from 30 December 2005 a new s 4A providing for the acquisition of parental responsibility by step-parents. Section 6 sets out the circumstances in which the appointment of a guardian may be revoked or disclaimed. One additional important feature of the ChA 1989 is that s 3(3) extends to a parent (and now a step-parent) with parental responsibility the right to call for and deal with all property belonging to his minor child, a right which was formerly available under the Guardianship Act 1973, s 7 only to a guardian.

With effect from 6 April 2009 the ChA 1989 is amended by HFEA 2008 to cater for cases where a child is born as a result of one of the procedures regulated by HFEA 1990 and 2008 and the mother has agreed that another woman who is not her civil partner is to be treated as the other parent. In such cases the ChA 1989 is amended so as to extend parental responsibility to that other parent in appropriate circumstances.

For a more detailed account of these provisions, and for their practical implications for will drafting, see Vol 1, para **[28.1]** ff and para **[203.47]** ff above.

PART I
INTRODUCTORY

* * * * *

[244.113]

2. Parental responsibility for children.— (1) Where a child's father and mother were married to each other at the time of his birth, they shall each have parental responsibility for the child.

[(1A) Where a child—

(a) has a parent by virtue of section 42 of the Human Fertilisation and Embryology Act 2008; or

(b) has a parent by virtue of section 43 of that Act and is a person to whom section 1(3) of the Family Law Reform Act 1987 applies, the child's mother and the other parent shall each have parental responsibility for the child.][1]

(2) Where a child's father and mother were not married to each other at the time of his birth—

(a) the mother shall have parental responsibility for the child;

(b) the father shall not have parental responsibility for the child, unless he acquires it in accordance with the provisions of this Act.

[(2A) Where a child has a parent by virtue of section 43 of the Human Fertilisation and Embryology Act 2008 and is not a person to whom section 1(3) of the Family Law Reform Act 1987 applies—

(a) the mother shall have parental responsibility for the child;

(b) the other parent shall have parental responsibility for the child if she has acquired it (and has not ceased to have it) in accordance with the provisions of this Act.][2]

(3) References in this Act to a child whose father and mother were, or (as the case may be) were not, married to each other at the time of his birth must be read with section 1 of the Family Law Reform Act 1987 (which extends their meaning).
(4) The rule of law that a father is the natural guardian of his legitimate child is abolished.
(5) More than one person may have parental responsibility for the same child at the same time.
(6) A person who has parental responsibility for a child at any time shall not cease to have that responsibility solely because some other person subsequently acquires parental responsibility for the child.
(7) Where more than one person has parental responsibility for a child, each of them may act alone and without the other (or others) in meeting that responsibility; but nothing in this Part shall be taken to affect the operation of any enactment which requires the consent of more than one person in a matter affecting the child.
(8) The fact that a person has parental responsibility for a child shall not entitle him to act in any way which would be incompatible with any order made with respect to the child under this Act.
(9) A person who has parental responsibility for a child may not surrender or transfer any part of that responsibility to another but may arrange for some or all of it to be met by one or more persons acting on his behalf.
(10) The person with whom any such arrangement is made may himself be a person who already has parental responsibility for the child concerned.
(11) The making of any such arrangement shall not affect any liability of the person making it which may arise from any failure to meet any part of his parental responsibility for the child concerned.

1 Subsection (1A) inserted with effect from 6 April 2009 for certain purposes and from 1 Septemeber 2009 for all remaining puposes by the Human Fertilisation and Embryology Act 2008, s 56, Sch 6, para 26(1), (2) and the Human Fertilisation and Embryology Act 2008 (Commencement No 1 and Transitional Provisions) Order 2009, SI 2009/479, art 6(1)(e), (f), (2).
2 Subsection (2A) inserted with effect from 6 April 2009 for certain puposes and from 1 September 2009 for all remaining purposes by the Human Fertilisation and Embryology Act 2008, s 56, Sch 6, para 26(1), (3) and the Human Fertilisation and Embryology Act 2008 (Commencement No 1 and Transitional Provisions) Order 2009, SI 2009/479, art 6(1)(e), (f), (2).

[244.115A]
[4ZA Acquisition of parental responsibility by second female parent
(1) Where a child has a parent by virtue of section 43 of the Human Fertilisation and Embryology Act 2008 and is not a person to whom section 1(3) of the Family Law Reform Act 1987 applies, that parent shall acquire parental responsibility for the child if—

(a) she becomes registered as a parent of the child under any of the enactments specified in subsection (2);
(b) she and the child's mother make an agreement providing for her to have parental responsibility for the child; or
(c) the court, on her application, orders that she shall have parental responsibility for the child.

(2) The enactments referred to in subsection (1)(a) are—

(a) paragraphs (a), (b) and (c) of section 10(1B) and of section 10A(1B) of the Births and Deaths Registration Act 1953;
(b) paragraphs (a), (b) and (d) of section 18B(1) and sections 18B(3)(a) and 20(1)(a) of the Registration of Births, Deaths and Marriages (Scotland) Act 1965; and
(c) sub-paragraphs (a), (b) and (c) of Article 14ZA(3) of the Births and Deaths Registration (Northern Ireland) Order 1976.

(3) The Secretary of State may by order amend subsection (2) so as to add further enactments to the list in that subsection.
(4) An agreement under subsection (1)(b) is also a 'parental responsibility agreement', and section 4(2) applies in relation to such an agreement as it applies in relation to parental responsibility agreements under section 4.
(5) A person who has acquired parental responsibility under subsection (1) shall cease to have that responsibility only if the court so orders.
(6) The court may make an order under subsection (5) on the application—

(a) of any person who has parental responsibility for the child; or
(b) with the leave of the court, of the child himself, subject, in the case of parental responsibility acquired under subsection (1)(c), to section 12(4).

(7) The court may only grant leave under subsection (6)(b) if it is satisfied that the child has sufficient understanding to make theproposed application.][1]

1 Section 2ZA inserted with effect from 6 April 2009 for certain purposes and from 1 September 2009 for all remaining purposes by the Human Fertilisation and Embryology Act 2008, s 56, Sch 6, para 27 and the Human Fertilisation and Embryology Act 2008 (Commencement No 1 and Transitional Provisions) Order 2009, SI 2009/479, art 6(1)(e), (f), (2).

PART XII
MISCELLANEOUS AND GENERAL

* * * * *

GENERAL

* * * * *

[244.119]
105. Interpretation.— (1) In this Act—

* * * * *

'child' means … a person under the age of eighteen;

* * * * *

'guardian of a child' means a guardian (other than a guardian of the estate of a child) appointed in accordance with the provisions of section 5;

* * * * *

['parental responsibility' has the meaning given in section 3;
'parental responsibility agreement' has the meaning given in [sections 4(1)[, 4ZA(4)] and 4A(2)][1];
'prescribed' means prescribed by regulations made under this Act;

* * * * *

'residence order' has the meaning given by section 8(1);

* * * * *

(2) References in this Act to a child whose father and mother were, or (as the case may be) were not, married to each other at the time of his birth must be read with section 1 of the Family Law Reform Act 1987 (which extends the meaning of such references).

1 Words in outer set of square brackets substituted with effect from 30 December 2005 by the Adoption and Children Act 2002, ss 139, 148, Sch 3, para 70(c) (with Sch 4, paras 6–8) and the Adoption aand Children Act 2002 (Commencement No 9) Order 2005, SI 2005/2213, art 2(o) and reference in inner set of square brackets inserted with effect from 6 April 2009 by the Human Fertilisation and Embryology Act 2008, s 56, Sch 6, para 31 and the Human Fertilisation and Embryology Act 2008 (Commencement No 1 and Transitional Provisions) Order 2009, SI 2009/479, art 6(1)(e), (f).

INTESTATE SUCCESSION (INTEREST AND CAPITALISATION) ORDER 1977

SI 1977/1491

SCHEDULE

[244.129A]

Note. The schedules and tables below form part of the Intestate Succession (Interest and Capitalisation) Order 1977 which is printed at paras **[244.90]** ff above. The schedule set out in para **[244.129B]** below formed part of the original 1977 Order and in the case of an election to capitalise a life interest made under the AEA 1925, s 47A on or after 15 September 1977 (when the 1977 Order came into force) the capital value of the life interest was reckoned under art 3 in accordance with the tables contained in the Schedule. Article 3 of the 1977 Order was slightly amended (it is printed as amended in para **[244.93]** above) and the Schedule to the Order replaced with the Schedule to the Intestate Succession (Interest and Capitalisation) (Amendment) Order 2008, SI 2008/3162, which is printed at para **[244.129C]** below. The 2008 Order came into force on 1 February 2009 and in the case of an election made on or after that date the capital value of the life interest is calculated in accordance with the new Schedule.

Schedule

Table 1 Multiplier to be applied to the part of the residuary estate in respect of which the election is exercised to obtain the capital value of the life interest of a surviving husband [or a surviving male civil partner][1] when the average gross redemption yield on medium coupon fifteen-year Government Stocks is at the rate shown

Age Last Birthday of Husband [or a surviving male civil partner][2]	*Less than 8.50%*	*8.50% or between 8.50% and 9.50%*	*9.50% or between 9.50% and 10.50%*	*10.50% or between 10.50% and 11.50%*	*11.50% or between 11.50% and 12.50%*	*12.50% or between 12.50% and 13.50%*	*13.50% or between 13.50% and 14.50%*	*14.50% or between 14.50% and 15.50%*	*15.50% or more*
16	0.882	0.897	0.908	0.917	0.923	0.927	0.931	0.934	0.936
17	0.879	0.895	0.906	0.915	0.921	0.926	0.930	0.933	0.935
18	0.876	0.892	0.904	0.913	0.920	0.925	0.929	0.932	0.934
19	0.873	0.890	0.902	0.911	0.918	0.923	0.928	0.931	0.933
20	0.870	0.887	0.900	0.909	0.917	0.922	0.926	0.930	0.933
21	0.866	0.884	0.897	0.907	0.915	0.921	0.925	0.929	0.932
22	0.863	0.881	0.895	0.905	0.913	0.919	0.924	0.928	0.931
23	0.859	0.878	0.892	0.903	0.911	0.918	0.923	0.927	0.930
24	0.855	0.875	0.890	0.901	0.909	0.916	0.921	0.925	0.929
25	0.852	0.872	0.887	0.898	0.907	0.914	0.920	0.924	0.928
26	0.847	0.868	0.884	0.896	0.905	0.912	0.918	0.923	0.926

Age Last Birthday of Husband [or a surviving male civil partner][2]	*Less than 8.50%*	*8.50% or between 8.50% and 9.50%*	*9.50% or between 9.50% and 10.50%*	*10.50% or between 10.50% and 11.50%*	*11.50% or between 11.50% and 12.50%*	*12.50% or between 12.50% and 13.50%*	*13.50% or between 13.50% and 14.50%*	*14.50% or between 14.50% and 15.50%*	*15.50% or more*
27	0.843	0.864	0.880	0.893	0.903	0.910	0.916	0.921	0.925
28	0.838	0.860	0.877	0.890	0.900	0.908	0.914	0.919	0.923
29	0.834	0.856	0.873	0.887	0.897	0.905	0.912	0.917	0.922
30	0.828	0.851	0.869	0.883	0.894	0.903	0.910	0.915	0.920
31	0.823	0.847	0.865	0.879	0.891	0.900	0.907	0.913	0.918
32	0.818	0.842	0.861	0.876	0.887	0.897	0.904	0.911	0.916
33	0.812	0.837	0.856	0.871	0.884	0.893	0.901	0.908	0.913
34	0.806	0.831	0.851	0.867	0.880	0.890	0.898	0.905	0.911
35	0.799	0.825	0.846	0.862	0.875	0.886	0.895	0.902	0.908
36	0.792	0.819	0.840	0.857	0.871	0.882	0.891	0.899	0.905
37	0.785	0.813	0.834	0.852	0.866	0.878	0.887	0.895	0.902
38	0.778	0.806	0.828	0.846	0.861	0.873	0.883	0.891	0.898
39	0.771	0.799	0.822	0.840	0.856	0.868	0.879	0.887	0.894
40	0.763	0.792	0.815	0.834	0.850	0.863	0.874	0.883	0.890
41	0.755	0.784	0.808	0.828	0.844	0.857	0.869	0.878	0.886
42	0.746	0.776	0.801	0.821	0.838	0.852	0.863	0.873	0.881
43	0.737	0.768	0.793	0.814	0.831	0.845	0.857	0.868	0.876

Age Last Birthday of Husband [or a surviving male civil partner][2]	*Less than 8.50%*	*8.50% or between 8.50% and 9.50%*	*9.50% or between 9.50% and 10.50%*	*10.50% or between 10.50% and 11.50%*	*11.50% or between 11.50% and 12.50%*	*12.50% or between 12.50% and 13.50%*	*13.50% or between 13.50% and 14.50%*	*14.50% or between 14.50% and 15.50%*	*15.50% or more*
44	0.728	0.759	0.785	0.806	0.824	0.839	0.851	0.862	0.871
45	0.719	0.750	0.776	0.798	0.816	0.832	0.845	0.856	0.866
46	0.709	0.741	0.768	0.790	0.809	0.825	0.838	0.850	0.860
47	0.699	0.731	0.758	0.781	0.801	0.817	0.831	0.843	0.853
48	0.688	0.721	0.749	0.772	0.792	0.809	0.823	0.836	0.847
49	0.678	0.711	0.739	0.763	0.783	0.800	0.815	0.828	0.839
50	0.666	0.700	0.729	0.753	0.774	0.791	0.807	0.820	0.832
51	0.655	0.689	0.718	0.743	0.764	0.782	0.798	0.812	0.824
52	0.643	0.678	0.707	0.732	0.754	0.772	0.789	0.803	0.815
53	0.631	0.666	0.695	0.721	0.743	0.762	0.779	0.794	0.807
54	0.619	0.654	0.684	0.710	0.732	0.752	0.769	0.784	0.797
55	0.606	0.641	0.671	0.698	0.721	0.741	0.758	0.774	0.787
56	0.594	0.628	0.659	0.685	0.709	0.729	0.747	0.763	0.777
57	0.580	0.615	0.646	0.673	0.696	0.717	0.735	0.752	0.766
58	0.567	0.602	0.633	0.660	0.683	0.705	0.723	0.740	0.755
59	0.553	0.588	0.619	0.646	0.670	0.692	0.711	0.728	0.743
60	0.539	0.574	0.605	0.632	0.657	0.678	0.698	0.715	0.731

Age Last Birthday of Husband [or a surviving male civil partner][2]	*Less than 8.50%*	*8.50% or between 8.50% and 9.50%*	*9.50% or between 9.50% and 10.50%*	*10.50% or between 10.50% and 11.50%*	*11.50% or between 11.50% and 12.50%*	*12.50% or between 12.50% and 13.50%*	*13.50% or between 13.50% and 14.50%*	*14.50% or between 14.50% and 15.50%*	*15.50% or more*
61	0.525	0.560	0.590	0.618	0.642	0.664	0.684	0.702	0.718
62	0.510	0.545	0.576	0.603	0.628	0.650	0.670	0.688	0.704
63	0.496	0.530	0.561	0.588	0.613	0.636	0.656	0.674	0.691
64	0.481	0.515	0.546	0.573	0.598	0.621	0.641	0.659	0.676
65	0.466	0.500	0.530	0.558	0.583	0.605	0.626	0.644	0.661
66	0.451	0.485	0.515	0.542	0.567	0.590	0.610	0.629	0.646
67	0.436	0.469	0.499	0.526	0.551	0.574	0.594	0.613	0.631
68	0.421	0.454	0.483	0.510	0.535	0.557	0.578	0.597	0.615
69	0.407	0.438	0.467	0.494	0.518	0.541	0.562	0.581	0.598
70	0.392	0.423	0.452	0.478	0.502	0.524	0.545	0.564	0.582
71	0.377	0.407	0.436	0.462	0.485	0.508	0.528	0.547	0.565
72	0.362	0.392	0.420	0.445	0.469	0.491	0.511	0.530	0.548
73	0.348	0.377	0.404	0.429	0.452	0.474	0.494	0.513	0.531
74	0.333	0.362	0.388	0.413	0.436	0.457	0.477	0.496	0.513
75	0.319	0.347	0.373	0.397	0.419	0.441	0.460	0.479	0.496
76	0.305	0.332	0.357	0.381	0.403	0.424	0.443	0.461	0.479
77	0.292	0.318	0.342	0.365	0.387	0.407	0.426	0.444	0.461

Age Last Birthday of Husband [or a surviving male civil partner][2]	*Less than 8.50%*	*8.50% or between 8.50% and 9.50%*	*9.50% or between 9.50% and 10.50%*	*10.50% or between 10.50% and 11.50%*	*11.50% or between 11.50% and 12.50%*	*12.50% or between 12.50% and 13.50%*	*13.50% or between 13.50% and 14.50%*	*14.50% or between 14.50% and 15.50%*	*15.50% or more*
78	0.278	0.304	0.328	0.350	0.371	0.391	0.410	0.427	0.444
79	0.265	0.290	0.313	0.335	0.355	0.375	0.393	0.410	0.427
80	0.253	0.277	0.299	0.320	0.340	0.359	0.377	0.394	0.410
81	0.241	0.264	0.285	0.306	0.325	0.343	0.361	0.377	0.393
82	0.229	0.251	0.272	0.292	0.310	0.328	0.345	0.361	0.377
83	0.218	0.239	0.259	0.278	0.296	0.313	0.330	0.346	0.361
84	0.207	0.227	0.246	0.265	0.282	0.299	0.315	0.331	0.345
85	0.196	0.216	0.234	0.252	0.269	0.285	0.301	0.316	0.330
86	0.186	0.205	0.223	0.240	0.256	0.272	0.287	0.302	0.315
87	0.177	0.195	0.212	0.228	0.244	0.259	0.274	0.288	0.301
88	0.168	0.185	0.201	0.217	0.232	0.247	0.261	0.275	0.288
89	0.159	0.176	0.191	0.207	0.221	0.235	0.249	0.262	0.275
90	0.151	0.167	0.182	0.197	0.211	0.224	0.237	0.250	0.262
91	0.144	0.159	0.173	0.187	0.201	0.214	0.227	0.239	0.251
92	0.137	0.151	0.165	0.179	0.192	0.205	0.217	0.229	0.240
93	0.130	0.144	0.158	0.171	0.183	0.196	0.208	0.219	0.230
94	0.124	0.138	0.151	0.163	0.175	0.187	0.199	0.210	0.221

Age Last Birthday of Husband [or a surviving male civil partner][2]	*Less than 8.50%*	*8.50% or between 8.50% and 9.50%*	*9.50% or between 9.50% and 10.50%*	*10.50% or between 10.50% and 11.50%*	*11.50% or between 11.50% and 12.50%*	*12.50% or between 12.50% and 13.50%*	*13.50% or between 13.50% and 14.50%*	*14.50% or between 14.50% and 15.50%*	*15.50% or more*
95	0.119	0.132	0.144	0.156	0.168	0.179	0.190	0.201	0.212
96	0.113	0.126	0.138	0.149	0.161	0.172	0.182	0.193	0.203
97	0.108	0.120	0.132	0.143	0.154	0.164	0.175	0.185	0.195
98	0.103	0.115	0.126	0.137	0.147	0.157	0.167	0.177	0.187
99	0.098	0.109	0.119	0.130	0.140	0.150	0.159	0.169	0.178
100 and over	0.093	0.103	0.112	0.123	0.133	0.143	0.151	0.161	0.169

1 Words in square brackets in main heading inserted with effect from 5 December 2005 by Civil Partnership Act 2004, s 259 and Civil Partnership Act 2004 (Amendments to Subordinate Legislation) Order 2005, SI 2005/2114, arts 1, 2(6), Sch 6, para1(1), (3)(a).

2 Words in square brackets in first column heading inserted with effect from 5 December 2005 by Civil Partnership Act 2004, s 259 and Civil Partnership Act 2004 (Amendments to Subordinate Legislation) Order 2005, SI 2005/2114, arts 1, 2(6), Sch 6, para1(1), (3)(b).

[244.129C]

Table 2 Multiplier to be applied to the part or the residuary estate in respect of which the election is exercised to obtain the capital value of the life interest of a surviving wife [or a surviving female civil partner][1], when the average gross redemption yield on medium coupon fifteen-year Government Stocks is at the rate shown.

Age Last Birthday of Wife [or a surviving female civil partner][2]	*Less than 8.50%*	*8.50% or between 8.50% and 9.50%*	*9.50% or between 9.50% and 10.50%*	*10.50% or between 10.50% and 11.50%*	*11.50% or between 11.50% and 12.50%*	*12.50% or between 12.50% and 13.50%*	*13.50% or between 13.50% and 14.50%*	*14.50% or between 14.50% and 15.50%*	*15.50% or more*
16	0.892	0.905	0.915	0.922	0.927	0.930	0.933	0.936	0.937
17	0.889	0.903	0.913	0.920	0.925	0.929	0.933	0.935	0.937
18	0.887	0.901	0.911	0.919	0.924	0.929	0.932	0.934	0.936
19	0.884	0.899	0.910	0.917	0.923	0.928	0.931	0.934	0.936
20	0.882	0.897	0.908	0.916	0.922	0.927	0.930	0.933	0.935
21	0.879	0.895	0.906	0.915	0.921	0.926	0.929	0.932	0.934
22	0.877	0.893	0.904	0.913	0.920	0.925	0.928	0.931	0.934
23	0.874	0.890	0.902	0.911	0.918	0.923	0.927	0.931	0.933
24	0.871	0.888	0.900	0.910	0.917	0.922	0.926	0.930	0.932
25	0.868	0.885	0.898	0.908	0.915	0.921	0.925	0.929	0.932
26	0.864	0.882	0.896	0.906	0.914	0.920	0.924	0.928	0.931
27	0.861	0.879	0.893	0.904	0.912	0.918	0.923	0.927	0.930

Age Last Birthday of Wife [or a surviving female civil partner][2]	*Less than 8.50%*	*8.50% or between 8.50% and 9.50%*	*9.50% or between 9.50% and 10.50%*	*10.50% or between 10.50% and 11.50%*	*11.50% or between 11.50% and 12.50%*	*12.50% or between 12.50% and 13.50%*	*13.50% or between 13.50% and 14.50%*	*14.50% or between 14.50% and 15.50%*	*15.50% or more*
28	0.857	0.876	0.891	0.901	0.910	0.916	0.921	0.925	0.929
29	0.853	0.873	0.888	0.899	0.908	0.915	0.920	0.924	0.928
30	0.849	0.869	0.885	0.896	0.906	0.913	0.918	0.923	0.926
31	0.845	0.866	0.882	0.894	0.903	0.911	0.916	0.921	0.925
32	0.840	0.862	0.878	0.891	0.901	0.908	0.914	0.919	0.923
33	0.836	0.858	0.875	0.888	0.898	0.906	0.912	0.918	0.922
34	0.831	0.853	0.871	0.884	0.895	0.903	0.910	0.916	0.920
35	0.826	0.849	0.867	0.881	0.892	0.901	0.908	0.913	0.918
36	0.820	0.844	0.863	0.877	0.889	0.898	0.905	0.911	0.916
37	0.815	0.839	0.858	0.873	0.885	0.895	0.902	0.909	0.914
38	0.809	0.834	0.853	0.869	0.881	0.891	0.899	0.906	0.911
39	0.803	0.828	0.848	0.864	0.877	0.888	0.896	0.903	0.909
40	0.796	0.822	0.843	0.860	0.873	0.884	0.893	0.900	0.906
41	0.790	0.816	0.838	0.855	0.869	0.880	0.889	0.897	0.903
42	0.783	0.810	0.832	0.850	0.864	0.876	0.885	0.893	0.900
43	0.775	0.803	0.826	0.844	0.859	0.871	0.881	0.889	0.896
44	0.768	0.796	0.820	0.838	0.854	0.866	0.877	0.885	0.893

Age Last Birthday of Wife [or a surviving female civil partner][2]	*Less than 8.50%*	*8.50% or between 8.50% and 9.50%*	*9.50% or between 9.50% and 10.50%*	*10.50% or between 10.50% and 11.50%*	*11.50% or between 11.50% and 12.50%*	*12.50% or between 12.50% and 13.50%*	*13.50% or between 13.50% and 14.50%*	*14.50% or between 14.50% and 15.50%*	*15.50% or more*
45	0.760	0.789	0.813	0.832	0.848	0.861	0.872	0.881	0.889
46	0.752	0.782	0.806	0.826	0.842	0.856	0.867	0.876	0.885
47	0.744	0.774	0.799	0.819	0.836	0.850	0.862	0.872	0.880
48	0.735	0.766	0.791	0.812	0.829	0.844	0.856	0.866	0.875
49	0.726	0.757	0.783	0.804	0.822	0.837	0.850	0.861	0.870
50	0.716	0.748	0.775	0.797	0.815	0.831	0.844	0.855	0.865
51	0.707	0.739	0.766	0.788	0.807	0.823	0.837	0.849	0.859
52	0.697	0.729	0.757	0.780	0.799	0.816	0.830	0.842	0.853
53	0.686	0.719	0.747	0.771	0.791	0.808	0.822	0.835	0.846
54	0.676	0.709	0.737	0.761	0.782	0.799	0.814	0.827	0.839
55	0.664	0.698	0.727	0.751	0.772	0.790	0.806	0.820	0.831
56	0.653	0.687	0.716	0.741	0.763	0.781	0.797	0.811	0.823
57	0.641	0.676	0.705	0.730	0.752	0.771	0.788	0.802	0.815
58	0.629	0.664	0.693	0.719	0.741	0.761	0.778	0.793	0.806
59	0.616	0.651	0.681	0.707	0.730	0.750	0.767	0.783	0.796
60	0.603	0.638	0.669	0.695	0.718	0.739	0.757	0.772	0.786
61	0.590	0.625	0.656	0.683	0.706	0.727	0.745	0.761	0.776

Age Last Birthday of Wife [or a surviving female civil partner][2]	*Less than 8.50%*	*8.50% or between 8.50% and 9.50%*	*9.50% or between 9.50% and 10.50%*	*10.50% or between 10.50% and 11.50%*	*11.50% or between 11.50% and 12.50%*	*12.50% or between 12.50% and 13.50%*	*13.50% or between 13.50% and 14.50%*	*14.50% or between 14.50% and 15.50%*	*15.50% or more*
62	0.577	0.612	0.643	0.670	0.693	0.715	0.733	0.750	0.764
63	0.563	0.598	0.629	0.656	0.680	0.702	0.721	0.738	0.753
64	0.549	0.584	0.615	0.642	0.667	0.688	0.708	0.725	0.740
65	0.534	0.569	0.600	0.628	0.653	0.674	0.694	0.712	0.728
66	0.520	0.555	0.586	0.613	0.638	0.660	0.680	0.698	0.714
67	0.505	0.540	0.570	0.598	0.623	0.645	0.666	0.684	0.700
68	0.490	0.524	0.555	0.583	0.608	0.630	0.651	0.669	0.686
69	0.475	0.509	0.539	0.567	0.592	0.615	0.635	0.654	0.671
70	0.459	0.493	0.523	0.551	0.576	0.599	0.619	0.638	0.655
71	0.444	0.477	0.507	0.535	0.560	0.582	0.603	0.622	0.640
72	0.428	0.461	0.491	0.518	0.543	0.566	0.586	0.606	0.623
73	0.413	0.445	0.475	0.501	0.526	0.549	0.570	0.589	0.606
74	0.398	0.429	0.458	0.485	0.509	0.532	0.552	0.572	0.589
75	0.382	0.413	0.442	0.468	0.492	0.514	0.535	0.554	0.572
76	0.367	0.397	0.425	0.451	0.475	0.497	0.517	0.536	0.554
77	0.352	0.381	0.408	0.434	0.457	0.479	0.499	0.518	0.536
78	0.337	0.365	0.392	0.417	0.440	0.461	0.482	0.500	0.518

Age Last Birthday of Wife [or a surviving female civil partner][2]	*Less than 8.50%*	*8.50% or between 8.50% and 9.50%*	*9.50% or between 9.50% and 10.50%*	*10.50% or between 10.50% and 11.50%*	*11.50% or between 11.50% and 12.50%*	*12.50% or between 12.50% and 13.50%*	*13.50% or between 13.50% and 14.50%*	*14.50% or between 14.50% and 15.50%*	*15.50% or more*
79	0.322	0.350	0.376	0.400	0.423	0.444	0.464	0.482	0.500
80	0.307	0.334	0.360	0.383	0.406	0.426	0.446	0.464	0.482
81	0.293	0.319	0.344	0.367	0.389	0.409	0.428	0.446	0.463
82	0.279	0.304	0.328	0.351	0.372	0.392	0.410	0.428	0.445
83	0.265	0.290	0.313	0.335	0.355	0.375	0.393	0.410	0.427
84	0.252	0.276	0.298	0.319	0.339	0.358	0.376	0.393	0.409
85	0.239	0.262	0.284	0.304	0.323	0.342	0.359	0.376	0.392
86	0.227	0.249	0.269	0.289	0.308	0.326	0.343	0.359	0.374
87	0.215	0.236	0.256	0.275	0.293	0.310	0.327	0.342	0.357
88	0.204	0.224	0.243	0.261	0.279	0.295	0.311	0.327	0.341
89	0.193	0.212	0.230	0.248	0.265	0.281	0.296	0.311	0.325
90	0.182	0.201	0.218	0.235	0.251	0.267	0.282	0.296	0.310
91	0.173	0.190	0.207	0.223	0.239	0.254	0.268	0.282	0.296
92	0.164	0.180	0.197	0.212	0.227	0.242	0.256	0.269	0.282
93	0.155	0.171	0.187	0.202	0.216	0.230	0.243	0.256	0.269
94	0.147	0.162	0.177	0.192	0.205	0.219	0.232	0.244	0.256
95	0.139	0.154	0.168	0.182	0.195	0.208	0.221	0.233	0.244

Age Last Birthday of Wife [or a surviving female civil partner][2]	*Less than 8.50%*	*8.50% or between 8.50% and 9.50%*	*9.50% or between 9.50% and 10.50%*	*10.50% or between 10.50% and 11.50%*	*11.50% or between 11.50% and 12.50%*	*12.50% or between 12.50% and 13.50%*	*13.50% or between 13.50% and 14.50%*	*14.50% or between 14.50% and 15.50%*	*15.50% or more*
96	0.132	0.146	0.159	0.173	0.185	0.198	0.210	0.222	0.233
97	0.125	0.138	0.151	0.164	0.176	0.188	0.199	0.211	0.222
98	0.118	0.130	0.143	0.155	0.167	0.178	0.189	0.200	0.210
99	0.110	0.122	0.134	0.146	0.157	0.168	0.178	0.189	0.199
100 and over	0.102	0.114	0.125	0.137	0.147	0.158	0.167	0.178	0.188

1 Words in square brackets in main heading inserted with effect from 5 December 2005 by Civil Partnership Act 2004, s 259 and Civil Partnership Act 2004 (Amendments to Subordinate Legislation) Order 2005, SI 2005/2114, arts 1, 2(6), Sch 6, para1(1), (4)(a).

2 Words in square brackets in first column heading inserted with effect from 5 December 2005 by Civil Partnership Act 2004, s 259 and Civil Partnership Act 2004 (Amendments to Subordinate Legislation) Order 2005, SI 2005/2114, arts 1, 2(6), Sch 6, para1(1), (4)(b).

Table 1 Multiplier to be applied to the part of the residuary estate in respect of which the election is exercised to obtain the capital value of the life interest of a surviving husband or a surviving male civil partner when the gross redemption yield on fifteen-year Government Stocks is at the rate shown

Age last birthday of husband or male civil partner	*Less than 2.5%*	*2.5% or between 2.5% and 3.5%*	*3.5% or between 3.5% and 4.5%*	*4.5% or between 4.5% and 5.5%*	*5.5% or between 5.5% and 6.5%*	*6.5% or between 6.5% and 7.5%*	*7.5% or between 7.5% and 8.5%*	*8.5% or between 8.5% and 9.5%*	*9.5% or between 9.5% and 10.5%*	*10.5% or between 10.5% and 11.5%*	*11.5% or more*
16	0.630	0.761	0.836	0.881	0.907	0.922	0.932	0.938	0.942	0.944	0.946
17	0.625	0.756	0.833	0.878	0.905	0.921	0.931	0.937	0.941	0.944	0.945
18	0.620	0.752	0.829	0.875	0.903	0.920	0.930	0.936	0.941	0.943	0.945
19	0.615	0.747	0.825	0.872	0.901	0.918	0.929	0.936	0.940	0.943	0.945
20	0.610	0.743	0.822	0.870	0.899	0.917	0.928	0.935	0.939	0.942	0.945
21	0.604	0.738	0.818	0.867	0.896	0.915	0.927	0.934	0.939	0.942	0.944
22	0.599	0.733	0.814	0.863	0.894	0.913	0.925	0.933	0.938	0.941	0.944
23	0.594	0.728	0.809	0.860	0.891	0.911	0.924	0.932	0.937	0.941	0.943
24	0.588	0.723	0.805	0.857	0.889	0.909	0.922	0.931	0.936	0.940	0.943
25	0.582	0.717	0.801	0.853	0.886	0.907	0.921	0.930	0.936	0.940	0.942
26	0.577	0.712	0.796	0.849	0.883	0.905	0.919	0.928	0.935	0.939	0.942
27	0.571	0.706	0.791	0.846	0.880	0.903	0.917	0.927	0.934	0.938	0.941

Age last birthday of husband or male civil partner	*Less than 2.5%*	*2.5% or between 2.5% and 3.5%*	*3.5% or between 3.5% and 4.5%*	*4.5% or between 4.5% and 5.5%*	*5.5% or between 5.5% and 6.5%*	*6.5% or between 6.5% and 7.5%*	*7.5% or between 7.5% and 8.5%*	*8.5% or between 8.5% and 9.5%*	*9.5% or between 9.5% and 10.5%*	*10.5% or between 10.5% and 11.5%*	*11.5% or more*
28	0.565	0.701	0.786	0.842	0.877	0.900	0.915	0.926	0.932	0.937	0.940
29	0.559	0.695	0.781	0.837	0.874	0.898	0.913	0.924	0.931	0.936	0.940
30	0.553	0.689	0.776	0.833	0.870	0.895	0.911	0.922	0.930	0.935	0.939
31	0.546	0.683	0.771	0.829	0.867	0.892	0.909	0.920	0.928	0.934	0.938
32	0.540	0.676	0.765	0.824	0.863	0.889	0.907	0.918	0.927	0.933	0.937
33	0.533	0.670	0.759	0.819	0.859	0.886	0.904	0.916	0.925	0.931	0.936
34	0.527	0.663	0.753	0.814	0.854	0.882	0.901	0.914	0.923	0.930	0.935
35	0.520	0.657	0.747	0.809	0.850	0.879	0.898	0.912	0.922	0.928	0.933
36	0.514	0.650	0.741	0.803	0.845	0.875	0.895	0.909	0.919	0.927	0.932
37	0.507	0.643	0.734	0.798	0.841	0.871	0.892	0.907	0.917	0.925	0.931
38	0.500	0.636	0.728	0.792	0.836	0.867	0.888	0.904	0.915	0.923	0.929
39	0.493	0.628	0.721	0.785	0.830	0.862	0.885	0.901	0.912	0.921	0.927
40	0.485	0.621	0.714	0.779	0.825	0.858	0.881	0.897	0.910	0.918	0.925
41	0.478	0.613	0.706	0.773	0.819	0.853	0.877	0.894	0.907	0.916	0.923
42	0.471	0.605	0.699	0.766	0.813	0.847	0.872	0.890	0.903	0.913	0.921
43	0.463	0.597	0.691	0.759	0.807	0.842	0.867	0.886	0.900	0.910	0.918
44	0.456	0.589	0.683	0.751	0.800	0.836	0.863	0.882	0.896	0.907	0.916

Age last birthday of husband or male civil partner	*Less than 2.5%*	*2.5% or between 2.5% and 3.5%*	*3.5% or between 3.5% and 4.5%*	*4.5% or between 4.5% and 5.5%*	*5.5% or between 5.5% and 6.5%*	*6.5% or between 6.5% and 7.5%*	*7.5% or between 7.5% and 8.5%*	*8.5% or between 8.5% and 9.5%*	*9.5% or between 9.5% and 10.5%*	*10.5% or between 10.5% and 11.5%*	*11.5% or more*
45	0.448	0.580	0.675	0.744	0.794	0.830	0.857	0.877	0.893	0.904	0.913
46	0.440	0.572	0.666	0.736	0.786	0.824	0.852	0.873	0.888	0.900	0.910
47	0.432	0.563	0.658	0.728	0.779	0.817	0.846	0.868	0.884	0.896	0.906
48	0.424	0.554	0.649	0.719	0.771	0.811	0.840	0.862	0.879	0.892	0.903
49	0.416	0.545	0.640	0.711	0.763	0.803	0.834	0.856	0.874	0.888	0.899
50	0.408	0.536	0.630	0.702	0.755	0.796	0.827	0.850	0.869	0.883	0.895
51	0.400	0.526	0.621	0.692	0.746	0.788	0.820	0.844	0.863	0.878	0.890
52	0.392	0.517	0.611	0.683	0.738	0.780	0.812	0.837	0.857	0.873	0.885
53	0.383	0.507	0.601	0.673	0.728	0.771	0.804	0.830	0.851	0.867	0.880
54	0.375	0.497	0.591	0.663	0.719	0.762	0.796	0.823	0.844	0.861	0.875
55	0.366	0.487	0.580	0.653	0.709	0.753	0.788	0.815	0.837	0.855	0.869
56	0.357	0.477	0.569	0.642	0.698	0.743	0.779	0.807	0.829	0.848	0.863
57	0.349	0.467	0.558	0.631	0.688	0.733	0.769	0.798	0.821	0.840	0.856
58	0.340	0.456	0.547	0.620	0.677	0.723	0.759	0.789	0.813	0.833	0.849
59	0.331	0.445	0.536	0.608	0.665	0.712	0.749	0.779	0.804	0.824	0.841
60	0.322	0.435	0.524	0.596	0.654	0.701	0.738	0.769	0.795	0.816	0.833
61	0.313	0.424	0.512	0.584	0.641	0.689	0.727	0.759	0.785	0.806	0.825

Age last birthday of husband or male civil partner	*Less than 2.5%*	*2.5% or between 2.5% and 3.5%*	*3.5% or between 3.5% and 4.5%*	*4.5% or between 4.5% and 5.5%*	*5.5% or between 5.5% and 6.5%*	*6.5% or between 6.5% and 7.5%*	*7.5% or between 7.5% and 8.5%*	*8.5% or between 8.5% and 9.5%*	*9.5% or between 9.5% and 10.5%*	*10.5% or between 10.5% and 11.5%*	*11.5% or more*
62	0.304	0.413	0.500	0.571	0.629	0.677	0.716	0.748	0.774	0.797	0.815
63	0.295	0.401	0.488	0.558	0.616	0.664	0.704	0.736	0.764	0.786	0.806
64	0.286	0.390	0.475	0.545	0.603	0.651	0.691	0.724	0.752	0.776	0.796
65	0.277	0.379	0.462	0.532	0.590	0.638	0.678	0.712	0.740	0.765	0.785
66	0.268	0.367	0.450	0.519	0.576	0.624	0.665	0.699	0.728	0.753	0.774
67	0.259	0.356	0.437	0.505	0.562	0.610	0.651	0.685	0.715	0.740	0.762
68	0.250	0.344	0.424	0.491	0.547	0.596	0.637	0.671	0.701	0.727	0.750
69	0.240	0.333	0.410	0.476	0.533	0.581	0.622	0.657	0.687	0.714	0.737
70	0.231	0.321	0.397	0.462	0.517	0.565	0.606	0.642	0.673	0.699	0.723
71	0.222	0.309	0.383	0.447	0.502	0.549	0.590	0.626	0.657	0.684	0.708
72	0.213	0.297	0.369	0.432	0.486	0.533	0.574	0.610	0.641	0.669	0.693
73	0.204	0.285	0.355	0.417	0.470	0.516	0.557	0.593	0.624	0.652	0.677
74	0.195	0.273	0.341	0.401	0.453	0.499	0.540	0.575	0.607	0.635	0.660
75	0.186	0.261	0.327	0.385	0.436	0.482	0.522	0.557	0.589	0.617	0.642
76	0.177	0.249	0.313	0.370	0.419	0.464	0.503	0.539	0.570	0.598	0.624
77	0.168	0.237	0.299	0.354	0.402	0.446	0.485	0.519	0.551	0.579	0.604
78	0.159	0.225	0.284	0.337	0.385	0.427	0.465	0.500	0.531	0.559	0.585

Age last birthday of husband or male civil partner	*Less than 2.5%*	*2.5% or between 2.5% and 3.5%*	*3.5% or between 3.5% and 4.5%*	*4.5% or between 4.5% and 5.5%*	*5.5% or between 5.5% and 6.5%*	*6.5% or between 6.5% and 7.5%*	*7.5% or between 7.5% and 8.5%*	*8.5% or between 8.5% and 9.5%*	*9.5% or between 9.5% and 10.5%*	*10.5% or between 10.5% and 11.5%*	*11.5% or more*
79	0.150	0.214	0.270	0.321	0.367	0.409	0.446	0.480	0.510	0.538	0.564
80	0.142	0.202	0.256	0.305	0.349	0.390	0.426	0.459	0.490	0.517	0.543
81	0.133	0.191	0.242	0.289	0.332	0.371	0.406	0.439	0.468	0.496	0.521
82	0.125	0.179	0.228	0.273	0.314	0.352	0.386	0.418	0.447	0.473	0.498
83	0.117	0.168	0.215	0.257	0.297	0.333	0.366	0.397	0.425	0.451	0.475
84	0.109	0.157	0.201	0.242	0.279	0.314	0.346	0.376	0.403	0.429	0.453
85	0.102	0.147	0.188	0.227	0.262	0.296	0.326	0.355	0.381	0.406	0.429
86	0.095	0.137	0.176	0.212	0.246	0.278	0.307	0.334	0.360	0.384	0.406
87	0.088	0.127	0.164	0.198	0.230	0.260	0.288	0.314	0.339	0.362	0.384
88	0.081	0.118	0.152	0.185	0.215	0.243	0.270	0.295	0.318	0.340	0.362
89	0.075	0.110	0.142	0.172	0.200	0.227	0.252	0.276	0.299	0.320	0.340
90	0.070	0.102	0.132	0.160	0.187	0.212	0.236	0.259	0.280	0.301	0.320
91	0.065	0.094	0.122	0.149	0.174	0.198	0.221	0.242	0.263	0.282	0.301
92	0.060	0.088	0.114	0.139	0.162	0.185	0.207	0.227	0.247	0.265	0.283
93	0.056	0.082	0.106	0.130	0.152	0.173	0.194	0.213	0.231	0.249	0.266
94	0.052	0.076	0.099	0.121	0.142	0.162	0.181	0.200	0.217	0.234	0.251
95	0.048	0.071	0.092	0.113	0.133	0.152	0.170	0.188	0.204	0.221	0.236

Age last birthday of husband or male civil partner	*Less than 2.5%*	*2.5% or between 2.5% and 3.5%*	*3.5% or between 3.5% and 4.5%*	*4.5% or between 4.5% and 5.5%*	*5.5% or between 5.5% and 6.5%*	*6.5% or between 6.5% and 7.5%*	*7.5% or between 7.5% and 8.5%*	*8.5% or between 8.5% and 9.5%*	*9.5% or between 9.5% and 10.5%*	*10.5% or between 10.5% and 11.5%*	*11.5% or more*
96	0.045	0.066	0.086	0.106	0.124	0.143	0.160	0.176	0.192	0.208	0.223
97	0.042	0.062	0.081	0.099	0.117	0.134	0.150	0.166	0.181	0.196	0.210
98	0.039	0.058	0.075	0.093	0.109	0.125	0.141	0.156	0.170	0.184	0.198
99	0.037	0.054	0.071	0.087	0.102	0.118	0.132	0.146	0.160	0.173	0.186
100 and over	0.034	0.050	0.066	0.081	0.096	0.110	0.124	0.137	0.150	0.163	0.175

[244.129E]

Table 2 Multiplier to be applied to the part of the residuary estate in respect of which the election is exercised to obtain the capital value of the life interest of a surviving wife or a surviving female civil partner when the gross redemption yield on fifteen-year Government Stocks is at the rate shown

Age last birthday of wife or female civil partner	*Less than 2.5%*	*2.5% or between 2.5% and 3.5%*	*3.5% or between 3.5% and 4.5%*	*4.5% or between 4.5% and 5.5%*	*5.5% or between 5.5% and 6.5%*	*6.5% or between 6.5% and 7.5%*	*7.5% or between 7.5% and 8.5%*	*8.5% or between 8.5% and 9.5%*	*9.5% or between 9.5% and 10.5%*	*10.5% or between 10.5% and 11.5%*	*11.5% or more*
16	0.650	0.779	0.851	0.892	0.916	0.929	0.937	0.942	0.944	0.946	0.947
17	0.645	0.775	0.848	0.890	0.914	0.928	0.936	0.941	0.944	0.946	0.947
18	0.640	0.771	0.845	0.888	0.912	0.927	0.936	0.941	0.944	0.946	0.947
19	0.636	0.767	0.842	0.885	0.911	0.926	0.935	0.940	0.944	0.946	0.947
20	0.631	0.762	0.838	0.883	0.909	0.925	0.934	0.940	0.943	0.945	0.947
21	0.626	0.758	0.835	0.880	0.907	0.923	0.933	0.939	0.943	0.945	0.947
22	0.621	0.753	0.831	0.878	0.905	0.922	0.932	0.938	0.942	0.945	0.946
23	0.615	0.749	0.828	0.875	0.903	0.921	0.931	0.938	0.942	0.944	0.946
24	0.610	0.744	0.824	0.872	0.901	0.919	0.930	0.937	0.941	0.944	0.946
25	0.605	0.739	0.820	0.869	0.899	0.917	0.929	0.936	0.941	0.944	0.946
26	0.599	0.734	0.816	0.866	0.897	0.916	0.928	0.935	0.940	0.943	0.945
27	0.594	0.729	0.812	0.863	0.894	0.914	0.926	0.934	0.939	0.943	0.945

Age last birthday of wife or female civil partner	Less than 2.5%	2.5% or between 2.5% and 3.5%	3.5% or between 3.5% and 4.5%	4.5% or between 4.5% and 5.5%	5.5% or between 5.5% and 6.5%	6.5% or between 6.5% and 7.5%	7.5% or between 7.5% and 8.5%	8.5% or between 8.5% and 9.5%	9.5% or between 9.5% and 10.5%	10.5% or between 10.5% and 11.5%	11.5% or more
28	0.588	0.724	0.807	0.859	0.892	0.912	0.925	0.933	0.939	0.942	0.945
29	0.582	0.719	0.803	0.856	0.889	0.910	0.924	0.932	0.938	0.942	0.944
30	0.577	0.713	0.798	0.852	0.886	0.908	0.922	0.931	0.937	0.941	0.944
31	0.571	0.708	0.794	0.848	0.883	0.906	0.920	0.930	0.936	0.940	0.943
32	0.565	0.702	0.789	0.844	0.880	0.903	0.919	0.929	0.935	0.940	0.943
33	0.559	0.696	0.784	0.840	0.877	0.901	0.917	0.927	0.934	0.939	0.942
34	0.552	0.690	0.778	0.836	0.874	0.898	0.915	0.926	0.933	0.938	0.941
35	0.546	0.684	0.773	0.832	0.870	0.896	0.913	0.924	0.932	0.937	0.941
36	0.540	0.678	0.767	0.827	0.866	0.893	0.910	0.922	0.930	0.936	0.940
37	0.533	0.671	0.762	0.822	0.862	0.890	0.908	0.920	0.929	0.935	0.939
38	0.527	0.664	0.756	0.817	0.858	0.886	0.905	0.918	0.927	0.934	0.938
39	0.520	0.658	0.750	0.812	0.854	0.883	0.902	0.916	0.926	0.932	0.937
40	0.513	0.651	0.743	0.807	0.849	0.879	0.900	0.914	0.924	0.931	0.936
41	0.506	0.644	0.737	0.801	0.845	0.875	0.896	0.911	0.922	0.929	0.935
42	0.499	0.636	0.730	0.795	0.840	0.871	0.893	0.909	0.920	0.927	0.933
43	0.492	0.629	0.723	0.789	0.835	0.867	0.890	0.906	0.917	0.926	0.932
44	0.485	0.621	0.716	0.783	0.829	0.862	0.886	0.903	0.915	0.924	0.930

Age last birthday of wife or female civil partner	*Less than 2.5%*	*2.5% or between 2.5% and 3.5%*	*3.5% or between 3.5% and 4.5%*	*4.5% or between 4.5% and 5.5%*	*5.5% or between 5.5% and 6.5%*	*6.5% or between 6.5% and 7.5%*	*7.5% or between 7.5% and 8.5%*	*8.5% or between 8.5% and 9.5%*	*9.5% or between 9.5% and 10.5%*	*10.5% or between 10.5% and 11.5%*	*11.5% or more*
45	0.477	0.613	0.708	0.776	0.823	0.858	0.882	0.899	0.912	0.921	0.928
46	0.470	0.605	0.701	0.769	0.817	0.852	0.878	0.896	0.909	0.919	0.926
47	0.462	0.597	0.693	0.762	0.811	0.847	0.873	0.892	0.906	0.916	0.924
48	0.454	0.589	0.685	0.754	0.805	0.841	0.868	0.888	0.902	0.913	0.922
49	0.447	0.580	0.676	0.747	0.798	0.835	0.863	0.883	0.899	0.910	0.919
50	0.439	0.572	0.668	0.739	0.791	0.829	0.858	0.879	0.895	0.907	0.916
51	0.431	0.563	0.659	0.730	0.783	0.823	0.852	0.874	0.891	0.903	0.913
52	0.422	0.553	0.650	0.722	0.775	0.816	0.846	0.868	0.886	0.899	0.910
53	0.414	0.544	0.640	0.713	0.767	0.808	0.839	0.863	0.881	0.895	0.906
54	0.406	0.534	0.631	0.703	0.758	0.800	0.832	0.857	0.876	0.890	0.902
55	0.397	0.525	0.620	0.694	0.749	0.792	0.825	0.850	0.870	0.885	0.897
56	0.388	0.515	0.610	0.684	0.740	0.784	0.817	0.843	0.864	0.880	0.893
57	0.379	0.504	0.600	0.673	0.730	0.775	0.809	0.836	0.857	0.874	0.888
58	0.371	0.494	0.589	0.663	0.720	0.765	0.800	0.828	0.850	0.868	0.882
59	0.361	0.483	0.577	0.652	0.709	0.755	0.791	0.820	0.843	0.861	0.876
60	0.352	0.472	0.566	0.640	0.698	0.745	0.782	0.811	0.835	0.854	0.869
61	0.343	0.461	0.554	0.628	0.687	0.734	0.771	0.802	0.826	0.846	0.862

Age last birthday of wife or female civil partner	*Less than 2.5%*	*2.5% or between 2.5% and 3.5%*	*3.5% or between 3.5% and 4.5%*	*4.5% or between 4.5% and 5.5%*	*5.5% or between 5.5% and 6.5%*	*6.5% or between 6.5% and 7.5%*	*7.5% or between 7.5% and 8.5%*	*8.5% or between 8.5% and 9.5%*	*9.5% or between 9.5% and 10.5%*	*10.5% or between 10.5% and 11.5%*	*11.5% or more*
62	0.334	0.450	0.542	0.616	0.675	0.722	0.761	0.792	0.817	0.837	0.854
63	0.324	0.438	0.529	0.603	0.662	0.710	0.749	0.781	0.807	0.828	0.846
64	0.315	0.427	0.517	0.590	0.649	0.698	0.737	0.770	0.797	0.819	0.837
65	0.305	0.415	0.504	0.577	0.636	0.685	0.725	0.758	0.786	0.808	0.828
66	0.295	0.403	0.490	0.563	0.622	0.671	0.712	0.746	0.774	0.797	0.817
67	0.286	0.391	0.477	0.549	0.608	0.657	0.698	0.732	0.761	0.786	0.806
68	0.276	0.378	0.463	0.534	0.593	0.642	0.684	0.719	0.748	0.773	0.795
69	0.266	0.366	0.449	0.519	0.578	0.627	0.669	0.704	0.734	0.760	0.782
70	0.256	0.353	0.435	0.504	0.562	0.611	0.653	0.689	0.720	0.746	0.769
71	0.246	0.340	0.420	0.488	0.545	0.595	0.637	0.673	0.704	0.731	0.754
72	0.236	0.327	0.405	0.472	0.529	0.578	0.620	0.656	0.688	0.715	0.739
73	0.226	0.314	0.390	0.455	0.512	0.560	0.602	0.639	0.671	0.698	0.723
74	0.216	0.301	0.375	0.439	0.494	0.542	0.584	0.621	0.653	0.681	0.706
75	0.206	0.288	0.359	0.422	0.476	0.524	0.565	0.602	0.634	0.662	0.688
76	0.196	0.275	0.344	0.404	0.457	0.504	0.546	0.582	0.614	0.643	0.669
77	0.186	0.262	0.328	0.387	0.439	0.485	0.526	0.562	0.594	0.623	0.649
78	0.176	0.248	0.312	0.369	0.420	0.465	0.505	0.541	0.573	0.602	0.628

Age last birthday of wife or female civil partner	*Less than 2.5%*	*2.5% or between 2.5% and 3.5%*	*3.5% or between 3.5% and 4.5%*	*4.5% or between 4.5% and 5.5%*	*5.5% or between 5.5% and 6.5%*	*6.5% or between 6.5% and 7.5%*	*7.5% or between 7.5% and 8.5%*	*8.5% or between 8.5% and 9.5%*	*9.5% or between 9.5% and 10.5%*	*10.5% or between 10.5% and 11.5%*	*11.5% or more*
79	0.166	0.235	0.296	0.351	0.400	0.444	0.484	0.519	0.551	0.580	0.606
80	0.156	0.222	0.281	0.334	0.381	0.424	0.462	0.497	0.529	0.557	0.583
81	0.147	0.209	0.265	0.316	0.361	0.403	0.440	0.474	0.506	0.534	0.560
82	0.138	0.197	0.250	0.298	0.342	0.382	0.418	0.451	0.482	0.510	0.536
83	0.129	0.184	0.234	0.280	0.322	0.361	0.396	0.428	0.458	0.485	0.511
84	0.120	0.172	0.219	0.263	0.303	0.340	0.374	0.405	0.434	0.461	0.486
85	0.111	0.160	0.205	0.246	0.284	0.320	0.352	0.382	0.410	0.436	0.460
86	0.103	0.149	0.191	0.230	0.266	0.299	0.330	0.359	0.386	0.411	0.435
87	0.095	0.138	0.177	0.214	0.248	0.280	0.309	0.337	0.363	0.387	0.410
88	0.088	0.127	0.164	0.198	0.230	0.261	0.289	0.315	0.340	0.363	0.385
89	0.081	0.118	0.152	0.184	0.214	0.242	0.269	0.294	0.318	0.340	0.361
90	0.075	0.109	0.140	0.170	0.199	0.225	0.251	0.274	0.297	0.318	0.338
91	0.069	0.100	0.130	0.158	0.184	0.210	0.233	0.256	0.277	0.297	0.317
92	0.063	0.093	0.120	0.146	0.171	0.195	0.217	0.238	0.259	0.278	0.297
93	0.059	0.086	0.111	0.136	0.159	0.181	0.202	0.222	0.242	0.260	0.278
94	0.054	0.079	0.103	0.126	0.148	0.169	0.189	0.207	0.226	0.243	0.260
95	0.050	0.073	0.096	0.117	0.137	0.157	0.176	0.194	0.211	0.228	0.244

Age last birthday of wife or female civil partner	*Less than 2.5%*	*2.5% or between 2.5% and 3.5%*	*3.5% or between 3.5% and 4.5%*	*4.5% or between 4.5% and 5.5%*	*5.5% or between 5.5% and 6.5%*	*6.5% or between 6.5% and 7.5%*	*7.5% or between 7.5% and 8.5%*	*8.5% or between 8.5% and 9.5%*	*9.5% or between 9.5% and 10.5%*	*10.5% or between 10.5% and 11.5%*	*11.5% or more*
96	0.046	0.068	0.089	0.109	0.128	0.146	0.164	0.181	0.197	0.213	0.228
97	0.043	0.063	0.083	0.101	0.119	0.137	0.153	0.169	0.185	0.200	0.214
98	0.040	0.059	0.077	0.094	0.111	0.127	0.143	0.158	0.173	0.187	0.201
99	0.037	0.055	0.071	0.088	0.104	0.119	0.134	0.148	0.162	0.175	0.188
100 and over	0.034	0.051	0.066	0.082	0.097	0.111	0.125	0.138	0.152	0.164	0.177

SECTION 2

Succession rights and adoption, legitimation, illegitimacy and change of gender

[245.1]

Note. This Section reproduces in chronological order all the statutory provisions which have governed and now govern the property rights of adopted, legitimated, and illegitimate children under dispositions of property and the rules of intestate succession. They also of course govern the rights of such children's parents and other relatives. We have omitted the Adoption of Children Act 1949, the relevant provisions of which were replaced retrospectively from the same commencement date by the Adoption Act 1950, and the provisions of the Children Act 1975 concerning the effects of legitimation and adoption which were replaced, again with retrospective effect from the same commencement date, by the Legitimacy Act 1976 (LA 1976) and the Adoption Act 1976 (AA 1976).

The main effect of these statutes has been to reverse the common law presumptions as to the meaning of words descriptive of family relationships in dispositions of property, such as wills or settlements (for these presumptions see Vol 1, paras **[72.1]** and **[75.1]** ff) and to enlarge the categories of issue who can take under the intestacy rules. With one exception, each change in the law has only applied to dispositions made after the change in the law has taken effect, and so the repealed statutes included here continue to be relevant to dispositions made when they were in force. The exception is to be found in the Human Fertilisation and Embryology Act 1990 (HFEA 1990), s 29(3) at para **[245.87]** below.

At common law references to children were presumed to be references to legitimate children, i e children born in lawful wedlock, and references to other relationships were likewise confined to persons who were legitimate and who claimed descent or kinship exclusively through persons who were legitimate. Not only were illegitimate persons excluded but also persons who were adopted or legitimated. Statute has made progressive inroads on the austerity of the common law rule. As regards adopted and legitimated children this process culminated in the Children Act 1975 which provided that in relation to instruments made on or after 1 January 1976 (including the wills whenever made of persons dying on or after that date) references to children (or persons related in any other way) were to be deemed in the absence of a contrary intention to include references to adopted and legitimated children (or persons who were adopted or legitimated and claimed descent or kinship through adopted or legitimated persons) and to be deemed to do so whether the adoption or legitimation occurred before or after the date of the instrument or death. The relevant provisions of the Children Act 1975 are not reproduced in this section as they were replaced (with effect from the same commencement date) by the identical provisions of the LA 1976 and the AA 1976.

As regards illegitimate persons the process of development culminated in the comprehensive provisions contained in the Family Law Reform Act 1987 (FLRA 1987) which provides that in relation to instruments made on or after the commencement of the Act (which in the case of wills means wills actually made and not merely confirmed by codicil on or after that time) references to children (or other relatives) are to be deemed to include illegitimate children (or persons claiming kinship through illegitimate persons). This Act (which replaced the more limited provisions of the Family Law Reform Act 1969 (FLRA 1969) was brought into force on 4 April 1988. (For the background to the Act see the Law Commission's Second Report on Illegitimacy, October 1986 (Law Com No 157, Cmnd 9913).)

Mention should also be made of the HFEA 1990 which made special provision in relation to persons born as a result of artificial insemination, in vitro fertilisation or other artificial means and for succession rights to be conferred on such persons. This Act was amended by the Human Fertilisation and Embryology (Deceased Fathers) Act 2003 and has recently been amended by the Human Fertilisation and Embryology Act 2008 which replaces the succession provisions in the earlier legislation in relation to children born as a result of treatment received on or after 6 April 2009.

In relation to older instruments, however, the former rules of construction which have now been superseded by statute may still be relevant. This section therefore reproduces all the relevant statutory provisions.

For an account of the law governing the property rights of adopted, legitimated and illegimate children see Vol 1, paras **[72.1]** ff and **[75.1]** ff.

Mention should finally be made of the Gender Recognition Act 2004 (paras **[245.102]** ff below) which was brought into force on 4 April 2005 and the Civil Partnership Act 2004 (paras **[244.130]** ff above) which was brought into force on 5 December 2005. The former Act makes provision for changes of gender to be legally recognised. The latter Act gives statutory recognition to same-sex relationships by permitting two persons of the same sex to register their partnership as a civil partnership and by conferring on that relationship a status similar to that of marriage. Both Acts affect succession rights: see Notes at paras **[245.102]** below and **[244.130]** above.

LEGITIMACY ACT 1976

(1976 c 31)

[22 July 1976]

[245.43]

Note. This Act currently governs the property rights of legitimated children. In effect, the Act protects the rights of legitimated children by treating them as if they had been born legitimate. The rules of construction reflecting this policy are contained in s 5 (para **[245.48]**) and apply to instruments made on or after 1 January 1976, replacing the corresponding rules introduced by the Children Act 1975 from the same commencement date. The new rules apply to a will made before 1 January 1976 if the testator dies on or after that date and apply whether the legitimation takes place before or after the death. The Act has been amended by AA 1976 and FLRA 1987 and more recently by HFEA 2008 to cater for the legitimation of the children of same-sex couples who subsequently form a civil partnership. The relevant provisions of the Act as so amended are printed below.

[245.45A]

[2A Legitimation by subsequent civil partnership of parents. Subject to the following provisions of this Act, where—

- (a) a person ('the child') has a parent ('the female parent') by virtue of section 43 of the Human Fertilisation and Embryology Act 2008 (treatment provided to woman who agrees that second woman to be parent),
- (b) at the time of the child's birth, the female parent and the child's mother are not civil partners of each other,
- (c) the female parent and the child's mother subsequently enter into a civil partnership, and
- (d) the female parent is at the date of the formation of the civil partnership domiciled in England and Wales, the civil partnership shall render the child, if living, legitimate from the date of the formation of the civil partnership.][1]

1 Section 2A inserted with effect from 6 April 2009 for certain purposes and from 1 September 2009 for remaining purposes by the Human Fertilisation and Embryology Act 2008, s 56, Sch 6, para 16 and the Human Fertilisation and Embryology Act 2008 (Commencement No 1 and Transitional Provisions) Order 2009, SI 2009/479, art 6(1)(e), (f), (2).

[245.46]

3. Legitimation by extraneous law. [(1)][1] Subject to the following provisions of this Act, where the parents of an illegitimate person marry one another and the father of the illegitimate person is not at the time of the marriage domiciled in England and Wales but is domiciled in a country by the law of which the illegitimate person became legitimated by virtue of such subsequent marriage, that person, if living, shall in England and Wales be recognised as having been so legitimated from the date of the marriage notwithstanding that, at the time of his birth, his father was domiciled in a country the law of which did not permit legitimation by subsequent marriage.

[(2) Subject to the following provisions of this Act, where—

(a) a person ('the child') has a parent ('the female parent') by virtue of section 43 of the Human Fertilisation and Embryology Act 2008 (treatment provided to woman who agrees that second woman to be parent),

(b) at the time of the child's birth, the female parent and the child's mother are not civil partners of each other,

(c) the female parent and the child's mother subsequently enter into a civil partnership, and

(d) the female parent is not at the time of the formation of the civil partnership domiciled in England and Wales but is domiciled in a country by the law of which the child became legitimated by virtue of the civil partnership,

the child, if living, shall in England and Wales be recognised as having been so legitimated from the date of the formation of the civil partnership notwithstanding that, at the time of the child's birth, the female parent was domiciled in a country the law of which did not permit legitimation by subsequent civil partnership.][1]

1 The existing section was renumbered sub-s (1) and sub-s (2) was added with effect from 6 April 2009 for certain purposes and from 1 September 2009 for remaining purposes by the Human Fertilisation and Embryology Act 2008, s 56, Sch 6, para 17 and the Human Fertilisation and Embryology Act 2008 (Commencement No 1 and Transitional Provisions) Order 2009, SI 2009/479, art 6(1)(e), (f), (2).

[245.51]

10. Interpretation.— (1) In this Act, except where the context otherwise requires—

'disposition' includes the conferring of a power of appointment and any other disposition of an interest in or right over property;

'existing', in relation to an instrument, means one made before 1st January 1976;

'legitimated person' means a person legitimated or recognised as legitimated—

(a) under section 2[, 2A][1] or 3 above;

(b) under section 1 or 8 of the Legitimacy Act 1926; or

(c) except in section 8, by legitimation (whether or not by virtue of the subsequent marriage of his parents) recognised by the law of England and Wales and effected under the law of any other country;

and cognate expressions shall be construed accordingly;

'power of appointment' includes any discretionary power to transfer a beneficial interest in property without the furnishing of valuable consideration;

'void marriage' means a marriage, not being voidable only, in respect of which the High Court has or had jurisdiction to grant a decree of nullity, or would have or would have had such jurisdiction if the parties were domiciled in England and Wales.

(2) For the purposes of this Act 'legitimated person' includes, where the context admits, a person legitimated, or recognised as legitimated, before the passing of the Children Act 1975.

(3) For the purpose of this Act, except where the context otherwise requires—

(a) the death of the testator is the date at which a will or codicil is to be regarded as made;

(b) an oral disposition of property shall be deemed to be contained in an instrument made when the disposition was made.

(4) It is hereby declared that references in this Act to dispositions of property include references to a disposition by the creation of an entailed interest.

(5) Except in so far as the context otherwise requires, any reference in this Act to an enactment shall be construed as a reference to that enactment as amended by or under any other enactment, including this Act.

1 Reference to the new s 2A in para (a) of the definition of 'legitimated person' in sub-s (1) was inserted with effect from 6 April 2009 for certain purposes and from 1 September 2009 for remaining purposes by the Human Fertilisation and Embryology Act 2008, s 56, Sch 6, para 17 and the Human Fertilisation and Embryology Act 2008 (Commencement No 1 and Transitional Provisions) Order 2009, SI 2009/479, art 6(1)(e), (f), (2).

FAMILY LAW REFORM ACT 1987

(1987 c 42)

[15 May 1987]

[245.69]

Note. This Act implements a number of Law Commission recommendations for the removal of the legal disadvantages attaching to illegitimacy. The general principle established by s 1 is embodied in the rule of construction set out in sub-s (1) thereof that both in the 1987 Act itself and in all enactments passed and instruments made after the coming into force of the section, references to any relationship between two persons shall, in the absence of a contrary intention, be construed without regard to whether or not the parents of either of them have or had been married to each other at any time. Subsections (2) and (3) exclude the primary rule of construction in relation to any person who is treated as legitimate by statute or who is legitimated or adopted or is otherwise treated in law as legitimate. This qualification of the primary rule of construction preserves the rights of these categories of person, who are otherwise catered for under the general law or under existing legislation (ie the LA 1976 and the AA 1976). Section 1 was brought into force on 4 April 1988 by the Family Law Reform Act 1987 (Commencement No 1) Order 1988 (SI 1988/425).

Part II of the 1987 Act amended, inter alia, the Guardianship of Minors Act 1971, ss 3 and 4; as from 1 April 1989 (SI 1989/382). These provisions were themselves replaced by the ChA 1989, ss 5 and 6, as from 14 October 1991 (ss 5(1) to (10), (13) and 6) and 1 February 1992 (s 5(11), (12)) (SI 1991/828, as amended by SI 1991/1990), which are the provisions currently in force (see paras **[244.116]** ff above).

Part III of the 1987 Act is concerned with property rights. Section 18 (which replaced the more limited provisions of the Family Law Reform Act 1969, s 14) expressly extends the general principle established by s 1 to the rules of intestate succession as they apply to the estates of persons dying after the coming into force of that section. Section 18(2) provides that for the purposes of the intestacy rules an illegitimate person (not being a person treated as legitimate or a legitimated or adopted person) is to be presumed not to have been survived by his father or any person related to him only through his father, unless the contrary is shown. (Compare the more limited presumption contained in s 14(4) of the 1969 Act: para **[245.38]** above). Section 19 (which replaced s 15 of the 1969 Act: para **[245.39]** above) makes more detailed provision for the application of the general principle to inter vivos dispositions and wills and codicils made on or after the date on which that section comes into force. It should be noted that s 19(7) (like s 15(8) of the 1969 Act) provides that a will or codicil made before that date is not to be treated as made on or after that date by reason only that it is confirmed by a codicil made on or after that date. However, the 1987 Act differs from the 1969 Act in the following respects:—

(i) Unlike s 15 of the 1969 Act, it applies to words creating an entailed interest unless a contrary intention appears (see s 19(2) of the 1987 Act, and compare s 15(2) of the 1969 Act). However, like s 15 of the 1969 Act, it does not apply to property limited to devolve with a dignity or title of honour (s 19(4) of the 1987 Act, s 15(5) of the 1969 Act).

(ii) Section 15(1) of the 1969 Act would not have applied if the only illegitimacy causing difficulty was that of the person from whom the relationship had to be traced, e g 'the uncles of R', where R, but not his father, mother or uncles, was illegitimate. The 1987 Act (see in particular s 1(1)) applies to such a case. However, in this type of case the common law presumption that words of relationship were confined to legitimate relations would usually have been displaced because the gift could only have any meaning if the presumption were to be displaced.

(iii) Section 15 of the 1969 Act only applied to references to a relationship where it had the effect of benefiting or rendering capable of benefit someone who was either himself illegitimate or claimed to be related through a person who was illegitimate (s 15(2)); there is no such restriction in the 1987 Act. Thus the descendants of a named monarch for the purposes of a royal lives perpetuity period, in a post-3 April 1988 disposition, will include illegitimate descendants if no contrary intention is shown. To avoid the risk of uncertainty in such a perpetuity period the 1987 Act should be excluded in relation to it. Another example to which the 1987 Act applies but s 15 of the 1969 Act would not have so applied is 'issue' in the precondition of a conditional gift such as 'If X shall predecease me leaving issue', where the gift does not confer any benefit on the issue of X (see e g Form B19.11 at para **[219.24]**).

(iv) Unlike s 15 of the 1969 Act, the general principle embodied in s 1 of the 1987 Act applies in relation to the construction of statutes and statutory instruments passed or made after the coming into force of the section. (See also the corresponding provision added to the Interpretion Act 1978, Sch 1.) Previously specific provision was often made in statutes to cater for illegitimate children. This will no longer be necessary.

Section 20 repeals (without replacing) s 17 of the 1969 Act (para **[245.41]** above) which enabled personal representatives and trustees to distribute property without having ascertained whether or not illegitimate persons were entitled to the property or a share of it under ss 14, 15 or 16 of the 1969 Act (paras **[245.38]**–**[245.40]** above). It should be noted the repeal takes effect in relation to all distributions made after the date on which s 20 of the 1987 Act comes into force, including distributions out of the estates of persons dying before that date and of trust property settled before that date. In all such cases personal representatives and trustees will need to protect themselves by giving notice by advertisement pursuant to the Trustee Act 1925 (TA 1925), s 27 (para **[246.25]** below); see *Re Aldhous* [1955] 2 All ER 80, [1955] 1 WLR 459. The provisions of Pt III of the 1987 Act were bought into force on 4 April 1988 at the same time as s 1 (SI 1988/425).

The 1987 Act also effects certain minor and consequential amendments to other statutory provisions, in particular the TA 1925, s 33 and the AEA 1925, s 50: see paras **[246.31]** below and **[244.67]** above.

The 1987 Act has been amended by the ACA 2002 and more recently by the HFEA 2008 so as to cater for the position of a child born as a result of in vitro fertilisation or other procedure regulated by the 1990 Act where the mother agrees that another woman who is not her civil partner shall be treated as the other parent. The relevant provisions of the 1987 Act as amended are printed below.

PART I
GENERAL PRINCIPLE

[245.70]
1. General principle.— (1) In this Act and enactments passed and instruments made after the coming into force of this section, references (however expressed) to any relationship between two persons shall, unless the contrary intention appears, be construed without regard to whether or not the father and mother of either of them, or the father and mother of any person through whom the relationship is deduced, have or had been married to each other at any time.
(2) In this Act and enactments passed after the coming into force of this section, unless the contrary intention appears—

- (a) references to a person whose father and mother were married to each other at the time of his birth include; and
- (b) references to a person whose father and mother were not married to each other at the time of his birth do not include,

references to any person to whom subsection (3) below applies, and cognate references shall be construed accordingly.
(3) This subsection applies to any person who—

- (a) is treated as legitimate by virtue of section 1 of the Legitimacy Act 1976;
- (b) is a legitimated person within the meaning of section 10 of that Act;
- [(ba) has a parent by virtue of section 42 of the Human Fertilisation and Embryology Act 2008 (which relates to treatment provided to a woman who is at the time of treatment a party to a civil partnership or, in certain circumstances, a void civil partnership);
- (bb) has a parent by virtue of section 43 of that Act (which relates to treatment provided to woman who agrees that second woman to be parent) who—
  - (i) is the civil partner of the child's mother at the time of the child's birth, or
  - (ii) was the civil partner of the child's mother at any time during the period beginning with the time mentioned in section 43(b) of that Act and ending with the child's birth;][1]
- [(c) is an adopted child within the meaning of the Adoption and Children Act 2002][2]; or
- (d) is otherwise treated in law as legitimate.

(4) For the purpose of construing references falling within subsection (2) above, the time of a person's birth shall be taken to include any time during the period beginning with—

- (a) the insemination resulting in his birth; or
- (b) where there was no such insemination, his conception,

and (in either case) ending with his birth.
[(5) A child whose parents are parties to a void civil partnership shall, subject to subsection (6), be treated as falling within subsection (3)(bb) if at the time when the parties registered as civil partners of each other both or either of the parties reasonably believed that the civil partnership was valid.

(6) Subsection (5) applies only where the woman who is a parent by virtue of section 43 was domiciled in England and Wales at the time of the birth or, if she died before the birth, was so domiciled immediately before her death.
(7) Subsection (5) applies even though the belief that the civil partnership was valid was due to a mistake as to law.
(8) It shall be presumed for the purposes of subsection (5), unless the contrary is shown, that one of the parties to a void civil partnership reasonably believed at the time of the formation of the civil partnership that the civil partnership was valid.][3]

1 Paragraphs (ba) and (bb) of sub-s (3) were inserted with effect from 6 April 2009 by the Human Fertilisation and Embryology Act 2008, s 56, Sch 6, para 24(1), (2) and the Human Fertilisation and Embryology Act 2008 (Commencement No 1 and Transitional Provisions) Order 2009, SI 2009/479, art 6(1)(d), (f).
2 Paragraph (c) of sub-s (3) substituted with effect from 30 December 2005: ACA 2002, s 139(1), Sch 3, paras 50 and 51 and Adoption and Children Act 2002 (Commencement No 9) Order 2005, SI 2005/2213, art 2(o).
3 Subsections (5) to (8) were inserted with effect from 6 April 2009 by the Human Fertilisation and Embryology Act 2008, s 56, Sch 6, para 24(1), (3) and the Human Fertilisation and Embryology Act 2008 (Commencement No 1 and Transitional Provisions) Order 2009, SI 2009/479, art 6(1)(d), (f).

PART III
PROPERTY RIGHTS

[245.71]
18. Succession on intestacy.— (1) In Part IV of the Administration of Estates Act 1925 (which deals with the distribution of the estate of an intestate), references (however expressed) to any relationship between two persons shall be construed in accordance with section 1 above.
(2) For the purposes of subsection (1) above and that Part of that Act, a person whose father and mother were not married to each other at the time of his birth shall be presumed not to have been survived by his father, or by any person related to him only through his father, unless the contrary is shown.
[(2A) In the case of a person who has a parent by virtue of section 43 of the Human Fertilisation and Embryology Act 2008 (treatment provided to woman who agrees that second woman to be parent), the second and third references in subsection (2) to the person's father are to be read as references to the woman who is a parent of the person by virtue of that section.][1]
(3) In [section 50(1) of the Administration of Estates Act 1925][2] (which relates to the construction of documents), the reference to Part IV of that Act, or to the foregoing provisions of that Part, shall in relation to an instrument inter vivos made, or a will or codicil coming into operation, after the coming into force of this section (but not in relation to instruments inter vivos made or wills or codicils coming into operation earlier) be construed as including references to this section.
(4) This section does not affect any rights under the intestacy of a person dying before the coming into force of this section.

1 Subsection (2A) inserted with effect from 6 April 2009 by the Human Fertilisation and Embryology Act 2008, s 56, Sch 6, para 25(1), (2) and the Human Fertilisation and Embryology Act 2008 (Commencement No 1 and Transitional Provisions) Order 2009, SI 2009/479, art 6(1)(d), (f).

2 Words in brackets in sub-s (3) substituted for 'section 50(1) of that Act' with effect from 6 April 2009 by the Human Fertilisation and Embryology Act 2008, s 56, Sch 6, para 25(1), (3) and the Human Fertilisation and Embryology Act 2008 (Commencement No 1 and Transitional Provisions) Order 2009, SI 2009/479, art 6(1)(d), (f).

HUMAN FERTILISATION AND EMBRYOLOGY ACT 1990

(1990 c 37)

[1 November 1990]

[245.82]

Note. This Act introduces a new system of control for the treatment of infertility and for research involving human embryos. It also contains provisions identifying the persons who are to be treated in law as the father (if any) and mother of persons coming into existence as a consequence of artificial insemination or other techniques to deal with infertility that are regulated by the Act (ss 27 and 28). These provisions will affect the construction of wills and other dispositions (even if made before the commencement of the relevant provision), and the operation of the intestacy rules (s 29(3)). There is also provision (s 30) for the courts to make orders, inter alia applying the adoption legislation, in cases of surrogate motherhood. Sections 1, 2, 27 to 29 came into force on 1 August 1991 (SI 1991/1400), and the ancillary provisions in ss 47 to 49 came into force on or before that date. Section 30 was brought into force on dates in 1994 (SI 1994/1776). The Act was slightly amended by the Adoption and Children Act 2002 and was further amended with effect from 1 December 2003 by the Human Fertilisation and Embryology (Deceased Fathers) Act 2003. The Act has recently been more substantially amended by the Human Fertilisation and Embryology Act 2008 and the provisions of s 29 (which relate to status and succession) have been largely superseded as regards children born as a result of treatment received on or after 6 April 2009 by the provisions of Part 2 of the 2008 Act. The provisions of ss 54 and 55 of the 2008 (relating to parental orders) have not yet been activated and s 30 of the 1990 Act remains in force. The relevant sections of the 1990 Act are printed as amended below.

PRINCIPAL TERMS USED

[245.83]

1. Meaning of 'embryo', 'gamete' and associated expressions.— [(1) In this Act, except where otherwise stated—

- (a) embryo means a live human embryo where fertilisation is complete, and
- (b) references to an embryo include an egg in the process of fertilisation,

and, for this purpose, fertilisation is not complete until the appearance of a two cell zygote.][1]

[(1) In this Act (except in section 4A[2] or in the term 'human admixed embryo')—

- (a) embryo means a live human embryo and does not include a human admixed embryo (as defined by section 4A(6)), and
- (b) references to an embryo include an egg that is in the process of fertilisation or is undergoing any other process capable of resulting in an embryo.][3]

(2)This Act, so far as it governs bringing about the creation of an embryo, applies only to bringing about the creation of an embryo outside the human body; and in this Act—

[(a) references to embryos the creation of which was brought about *in vitro* (in their application to those where fertilisation is complete) are to those where fertilisation began outside the human body whether or not it was completed there, and][4]

[(a) references to embryos the creation of which was brought about in vitro (in their application to those where fertilisation or any other process by which an embryo is created is complete) are to those where fertilisation or any other process by which the embryo was created began outside the human body whether or not it was completed there, and][5]

(b) references to embryos taken from a woman do not include embryos whose creation was brought about *in vitro*.

(3) This Act, so far as it governs the keeping or use of an embryo, applies only to keeping or using an embryo outside the human body.

[(4) References in this Act to gametes, eggs or sperm, except where otherwise stated, are to live human gametes, eggs or sperm but references below in this Act to gametes or eggs do not include eggs in the process of fertilisation.][6]

[(4) In this Act (except in section 4A)—

(a) references to eggs are to live human eggs, including cells of the female germ line at any stage of maturity, but (except in subsection (1)(b)) not including eggs that are in the process of fertilisation or are undergoing any other process capable of resulting in an embryo,

(b) references to sperm are to live human sperm, including cells of the male germ line at any stage of maturity, and

(c) references to gametes are to be read accordingly.][7]

[(5) For the purposes of this Act, sperm is to be treated as partner-donated if the donor of the sperm and the recipient of the sperm declare that they have an intimate physical relationship.][8]

[(6) If it appears to the Secretary of State necessary or desirable to do so in the light of developments in science or medicine, regulations may provide that in this Act (except in section 4A) 'embryo', 'eggs', 'sperm' or 'gametes' includes things specified in the regulations which would not otherwise fall within the definition.

(7) Regulations made by virtue of subsection (6) may not provide for anything containing any nuclear or mitochondrial DNA that is not human to be treated as an embryo or as eggs, sperm or gametes.][9]

1 Subsection (1) is to be replaced by the Human Fertilisation and Embryology Act 2008, s 1(1), (2) with the subsection next following from a date to be appointed. No date has yet been appointed.

2 Section 4A, which is to be inserted in the 1990 Act by s 4 of the 2008 Act from a date which has not yet been appointed, contains certain prohibitions on the use of genetic material not of human origin.

3 See note 1 above.

4 Paragraph (a) of sub-s (2) is to be replaced by the Human Fertilisation and Embryology Act 2008, s 1(1), (3) with the paragraph next following from a date to be appointed. No date has yet been appointed.

5 See note 4 above.

6 Subsection (4) is to be replaced by the Human Fertilisation and Embryology Act 2008, s 1(1), (4) with the subsection next following from a date to be appointed. No date has yet been appointed.
7 See note 6 above.
8 Subsection (5) is to be inserted with effect from 5 July 2007 by regs 1(2), 3 and 4 of the Human Fertilisation and Embryology (Quality and Safety) Regulations 2007, SI 2007/1522, which were made under powers conferred by the European Communities Act 1972, s 2(2) to give effect to Directive 2004/23/EC of the European Parliament and of the Council of 31 March 2004 and Commission Directives 2006/17/EC and 2006/86/EC.
9 Subsections (6) and (7) are to be replaced by the Human Fertilisation and Embryology Act 2008, s 1(1), (5) from a date to be appointed. No date has yet been appointed. The term 'nuclear DNA' is defined by s 2 of the Act and the term 'mitochondrial DNA' is defined by s 35A of the Human Fertilisation and Embryology Act 1990 as inserted by s 26 of the 2008 Act.

STATUS

[245.85]
27. Meaning of 'mother'[1].— (1) The woman who is carrying or has carried a child as a result of the placing in her of an embryo or of sperm and eggs, and no other woman, is to be treated as the mother of the child.
(2) Subsection (1) above does not apply to any child to the extent that the child is treated by virtue of adoption as not being the [woman's child][2].
(3) Subsection (1) above applies whether the woman was in the United Kingdom or elsewhere at the time of the placing in her of the embryo or the sperm and eggs.

1 This section has been superseded in so far as it relates to children carried by women as a result of the placing in them of embryos or of sperm and eggs on or after 6 April 2009, the date on which ss 33–38 of HFEA 2008 came into force: see s 57(2) and Human Fertilisation and Embryology Act 2008 (Commencement No 1 and Transitional Provisions) Order 2009, SI 2009/479, art 6(1)(b). But the section continues to apply to children carried by women as a result of these procedures prior to that date.
2 Words substituted in sub-s (2) with effect from 30 December 2005: ACA 2002, s 139(1), Sch 3, paras 76 and 77 and Adoption and Children Act 2002 (Commencement No 9) Order 2005, SI 2005/2213, art 2(o).

[245.86]
28. Meaning of 'father'[1].— (1) [Subject to subsections (5A) to (5I) below,][2] This section applies in the case of a child who is being or has been carried by a woman as the result of the placing in her of an embryo or of sperm and eggs or her artificial insemination.
(2) If—

(a) at the time of the placing in her of the embryo or the sperm and eggs or of her insemination, the woman was a party to a marriage, and
(b) the creation of the embryo carried by her was not brought about with the sperm of the other party to the marriage,

then, subject to subsection (5) below, the other party to the marriage shall be treated as the father of the child unless it is shown that he did not consent to the placing in her of the embryo or the sperm and eggs or to her insemination (as the case may be).
(3) If no man is treated, by virtue of subsection (2) above, as the father of the child but—

(a) the embryo or the sperm and eggs were placed in the woman, or she was artificially inseminated, in the course of treatment services provided for her and a man together by a person to whom a licence applies, and
(b) the creation of the embryo carried by her was not brought about with the sperm of that man,

then, subject to subsection (5) below, that man shall be treated as the father of the child.
(4) Where a person is treated as the father of the child by virtue of subsection (2) or (3) above, no other person is to be treated as the father of the child.
(5) Subsections (2) and (3) above do not apply—

(a) in relation to England and Wales and Northern Ireland, to any child who, by virtue of the rules of common law, is treated as the legitimate child of the parties to a marriage,
(b) (*applies to Scotland only*), or
(c) to any child to the extent that the child is treated by virtue of adoption as not being the child of any person other than the adopter or adopters [man's child][3].

[(5A) If—

(a) a child has been carried by a woman as the result of the placing in her of an embryo or of sperm and eggs or her artificial insemination,
(b) the creation of the embryo carried by her was brought about by using the sperm of a man after his death, or the creation of the embryo was brought about using the sperm of a man before his death but the embryo was placed in the woman after his death,
(c) the woman was a party to a marriage with the man immediately before his death,
(d) the man consented in writing (and did not withdraw the consent)—
   (i) to the use of his sperm after his death which brought about the creation of the embryo carried by the woman or (as the case may be) to the placing in the woman after his death of the embryo which was brought about using his sperm before his death, and
   (ii) to being treated for the purpose mentioned in subsection (5I) below as the father of any resulting child,
(e) the woman has elected in writing not later than the end of the period of 42 days from the day on which the child was born for the man to be treated for the purpose mentioned in subsection (5I) below as the father of the child, and
(f) no-one else is to be treated as the father of the child by virtue of subsection (2) or (3) above or by virtue of adoption or the child being treated as mentioned in paragraph (a) or (b) of subsection (5) above,

then the man shall be treated for the purpose mentioned in subsection (5I) below as the father of the child.

(5B) If—

(a) a child has been carried by a woman as the result of the placing in her of an embryo or of sperm and eggs or her artificial insemination,

(b) the creation of the embryo carried by her was brought about by using the sperm of a man after his death, or the creation of the embryo was brought about using the sperm of a man before his death but the embryo was placed in the woman after his death,

(c) the woman was not a party to a marriage with the man immediately before his death but treatment services were being provided for the woman and the man together before his death either by a person to whom a licence applies or outside the United Kingdom,

(d) the man consented in writing (and did not withdraw the consent)—

(i) to the use of his sperm after his death which brought about the creation of the embryo carried by the woman or (as the case may be) to the placing in the woman after his death of the embryo which was brought about using his sperm before his death, and

(ii) to being treated for the purpose mentioned in subsection (5I) below as the father of any resulting child,

(e) the woman has elected in writing not later than the end of the period of 42 days from the day on which the child was born for the man to be treated for the purpose mentioned in subsection (5I) below as the father of the child, and

(f) no-one else is to be treated as the father of the child by virtue of subsection (2) or (3) above or by virtue of adoption or the child being treated as mentioned in paragraph (a) or (b) of subsection (5) above,

then the man shall be treated for the purpose mentioned in subsection (5I) below as the father of the child.

(5C) If—

(a) a child has been carried by a woman as the result of the placing in her of an embryo,

(b) the embryo was created at a time when the woman was a party to a marriage,

(c) the creation of the embryo was not brought about with the sperm of the other party to the marriage,

(d) the other party to the marriage died before the placing of the embryo in the woman,

(e) the other party to the marriage consented in writing (and did not withdraw the consent)—

(i) to the placing of the embryo in the woman after his death, and

(ii) to being treated for the purpose mentioned in subsection (5I) below as the father of any resulting child,

(f) the woman has elected in writing not later than the end of the period of 42 days from the day on which the child was born for the other party to the marriage to be treated for the purpose mentioned in subsection (5I) below as the father of the child, and

(g) no-one else is to be treated as the father of the child by virtue of subsection (2) or (3) above or by virtue of adoption or the child being treated as mentioned in paragraph (a) or (b) of subsection (5) above,

then the other party to the marriage shall be treated for the purpose mentioned in subsection (5I) below as the father of the child.

(5D) If—

(a) a child has been carried by a woman as the result of the placing in her of an embryo,
(b) the embryo was not created at a time when the woman was a party to a marriage but was created in the course of treatment services provided for the woman and a man together either by a person to whom a licence applies or outside the United Kingdom,
(c) the creation of the embryo was not brought about with the sperm of that man,
(d) the man died before the placing of the embryo in the woman,
(e) the man consented in writing (and did not withdraw the consent)—
  (i) to the placing of the embryo in the woman after his death, and
  (ii) to being treated for the purpose mentioned in subsection (5I) below as the father of any resulting child,
(f) the woman has elected in writing not later than the end of the period of 42 days from the day on which the child was born for the man to be treated for the purpose mentioned in subsection (5I) below as the father of the child, and
(g) no-one else is to be treated as the father of the child by virtue of subsection (2) or (3) above or by virtue of adoption or the child being treated as mentioned in paragraph (a) or (b) of subsection (5) above,

then the man shall be treated for the purpose mentioned in subsection (5I) below as the father of the child.

(5E) (*Applies to Scotland only*).

(5F) The requirement under subsection (5A), (5B), (5C) or (5D) above as to the making of an election (which requires an election to be made either on or before the day on which the child was born or within the period of 42 or, as the case may be, 21 days from that day) shall nevertheless be treated as satisfied if the required election is made after the end of that period but with the consent of the Registrar General under subsection (5G) below.

(5G) The Registrar General may at any time consent to the making of an election after the end of the period mentioned in subsection (5F) above if, on an application made to him in accordance with such requirements as he may specify, he is satisfied that there is a compelling reason for giving his consent to the making of such an election.

(5H) In subsections (5F) and (5G) above 'the Registrar General' means the Registrar General for England and Wales, the Registrar General of Births, Deaths and Marriages for Scotland or (as the case may be) the Registrar General for Northern Ireland.

(5I) The purpose referred to in subsections (5A) to (5D) above is the purpose of enabling the man's particulars to be entered as the particulars of the child's father in (as the case may be) a register of livebirths or still-births kept under the Births and Deaths Registration Act 1953 or the Births and Deaths Registration (Northern Ireland) Order 1976 or a register of births or still-births kept under the Registration of Births, Deaths and Marriages (Scotland) Act 1965.][4]
(6) Where—

(a) the sperm of a man who had given such consent as is required by paragraph 5 of Schedule 3 to this Act was used for a purpose for which such consent was required, or
(b) the sperm of a man, or any embryo the creation of which was brought about with his sperm, was used after his death,

he is not[, subject to subsections (5A) and (5B) above,][5] to be treated as the father of the child.
(7) The references in subsection (2) above [and subsections (5A) to (5D) above][6] to the parties to a marriage at the time there referred to—

(a) are to the parties to a marriage subsisting at that time, unless a judicial separation was then in force, but
(b) include the parties to a void marriage if either or both of them reasonably believed at that time that the marriage was valid; and for the purposes of this subsection it shall be presumed, unless the contrary is shown, that one of them reasonably believed at that time that the marriage was valid.

(8) This section applies whether the woman was in the United Kingdom or elsewhere at the time of the placing in her of the embryo or the sperm and eggs or her artificial insemination.
(9) In subsection (7)(a) above, 'judicial separation' includes a legal separation obtained in a country outside the British Islands and recognised in the United Kingdom.

1 This section has been superseded in so far as it relates to children carried by women as a result of the placing in them of embryos or of sperm and eggs on or after 6 April 2009, the date on which ss 33–38 of HFEA 2008 came into force: see s 57(2) and Human Fertilisation and Embryology Act 2008 (Commencement No 1 and Transitional Provisions) Order 2009, SI 2009/479, art 6(1)(b). But the section continues to apply to children carried by women as a result of these procedures prior to that date.
2 Words in square brackets in sub-s (1) inserted with effect from 1 December 2003 by Human Fertilisation and Embryology (Deceased Fathers) Act 2003, s 2(1), Sch, para 13 and Human Fertilisation and Embryology (Deceased Fathers) Act 2003 (Commencement) Order 2003, SI 2003/3095, art 2.
3 Words substituted in sub-s (5) with effect from 30 December 2005: ACA 2002, s 139(1), Sch 3, paras 76 and 78 and Adoption and Children Act 2002 (Commencement No 9) Order 2005, SI 2005/2213, art 2(o).
4 Subsections (5A)–(5I) inserted with effect from 1 December 2003 by Human Fertilisation and Embryology (Deceased Fathers) Act 2003, s 1(1) and Human Fertilisation and Embryology (Deceased Fathers) Act 2003 (Commencement) Order 2003, SI 2003/3095, art 2.
5 Words in square brackets in sub-s (6) inserted with effect from 1 December 2003 by Human Fertilisation and Embryology (Deceased Fathers) Act 2003, s 2(1), Sch, para 14 and Human Fertilisation and Embryology (Deceased Fathers) Act 2003 (Commencement) Order 2003, SI 2003/3095, art 2.

6 Words in square brackets in sub-s (7) inserted with effect from 1 December 2003 by Human Fertilisation and Embryology (Deceased Fathers) Act 2003, s 2(1), Sch, para 15 and Human Fertilisation and Embryology (Deceased Fathers) Act 2003 (Commencement) Order 2003, SI 2003/3095, art 2.

[245.87]
29. Effect of sections 27 and 28[1].— (1) Where by virtue of section 27 or 28 of this Act a person is to be treated as the mother or father of a child, that person is to be treated in law as the mother or, as the case may be, father of the child for all purposes.
(2) Where by virtue of section 27 or 28 of this Act a person is not to be treated as the mother or father of a child, that person is to be treated in law as not being the mother or, as the case may be, father of the child for any purpose.
(3) Where subsection (1) or (2) above has effect, references to any relationship between two people in any enactment, deed or other instrument or document (whenever passed or made) are to be read accordingly.
[(3A) Subsections (1) to (3) above do not apply in relation to the treatment in law of a deceased man in a case to which section 28(5A), (5B), (5C) or (5D) of this Act applies.
(3B) Where subsection (5A), (5B), (5C) or (5D) of section 28 of this Act applies, the deceased man—

(a) is to be treated in law as the father of the child for the purpose referred to in that subsection, but
(b) is to be treated in law as not being the father of the child for any other purpose.

(3C) Where subsection (3B) above has effect, references to any relationship between two people in any enactment, deed or other instrument or document (whenever passed or made) are to be read accordingly.
(3D) In subsection (3C) above 'enactment' includes an enactment comprised in, or in an instrument made under, an Act of the Scottish Parliament or Northern Ireland legislation.][2]
(4) In relation to England and Wales and Northern Ireland, nothing in the provisions of section 27(1) or 28(2) to (4) [or (5A) to (5I)][3], read with this section, affects—

(a) the succession to any dignity or title of honour or renders any person capable of succeeding to or transmitting a right to succeed to any such dignity or title, or
(b) the devolution of any property limited (expressly or not) to devolve (as nearly as the law permits) along with any dignity or title of honour.

(5) (*Applies to Scotland only.*)

1 This section has been superseded in so far as it relates to children carried by women as a result of the placing in them of embryos or of sperm and eggs on or after 6 April 2009, the date on which ss 33–38 of HFEA 2008 came into force: see s 57(2) and Human Fertilisation and Embryology Act 2008 (Commencement No 1 and Transitional Provisions) Order 2009, SI 2009/479, art 6(1)(b). But the section continues to apply to children carried by women as a result of these procedures prior to that date.

2 Subsections (3A)–(3D) inserted with effect from 1 December 2003 by Human Fertilisation and Embryology (Deceased Fathers) Act 2003, s 1(2) and Human Fertilisation and Embryology (Deceased Fathers) Act 2003 (Commencement) Order 2003, SI 2003/3095, art 2.

3 Words in square brackets in sub-s (4) inserted with effect from 1 December 2003 by Human Fertilisation and Embryology (Deceased Fathers) Act 2003, s 2(1), Sch, para 16 and Human Fertilisation and Embryology (Deceased Fathers) Act 2003 (Commencement) Order 2003, SI 2003/3095, art 2.

[245.88]
30. Parental orders in favour of gamete donors[1].— (1) The court may make an order providing for a child to be treated in law as the child of the parties to a marriage (referred to in this section as 'the husband' and 'the wife') if—

(a) the child has been carried by a woman other than the wife as the result of the placing in her of an embryo or sperm and eggs or her artificial insemination,
(b) the gametes of the husband or the wife, or both, were used to bring about the creation of the embryo, and
(c) the conditions in subsections (2) to (7) below are satisfied.

(2) The husband and the wife must apply for the order within six months of the birth of the child or, in the case of a child born before the coming into force of this Act, within six months of such coming into force.
(3) At the time of the application and of the making of the order—

(a) the child's home must be with the husband and the wife, and
(b) the husband or the wife, of both of them, must be domiciled in a part of the United Kingdom or in the Channel Islands or the Isle of Man.

(4) At the time of the making of the order both the husband and the wife must have attained the age of eighteen.
(5) The court must be satisfied that both the father of the child (including a person who is the father by virtue of section 28 of this Act), where he is not the husband, and the woman who carried the child have freely, and with full understanding of what is involved, agreed unconditionally to the making of the order.
(6) Subsection (5) above does not require the agreement of a person who cannot be found or is incapable of giving agreement and the agreement of the woman who carried the child is ineffective for the purposes of that subsection if given by her less than six weeks after the child's birth.
(7) The court must be satisfied that no money or other benefit (other than for expenses reasonably incurred) has been given or received by the husband or the wife for or in consideration of—

(a) the making of the order,
(b) any agreement required by subsection (5) above,
(c) the handing over of the child to the husband and the wife, or
(d) the making of any arrangements with a view to the making of the order, unless authorised by the court.

(8) For the purposes of an application under this section—

(a) in relation to England and Wales, section 92(7) to (10) of, and Part I of Schedule 11 to, the Children Act 1989 (jurisdiction of courts) shall apply for the purposes of this section to determine the meaning of 'the court' as they apply for the purposes of that Act and proceedings on the application shall be 'family proceedings' for the purposes of that Act,

(b) (*applies to Scotland only*), and

(c) in relation to Northern Ireland, 'the court' means the High Court or any county court within whose division the child is.

(9) Regulations may provide—

(a) for any provision of the enactments about adoption to have effect, with such modifications (if any) as may be specified in the regulations, in relation to orders under this section, and applications for such orders, as it has effect in relation to adoption, and applications for adoption orders, and

(b) for references in any enactment[2] to adoption, an adopted child or an adoptive relationship to be read (respectively) as references to the effect of an order under this section, a child to whom such an order applies and a relationship arising by virtue of the enactments about adoption, as applied by the regulations, and for similar expressions in connection with adoption to be read accordingly,

and the regulations may include such incidental or supplemental provision as appears to the Secretary of State necessary or desirable in consequence of any provision made by virtue of paragraph (a) or (b) above.

(10) In this section 'the enactments about adoption' means the [Adoption and Children Act 2002][3], the Adoption (Scotland) Act 1978 and the Adoption (Northern Ireland) Order 1987.

(11) Subsection (1)(a) above applies whether the woman was in the United Kingdom or elsewhere at the time of the placing in her of the embryo or the sperm and eggs or her artificial insemination.

1 This section will cease to have effect from a date to be appointed: Human Fertilisation and Embryology Act 2008, ss 57(3), 66, 68(2), Sch 8, Pt 1. No date has yet been appointed. Orders made under this section prior to that date will continue to have effect: see s 57(4) of the 2008 Act.

2 References to 'any enactment' in this paragraph are to be read with effect from 1 December 2003 as including a reference to any enactment contained in s 28(5A) to (5I) of this Act: Human Fertilisation and Embryology (Deceased Fathers) Act 2003, s 2(1), Sch, para 17 and SI 2003/3095, art 2.

3 Words substituted in sub-s (10) with effect from 30 December 2005: ACA 2002, s 139(1), Sch 3, paras 76 and 79 and Adoption and Children Act 2002 (Commencement No 9) Order 2005, SI 2005/2213, art 2(o).

HUMAN FERTILISATION AND EMBRYOLOGY (DECEASED FATHERS) ACT 2003

(2003 c 24)

[18th September 2003]

[245.102A]

Note. This Act makes provision about the circumstances in which, and the extent to which, a man is to be treated in law as the father of a child where the child has resulted from fertility treatment of the nature specified in the Human Fertilisation and Embryology Act 1990 which is undertaken after the man's death. Sections 1 and 2 and the Schedule make amendments to the 1990 Act, the relevant provisions of which are printed as so amended at paras **[245.83]** ff above. Section 3 of the 2003 Act which is set out below provides (with certain qualifications) for those amendments to have retrospective effect.

[245.102B]

3 Retrospective, transitional and transitory provision.— (1) This Act shall (in addition to any case where the sperm or embryo is used on or after the coming into force of section 1) apply to any case where the sperm of a man, or any embryo the creation of which was brought about with the sperm of a man, was used on or after 1st August 1991 and before the coming into force of that section.

(2) Where the child concerned was born before the coming into force of section 1 of this Act, section 28(5A) or (as the case may be) (5B) of the Human Fertilisation and Embryology Act 1990 (c. 37) shall have effect as if for paragraph (e) there were substituted—

> '(e) the woman has elected in writing not later than the end of the period of six months beginning with the coming into force of this subsection for the man to be treated for the purpose mentioned in subsection (5I) below as the father of the child,'.

(3) Where the child concerned was born before the coming into force of section 1 of this Act, section 28(5C) of the Act of 1990 shall have effect as if for paragraph (f) there were substituted—

> '(f) the woman has elected in writing not later than the end of the period of six months beginning with the coming into force of this subsection for the other party to the marriage to be treated for the purpose mentioned in subsection (5I) below as the father of the child,'.

(4) Where the child concerned was born before the coming into force of section 1 of this Act, section 28(5D) of the Act of 1990 shall have effect as if for paragraph (f) there were substituted—

> '(f) the woman has elected in writing not later than the end of the period of six months beginning with the coming into force of this subsection for the man to be treated for the purpose mentioned in subsection (5I) below as the father of the child,'.

(5) Where the child concerned was born before the coming into force of section 1 of this Act, section 28 of the Act of 1990 shall have effect as if—

(a) subsection (5E) were omitted; and
(b) in subsection (5F) for the words from '(which requires' to 'that day)' there were substituted '(which requires an election to be made not later than the end of a period of six months)'.

(6) Where the man who might be treated as the father of the child died before the passing of this Act—

(a) subsections (5A) and (5B) of section 28 of the Act of 1990 shall have effect as if paragraph (d) of each subsection were omitted;
(b) subsections (5C) and (5D) of that section of that Act shall have effect as if paragraph (e) of each subsection were omitted ...

* * * * *

HUMAN FERTILISATION AND EMBRYOLOGY ACT 2008

(2008 c 22)

[13th November 2003]

[245.111]

Note. This Act makes further and more comprehensive provision for the control of the treatment of infertility and research involving human embryos and the use of genetic material not of human origin and, in Part 2, for the identification of the persons who are to be treated as the 'mother', 'father' or 'parent' of a child who is born as a result of assisted reproduction. Part 2 largely supersedes the corresponding provisions the Human Fertilisation and Embryology Act 1990 (or will do so when fully brought into force) but only in relation to a children carried by women as a result of treatment received after the commencement of the relevant provisions on 6 April 2009. But the 2008 Act does not repeal the 1990 Act which continues to apply in relation to children born as a result of treatment received before that date.

PART 2
PARENTHOOD IN CASES INVOLVING ASSISTED REPRODUCTION

Meaning of 'mother'

[245.112]
33 Meaning of 'mother'.— (1) The woman who is carrying or has carried a child as a result of the placing in her of an embryo or of sperm and eggs, and no other woman, is to be treated as the mother of the child.
(2) Subsection (1) does not apply to any child to the extent that the child is treated by virtue of adoption as not being the woman's child.
(3) Subsection (1) applies whether the woman was in the United Kingdom or elsewhere at the time of the placing in her of the embryo or the sperm and eggs.

Application of sections 35 to 47

[245.113]
34 Application of sections 35 to 47.— (1) Sections 35 to 47 apply, in the case of a child who is being or has been carried by a woman (referred to in those sections as 'W') as a result of the placing in her of an embryo or of

sperm and eggs or her artificial insemination, to determine who is to be treated as the other parent of the child.
(2) Subsection (1) has effect subject to the provisions of sections 39, 40 and 46 limiting the purposes for which a person is treated as the child's other parent by virtue of those sections.

Meaning of 'father'

[245.114]
35 Woman married at time of treatment.— (1) If—

(a) at the time of the placing in her of the embryo or of the sperm and eggs or of her artificial insemination, W was a party to a marriage, and
(b) the creation of the embryo carried by her was not brought about with the sperm of the other party to the marriage,

then, subject to section 38(2) to (4), the other party to the marriage is to be treated as the father of the child unless it is shown that he did not consent to the placing in her of the embryo or the sperm and eggs or to her artificial insemination (as the case may be).
(2) This section applies whether W was in the United Kingdom or elsewhere at the time mentioned in subsection (1)(a).

[245.115]
36 Treatment provided to woman where agreed fatherhood conditions apply. If no man is treated by virtue of section 35 as the father of the child and no woman is treated by virtue of section 42 as a parent of the child but—

(a) the embryo or the sperm and eggs were placed in W, or W was artificially inseminated, in the course of treatment services provided in the United Kingdom by a person to whom a licence applies,
(b) at the time when the embryo or the sperm and eggs were placed in W, or W was artificially inseminated, the agreed fatherhood conditions (as set out in section 37) were satisfied in relation to a man, in relation to treatment provided to W under the licence,
(c) the man remained alive at that time, and
(d) the creation of the embryo carried by W was not brought about with the man's sperm,

then, subject to section 38(2) to (4), the man is to be treated as the father of the child.

[245.116]
37 The agreed fatherhood conditions.— (1) The agreed fatherhood conditions referred to in section 36(b) are met in relation to a man ('M') in relation to treatment provided to W under a licence if, but only if,—

(a) M has given the person responsible a notice stating that he consents to being treated as the father of any child resulting from treatment provided to W under the licence,

(b) W has given the person responsible a notice stating that she consents to M being so treated,

(c) neither M nor W has, since giving notice under paragraph (a) or (b), given the person responsible notice of the withdrawal of M's or W's consent to M being so treated,

(d) W has not, since the giving of the notice under paragraph (b), given the person responsible—

(i) a further notice under that paragraph stating that she consents to another man being treated as the father of any resulting child, or

(ii) a notice under section 44(1)(b) stating that she consents to a woman being treated as a parent of any resulting child, and

(e) W and M are not within prohibited degrees of relationship in relation to each other.

(2) A notice under subsection (1)(a), (b) or (c) must be in writing and must be signed by the person giving it.

(3) A notice under subsection (1)(a), (b) or (c) by a person ('S') who is unable to sign because of illness, injury or physical disability is to be taken to comply with the requirement of subsection (2) as to signature if it is signed at the direction of S, in the presence of S and in the presence of at least one witness who attests the signature.

[245.117]

38 Further provision relating to sections 35 and 36.— (1) Where a person is to be treated as the father of the child by virtue of section 35 or 36, no other person is to be treated as the father of the child.

(2) In England and Wales and Northern Ireland, sections 35 and 36 do not affect any presumption, applying by virtue of the rules of common law, that a child is the legitimate child of the parties to a marriage.

(3) In Scotland, sections 35 and 36 do not apply in relation to any child who, by virtue of any enactment or other rule of law, is treated as the child of the parties to a marriage.

(4) Sections 35 and 36 do not apply to any child to the extent that the child is treated by virtue of adoption as not being the man's child.

[245.118]

39 Use of sperm, or transfer of embryo, after death of man providing sperm.— (1) If—

(a) the child has been carried by W as a result of the placing in her of an embryo or of sperm and eggs or her artificial insemination,

(b) the creation of the embryo carried by W was brought about by using the sperm of a man after his death, or the creation of the embryo was brought about using the sperm of a man before his death but the embryo was placed in W after his death,

(c) the man consented in writing (and did not withdraw the consent)—

(i) to the use of his sperm after his death which brought about the creation of the embryo carried by W or (as the case may be) to the placing in W after his death of the embryo which was brought about using his sperm before his death, and

(ii) to being treated for the purpose mentioned in subsection (3) as the father of any resulting child,

(d) W has elected in writing not later than the end of the period of 42 days from the day on which the child was born for the man to be treated for the purpose mentioned in subsection (3) as the father of the child, and

(e) no-one else is to be treated—

(i) as the father of the child by virtue of section 35 or 36 or by virtue of section 38(2) or (3), or

(ii) as a parent of the child by virtue of section 42 or 43 or by virtue of adoption,

then the man is to be treated for the purpose mentioned in subsection (3) as the father of the child.

(2) Subsection (1) applies whether W was in the United Kingdom or elsewhere at the time of the placing in her of the embryo or of the sperm and eggs or of her artificial insemination.

(3) The purpose referred to in subsection (1) is the purpose of enabling the man's particulars to be entered as the particulars of the child's father in a relevant register of births.

(4) In the application of this section to Scotland, for any reference to a period of 42 days there is substituted a reference to a period of 21 days.

[245.119]

40 Embryo transferred after death of husband etc who did not provide sperm.— (1) If—

(a) the child has been carried by W as a result of the placing in her of an embryo,

(b) the embryo was created at a time when W was a party to a marriage,

(c) the creation of the embryo was not brought about with the sperm of the other party to the marriage,

(d) the other party to the marriage died before the placing of the embryo in W,

(e) the other party to the marriage consented in writing (and did not withdraw the consent)—

(i) to the placing of the embryo in W after his death, and

(ii) to being treated for the purpose mentioned in subsection (4) as the father of any resulting child,

(f) W has elected in writing not later than the end of the period of 42 days from the day on which the child was born for the man to be treated for the purpose mentioned in subsection (4) as the father of the child, and

(g) no-one else is to be treated—

(i) as the father of the child by virtue of section 35 or 36 or by virtue of section 38(2) or (3), or

(ii) as a parent of the child by virtue of section 42 or 43 or by virtue of adoption,

then the man is to be treated for the purpose mentioned in subsection (4) as the father of the child.

(2) If—

(a) the child has been carried by W as a result of the placing in her of an embryo,

(b) the embryo was not created at a time when W was a party to a marriage or a civil partnership but was created in the course of treatment services provided to W in the United Kingdom by a person to whom a licence applies,

(c) a man consented in writing (and did not withdraw the consent)—

  (i) to the placing of the embryo in W after his death, and

  (ii) to being treated for the purpose mentioned in subsection (4) as the father of any resulting child,

(d) the creation of the embryo was not brought about with the sperm of that man,

(e) the man died before the placing of the embryo in W,

(f) immediately before the man's death, the agreed fatherhood conditions set out in section 37 were met in relation to the man in relation to treatment proposed to be provided to W in the United Kingdom by a person to whom a licence applies,

(g) W has elected in writing not later than the end of the period of 42 days from the day on which the child was born for the man to be treated for the purpose mentioned in subsection (4) as the father of the child, and

(h) no-one else is to be treated—

  (i) as the father of the child by virtue of section 35 or 36 or by virtue of section 38(2) or (3), or

  (ii) as a parent of the child by virtue of section 42 or 43 or by virtue of adoption,

then the man is to be treated for the purpose mentioned in subsection (4) as the father of the child.

(3) Subsections (1) and (2) apply whether W was in the United Kingdom or elsewhere at the time of the placing in her of the embryo.

(4) The purpose referred to in subsections (1) and (2) is the purpose of enabling the man's particulars to be entered as the particulars of the child's father in a relevant register of births.

(5) In the application of this section to Scotland, for any reference to a period of 42 days there is substituted a reference to a period of 21 days.

[245.120]

41 Persons not to be treated as father.— (1) Where the sperm of a man who had given such consent as is required by paragraph 5 of Schedule 3 to the 1990 Act (consent to use of gametes for purposes of treatment services or non-medical fertility services) was used for a purpose for which such consent was required, he is not to be treated as the father of the child.

(2) Where the sperm of a man, or an embryo the creation of which was brought about with his sperm, was used after his death, he is not, subject to section 39, to be treated as the father of the child.

(3) Subsection (2) applies whether W was in the United Kingdom or elsewhere at the time of the placing in her of the embryo or of the sperm and eggs or of her artificial insemination.

Cases in which woman to be other parent

[245.121]
42 Woman in civil partnership at time of treatment.— (1) If at the time of the placing in her of the embryo or the sperm and eggs or of her artificial insemination, W was a party to a civil partnership, then subject to section 45(2) to (4), the other party to the civil partnership is to be treated as a parent of the child unless it is shown that she did not consent to the placing in W of the embryo or the sperm and eggs or to her artificial insemination (as the case may be).
(2) This section applies whether W was in the United Kingdom or elsewhere at the time mentioned in subsection (1).

[245.122]
43 Treatment provided to woman who agrees that second woman to be parent. If no man is treated by virtue of section 35 as the father of the child and no woman is treated by virtue of section 42 as a parent of the child but—

- (a) the embryo or the sperm and eggs were placed in W, or W was artificially inseminated, in the course of treatment services provided in the United Kingdom by a person to whom a licence applies,
- (b) at the time when the embryo or the sperm and eggs were placed in W, or W was artificially inseminated, the agreed female parenthood conditions (as set out in section 44) were met in relation to another woman, in relation to treatment provided to W under that licence, and
- (c) the other woman remained alive at that time,

then, subject to section 45(2) to (4), the other woman is to be treated as a parent of the child.

[245.123]
44 The agreed female parenthood conditions.— (1) The agreed female parenthood conditions referred to in section 43(b) are met in relation to another woman ('P') in relation to treatment provided to W under a licence if, but only if,—

- (a) P has given the person responsible a notice stating that P consents to P being treated as a parent of any child resulting from treatment provided to W under the licence,
- (b) W has given the person responsible a notice stating that W agrees to P being so treated,
- (c) neither W nor P has, since giving notice under paragraph (a) or (b), given the person responsible notice of the withdrawal of P's or W's consent to P being so treated,
- (d) W has not, since the giving of the notice under paragraph (b), given the person responsible—
  - (i) a further notice under that paragraph stating that W consents to a woman other than P being treated as a parent of any resulting child, or

(ii) a notice under section 37(1)(b) stating that W consents to a man being treated as the father of any resulting child, and

(e) W and P are not within prohibited degrees of relationship in relation to each other.

(2) A notice under subsection (1)(a), (b) or (c) must be in writing and must be signed by the person giving it.
(3) A notice under subsection (1)(a), (b) or (c) by a person ('S') who is unable to sign because of illness, injury or physical disability is to be taken to comply with the requirement of subsection (2) as to signature if it is signed at the direction of S, in the presence of S and in the presence of at least one witness who attests the signature.

[245.124]
45 Further provision relating to sections 42 and 43.— (1) Where a woman is treated by virtue of section 42 or 43 as a parent of the child, no man is to be treated as the father of the child.
(2) In England and Wales and Northern Ireland, sections 42 and 43 do not affect any presumption, applying by virtue of the rules of common law, that a child is the legitimate child of the parties to a marriage.
(3) In Scotland, sections 42 and 43 do not apply in relation to any child who, by virtue of any enactment or other rule of law, is treated as the child of the parties to a marriage.
(4) Sections 42 and 43 do not apply to any child to the extent that the child is treated by virtue of adoption as not being the woman's child.

[245.125]
46 Embryo transferred after death of civil partner or intended female parent.— (1) If—

(a) the child has been carried by W as the result of the placing in her of an embryo,
(b) the embryo was created at a time when W was a party to a civil partnership,
(c) the other party to the civil partnership died before the placing of the embryo in W,
(d) the other party to the civil partnership consented in writing (and did not withdraw the consent)—
  (i) to the placing of the embryo in W after the death of the other party, and
  (ii) to being treated for the purpose mentioned in subsection (4) as the parent of any resulting child,
(e) W has elected in writing not later than the end of the period of 42 days from the day on which the child was born for the other party to the civil partnership to be treated for the purpose mentioned in subsection (4) as the parent of the child, and
(f) no one else is to be treated—
  (i) as the father of the child by virtue of section 35 or 36 or by virtue of section 45(2) or (3), or
  (ii) as a parent of the child by virtue of section 42 or 43 or by virtue of adoption,

then the other party to the civil partnership is to be treated for the purpose mentioned in subsection (4) as a parent of the child.

(2) If—

- (a) the child has been carried by W as the result of the placing in her of an embryo,
- (b) the embryo was not created at a time when W was a party to a marriage or a civil partnership, but was created in the course of treatment services provided to W in the United Kingdom by a person to whom a licence applies,
- (c) another woman consented in writing (and did not withdraw the consent)—
  - (i) to the placing of the embryo in W after the death of the other woman, and
  - (ii) to being treated for the purpose mentioned in subsection (4) as the parent of any resulting child,
- (d) the other woman died before the placing of the embryo in W,
- (e) immediately before the other woman's death, the agreed female parenthood conditions set out in section 44 were met in relation to the other woman in relation to treatment proposed to be provided to W in the United Kingdom by a person to whom a licence applies,
- (f) W has elected in writing not later than the end of the period of 42 days from the day on which the child was born for the other woman to be treated for the purpose mentioned in subsection (4) as the parent of the child, and
- (g) no one else is to be treated—
  - (i) as the father of the child by virtue of section 35 or 36 or by virtue of section 45(2) or (3), or
  - (ii) as a parent of the child by virtue of section 42 or 43 or by virtue of adoption,

then the other woman is to be treated for the purpose mentioned in subsection (4) as a parent of the child.

(3) Subsections (1) and (2) apply whether W was in the United Kingdom or elsewhere at the time of the placing in her of the embryo.

(4) The purpose referred to in subsections (1) and (2) is the purpose of enabling the deceased woman's particulars to be entered as the particulars of the child's other parent in a relevant register of births.

(5) In the application of subsections (1) and (2) to Scotland, for any reference to a period of 42 days there is substituted a reference to a period of 21 days.

[245.126]

47 Woman not to be other parent merely because of egg donation. A woman is not to be treated as the parent of a child whom she is not carrying and has not carried, except where she is so treated—

- (a) by virtue of section 42 or 43, or
- (b) by virtue of section 46 (for the purpose mentioned in subsection (4) of that section), or
- (c) by virtue of adoption.

Effect of sections 33 to 47

[245.127]
48 Effect of sections 33 to 47.— (1) Where by virtue of section 33, 35, 36, 42 or 43 a person is to be treated as the mother, father or parent of a child, that person is to be treated in law as the mother, father or parent (as the case may be) of the child for all purposes.
(2) Where by virtue of section 33, 38, 41, 45 or 47 a person is not to be treated as a parent of the child, that person is to be treated in law as not being a parent of the child for any purpose.
(3) Where section 39(1) or 40(1) or (2) applies, the deceased man—

(a) is to be treated in law as the father of the child for the purpose mentioned in section 39(3) or 40(4), but
(b) is to be treated in law as not being the father of the child for any other purpose.

(4) Where section 46(1) or (2) applies, the deceased woman—

(a) is to be treated in law as a parent of the child for the purpose mentioned in section 46(4), but
(b) is to be treated in law as not being a parent of the child for any other purpose.

(5) Where any of subsections (1) to (4) has effect, references to any relationship between two people in any enactment, deed or other instrument or document (whenever passed or made) are to be read accordingly.
(6) In relation to England and Wales and Northern Ireland, a child who—

(a) has a parent by virtue of section 42, or
(b) has a parent by virtue of section 43 who is at any time during the period beginning with the time mentioned in section 43(b) and ending with the time of the child's birth a party to a civil partnership with the child's mother,

is the legitimate child of the child's parents.
(7) In relation to England and Wales and Northern Ireland, nothing in the provisions of section 33(1) or sections 35 to 47, read with this section—

(a) affects the succession to any dignity or title of honour or renders any person capable of succeeding to or transmitting a right to succeed to any such dignity or title, or
(b) affects the devolution of any property limited (expressly or not) to devolve (as nearly as the law permits) along with any dignity or title of honour.

(8) In relation to Scotland—

(a) those provisions do not apply to any title, coat of arms, honour or dignity transmissible on the death of its holder or affect the succession to any such title, coat of arms or dignity or its devolution, and
(b) where the terms of any deed provide that any property or interest in

property is to devolve along with a title, coat of arms, honour or dignity, nothing in those provisions is to prevent that property or interest from so devolving.

References to parties to marriage or civil partnership

[245.128]
49 Meaning of references to parties to a marriage.— (1) The references in sections 35 to 47 to the parties to a marriage at any time there referred to—

(a) are to the parties to a marriage subsisting at that time, unless a judicial separation was then in force, but
(b) include the parties to a void marriage if either or both of them reasonably believed at that time that the marriage was valid; and for the purposes of those sections it is to be presumed, unless the contrary is shown, that one of them reasonably believed at that time that the marriage was valid.

(2) In subsection (1)(a) 'judicial separation' includes a legal separation obtained in a country outside the British Islands and recognised in the United Kingdom.

[245.129]
50 Meaning of references to parties to a civil partnership.— (1) The references in sections 35 to 47 to the parties to a civil partnership at any time there referred to—

(a) are to the parties to a civil partnership subsisting at that time, unless a separation order was then in force, but
(b) include the parties to a void civil partnership if either or both of them reasonably believed at that time that the civil partnership was valid; and for the purposes of those sections it is to be presumed, unless the contrary is shown, that one of them reasonably believed at that time that the civil partnership was valid.

(2) The reference in section 48(6)(b) to a civil partnership includes a reference to a void civil partnership if either or both of the parties reasonably believed at the time when they registered as civil partners of each other that the civil partnership was valid; and for this purpose it is to be presumed, unless the contrary is shown, that one of them reasonably believed at that time that the civil partnership was valid.
(3) In subsection (1)(a), 'separation order' means—

(a) a separation order under section 37(1)(d) or 161(1)(d) of the Civil Partnership Act 2004 (c 33),
(b) a decree of separation under section 120(2) of that Act, or
(c) a legal separation obtained in a country outside the United Kingdom and recognised in the United Kingdom.

Further provision about registration by virtue of section 39, 40 or 46

[245.130]
51 Meaning of 'relevant register of births'. For the purposes of this Part a 'relevant register of births', in relation to a birth, is whichever of the following is relevant—

(a) a register of live-births or still-births kept under the Births and Deaths Registration Act 1953 (c 20),
(b) a register of births or still-births kept under the Registration of Births, Deaths and Marriages (Scotland) Act 1965 (c 49), or
(c) a register of live-births or still-births kept under the Births and Deaths Registration (Northern Ireland) Order 1976 (SI 1976/1041 (NI 14)).

[245.131]
52 Late election by mother with consent of Registrar General.— (1) The requirement under section 39(1), 40(1) or (2) or 46(1) or (2) as to the making of an election (which requires an election to be made either on or before the day on which the child was born or within the period of 42 or, as the case may be, 21 days from that day) is nevertheless to be treated as satisfied if the required election is made after the end of that period but with the consent of the Registrar General under subsection (2).
(2) The Registrar General may at any time consent to the making of an election after the end of the period mentioned in subsection (1) if, on an application made to him in accordance with such requirements as he may specify, he is satisfied that there is a compelling reason for giving his consent to the making of such an election.
(3) In this section 'the Registrar General' means the Registrar General for England and Wales, the Registrar General of Births, Deaths and Marriages for Scotland or (as the case may be) the Registrar General for Northern Ireland.

Interpretation of references to father etc where woman is other parent

[245.132]
53 Interpretation of references to father etc.— (1) Subsections (2) and (3) have effect, subject to subsections (4) and (6), for the interpretation of any enactment, deed or any other instrument or document (whenever passed or made).
(2) Any reference (however expressed) to the father of a child who has a parent by virtue of section 42 or 43 is to be read as a reference to the woman who is a parent of the child by virtue of that section.
(3) Any reference (however expressed) to evidence of paternity is, in relation to a woman who is a parent by virtue of section 42 or 43, to be read as a reference to evidence of parentage.
(4) This section does not affect the interpretation of the enactments specified in subsection (5) (which make express provision for the case where a child has a parent by virtue of section 42 or 43).
(5) Those enactments are—

(a) the Legitimacy Act (Northern Ireland) 1928 (c 5 (NI)),
(b) the Schedule to the Population (Statistics) Act 1938 (c 12),
(c) the Births and Deaths Registration Act 1953 (c 20),
(d) the Registration of Births, Deaths and Marriages (Special Provisions) Act 1957 (c 58),
(e) Part 2 of the Registration of Births, Deaths and Marriages (Scotland) Act 1965 (c 49),
(f) the Congenital Disabilities (Civil Liability) Act 1976 (c 28),
(g) the Legitimacy Act 1976 (c 31),
(h) the Births and Deaths Registration (Northern Ireland) Order 1976 (SI 1976/1041 (NI 14)),
(i) the British Nationality Act 1981 (c 61),
(j) the Family Law Reform Act 1987 (c 42),
(k) Parts 1 and 2 of the Children Act 1989 (c 41),
(l) Part 1 of the Children (Scotland) Act 1995 (c 36),
(m) section 1 of the Criminal Law (Consolidation) (Scotland) Act 1995 (c 39), and
(n) Parts 2, 3 and 14 of the Children (Northern Ireland) Order 1995 (SI 1995/755 (NI 2)).

(6) This section does not affect the interpretation of references that fall to be read in accordance with section 1(2)(a) or (b) of the Family Law Reform Act 1987 or Article 155(2)(a) or (b) of the Children (Northern Ireland) Order 1995 (references to a person whose father and mother were, or were not, married to each other at the time of the person's birth).

Parental orders

[245.133]
54 Parental orders.— (1) On an application made by two people ('the applicants'), the court may make an order providing for a child to be treated in law as the child of the applicants if—

(a) the child has been carried by a woman who is not one of the applicants, as a result of the placing in her of an embryo or sperm and eggs or her artificial insemination,
(b) the gametes of at least one of the applicants were used to bring about the creation of the embryo, and
(c) the conditions in subsections (2) to (8) are satisfied.

(2) The applicants must be—

(a) husband and wife,
(b) civil partners of each other, or
(c) two persons who are living as partners in an enduring family relationship and are not within prohibited degrees of relationship in relation to each other.

(3) Except in a case falling within subsection (11), the applicants must apply for the order during the period of 6 months beginning with the day on which the child is born.
(4) At the time of the application and the making of the order—

(a) the child's home must be with the applicants, and
(b) either or both of the applicants must be domiciled in the United Kingdom or in the Channel Islands or the Isle of Man.

(5) At the time of the making of the order both the applicants must have attained the age of 18.
(6) The court must be satisfied that both—

(a) the woman who carried the child, and
(b) any other person who is a parent of the child but is not one of the applicants (including any man who is the father by virtue of section 35 or 36 or any woman who is a parent by virtue of section 42 or 43),

have freely, and with full understanding of what is involved, agreed unconditionally to the making of the order.
(7) Subsection (6) does not require the agreement of a person who cannot be found or is incapable of giving agreement; and the agreement of the woman who carried the child is ineffective for the purpose of that subsection if given by her less than six weeks after the child's birth.
(8) The court must be satisfied that no money or other benefit (other than for expenses reasonably incurred) has been given or received by either of the applicants for or in consideration of—

(a) the making of the order,
(b) any agreement required by subsection (6),
(c) the handing over of the child to the applicants, or
(d) the making of arrangements with a view to the making of the order,

unless authorised by the court.
(9) For the purposes of an application under this section—

(a) in relation to England and Wales, section 92(7) to (10) of, and Part 1 of Schedule 11 to, the Children Act 1989 (c 41) (jurisdiction of courts) apply for the purposes of this section to determine the meaning of 'the court' as they apply for the purposes of that Act and proceedings on the application are to be 'family proceedings' for the purposes of that Act,
(b) in relation to Scotland, 'the court' means the Court of Session or the sheriff court of the sheriffdom within which the child is, and
(c) in relation to Northern Ireland, 'the court' means the High Court or any county court within whose division the child is.

(10) Subsection (1)(a) applies whether the woman was in the United Kingdom or elsewhere at the time of the placing in her of the embryo or the sperm and eggs or her artificial insemination.
(11) An application which—

(a) relates to a child born before the coming into force of this section, and
(b) is made by two persons who, throughout the period applicable under subsection (2) of section 30 of the 1990 Act, were not eligible to apply for an order under that section in relation to the child as husband and wife,

may be made within the period of six months beginning with the day on which this section comes into force.

[245.134]
55 Parental orders: supplementary provision.— (1) The Secretary of State may by regulations provide—

- (a) for any provision of the enactments about adoption to have effect, with such modifications (if any) as may be specified in the regulations, in relation to orders under section 54, and applications for such orders, as it has effect in relation to adoption, and applications for adoption orders, and
- (b) for references in any enactment to adoption, an adopted child or an adoptive relationship to be read (respectively) as references to the effect of an order under section 54, a child to whom such an order applies and a relationship arising by virtue of the enactments about adoption, as applied by the regulations, and for similar expressions in connection with adoption to be read accordingly.

(2) The regulations may include such incidental or supplemental provision as appears to the Secretary of State to be necessary or desirable in consequence of any provision made by virtue of subsection (1)(a) or (b).
(3) In this section 'the enactments about adoption' means—

- (a) the Adoption (Scotland) Act 1978 (c 28),
- (b) the Adoption and Children Act 2002 (c 38),
- (c) the Adoption and Children (Scotland) Act 2007 (asp 4), and
- (d) the Adoption (Northern Ireland) Order 1987 (SI 1987/2203 (NI 22)).

Amendments of enactments

[245.135]
56 Amendments relating to parenthood in cases involving assisted reproduction. Schedule 6 contains amendments related to the provisions of this Part.

General

[245.136]
57 Repeals and transitional provision relating to Part 2.— (1) Sections 33 to 48 have effect only in relation to children carried by women as a result of the placing in them of embryos or of sperm and eggs, or their artificial insemination (as the case may be), after the commencement of those sections.
(2) Sections 27 to 29 of the 1990 Act (which relate to status) do not have effect in relation to children carried by women as a result of the placing in them of embryos or of sperm and eggs, or their artificial insemination (as the case may be), after the commencement of sections 33 to 48.

(3) Section 30 of the 1990 Act (parental orders in favour of gamete donors) ceases to have effect.
(4) Subsection (3) does not affect the validity of any order made under section 30 of the 1990 Act before the coming into force of that subsection.

[245.137]
58 Interpretation of Part 2.— (1) In this Part 'enactment' means an enactment contained in, or in an instrument made under—

- (a) an Act of Parliament,
- (b) an Act of the Scottish Parliament,
- (c) a Measure or Act of the National Assembly for Wales, or
- (d) Northern Ireland legislation.

(2) For the purposes of this Part, two persons are within prohibited degrees of relationship if one is the other's parent, grandparent, sister, brother, aunt or uncle; and in this subsection references to relationships—

- (a) are to relationships of the full blood or half blood or, in the case of an adopted person, such of those relationships as would subsist but for adoption, and
- (b) include the relationship of a child with his adoptive, or former adoptive, parents,

but do not include any other adoptive relationships.
(3) Other expressions used in this Part and in the 1990 Act have the same meaning in this Part as in that Act.

PART 3
MISCELLANEOUS AND GENERAL

* * * * *

General

* * * * *

[245.138]
63 Meaning of 'the 1990 Act'. In this Act, 'the 1990 Act' means the Human Fertilisation and Embryology Act 1990 (c 37).

* * * * *

[245.139]
67 Extent (1) Subject to the following provisions, this Act extends to England and Wales, Scotland and Northern Ireland.
(2) Any amendment or repeal made by this Act has the same extent as the enactment to which it relates (ignoring extent by virtue of an Order in Council).[1]

1 The remaining subsections are not relevant.

[245.140]
68 Commencement.— (1) The following provisions of this Act come into force on the day on which this Act is passed—

sections 61 to 64;
section 67, this section and section 69.

(2) The remaining provisions of this Act come into force in accordance with provision made by the Secretary of State by order.[1]

1 The provisions of ss 33 to 53, 56 (for certain purposes), 57(1), (2) and 58 were brought into force on 6 April 2009 by the Human Fertilisation and Embryology Act 2008 (Commencement No 1 and Transitional Provisions) Order 2009, SI 2009/479, art 6(1)(a), (b), (c), and (f). No commencement date has been appointed for ss 54, 55, 57(3), (4) or the remaining purposes of s 56.

[245.141]
69 Short title. This Act may be cited as the Human Fertilisation and Embryology Act 2008.
… .